Vital Signs

Real-life medical dramas of doctors and patients, pain and compassion, hope and healing

Dennis L. Breo

Bonus Books, Inc., Chicago

Dramatic stories of doctors and patients, first published in the *Chicago Tribune Magazine* and *The Journal of the American Medical Association*, are presented to provide an inside look at the real world of medicine.

99 98 97 96 95 5 4 3 2 1

Library of Congress Cataloging-in-Publication Data

Breo, Dennis L., 1942–
Vital signs : real-life medical dramas of doctors and patients, pain and compassion, hope and healing / Dennis L. Breo.
p. cm.
Includes index.
ISBN 1-56625-034-X : $19.95
1. Physicians—United States—Biography. 2. Medicine. I. Title.
R153.B63 1995
610'.69—dc20 95-62
CIP

Bonus Books, Inc.
160 East Illinois Street
Chicago, Illinois 60611

Printed in the United States of America

For Julie

Contents

ACTS OF COURAGE

TOMORROW'S MEDICINE

Foreword

Several years ago Frank Slaughter, M.D., wrote a book about a physician having an affair that could not be denied. The passion and dedication to the mistress was all consuming. It was not long into the book when the reader realized that the mistress was the profession of medicine. The book was entitled *The Divine Mistress*.

In those days about all that physicians could offer was a diagnosis, a prognosis, and compassion. The pursuit of those capabilities was all-consuming for most physicians as they tried to do the best they could, frustrated by knowing that the tools they had were all too inadequate. Because of this the quest for knowledge was strong and every case presented an opportunity to learn. Science was lacking and there had to be more than observing illness. Prior to this time most medical advances had little to do with medicine, but rather were the results of societal changes in sanitation, contagion control, and better personal hygiene. What research there was tended to be clinical, identifying a disease and then trying to find a cure. Doctors desperately wanted to do better, as they do today.

It was from this foundation, aided by advances in other areas of science, that medicine and physicians pressed forward toward the health care we enjoy today. Early on, most of the advances were serendipitous; in many respects they still are. If Alexander Fleming had maintained a spotless laboratory, for example, penicillin might not have been discovered for many more years.

Sad but true, medical advances were also aided by warfare. The Second World War saw the advent of antibiotics and the control of infection. The Korean War opened up the field of vascular surgery, and the Vietnam War produced techniques for the maintenance of nutrition solely through intravenous routes. Each of these capabilities was developed in response to an urgent need, and demonstrated the ingenuity of physicians when faced with critical unsolved problems.

For many years medical progress was measured by how well needs were met. From these early steps physicians came to realize the potential for clinical research. A whole new era began. Aided by the federal government, the research establishment became a reality, and physicians tried to anticipate medical needs using the tools of basic science. For the first time, there were physicians who didn't just see patients, but saw possibilities.

The *Divine Mistress* became more demanding with each passing year. Whereas previously, social and industrial advances had contributed to health, whole new concerns now surfaced over toxic wastes and environmental pollution. Lifestyles were changing. Initially no one could foresee the consequences of the affluent society. With the acceptance, indeed the necessity, of women in the workforce, the family structure began to deteriorate with predictable results. For the first time it was possible to have five generations of the same family all alive at the same time. This presented further responsibilities to the individual and society that neither was ready to assume.

Also, the patient-doctor relationship was changing. Health insurance began to grow as workers preferred tax-free medical protection to taxable income. Insurance isolated patients from the economic consequences of their health care decisions. The neat one-on-one relationship of mutual responsibility was destroyed, and demand for care exploded. With the rapid aging of the population and pockets of abject poverty, in 1965 the Federal Government enacted what were to become the first entitlements in health care known as Medicaid and Medicare. As might be expected, demand for care among these groups mushroomed.

The medical profession during this period did exactly what it was being rewarded to do both medically and financially. It grew and prospered. Who could have imagined that the medical profession was to become the victim of its own success, and that society would be unable to sustain that level of success? The tyranny of technology drove both the public and the physician to want more and better treatment for more people. Death became the ultimate defeat for physicians, and people expected medicine to assure disease-free perfect bodies and lives.

All of these changes had subtle—and sometimes not so subtle—effects on the attitude of physicians and how they saw their role. Their clinical and professional independence was being challenged and circumscribed. Despite all these changes, though, physicians still care deeply for their patients, and for society in general. The medical profession today is solidly balanced on the tripod of education, research, and patient care with ever-expanding knowledge whose consequences are beyond most imagination.

Naturally, this sequence of events has not been without consequences. While more than ever, in most polls, the medical profession is under siege, the individual physician still ranks as one of the most respected and trusted individuals in society. Yet the profession is suspect in its goals. This should not be surprising; in a sense it has always been so. George Bernard Shaw in his treatise *The Doctor's Dilemma* said it best, asking, "Why should I pay a physician to take my leg off? I should pay him to keep it on."

There has always been a gap between the image of the profession and the individual physician. The profession is impersonal and distant, while the physician is real and near. The patient-physician relationship is probably the closest affirmation of faith that exists. Patients every day place their faith in the physician to do what is best for them. Confounding this relationship is the fact that the rapid advance of medical science sometimes makes it difficult to know what is really in the best interest of the patient. There are no standard patients, no standard diseases, no standard doctors and, therefore, no standard outcomes of care. No wonder the practice of medicine is difficult.

Complicating this natural variation is the consumerism movement: people want the maximum information so as to be involved in their own health care decisions, but it stands to reason that unless one has gone through a medical education, one cannot make decisions on the same footing with physicians. Paternalism should not be tolerated, but it must be recognized that medicine will always be an inexact science and the best decisions will finally be made by dedicated physicians trying to sort out the benefits for each individual patient. Statistics are useful, but they say nothing about the individual case.

Medicine has never been more complicated and shows every indication of becoming more so. The horizons are limited only by the imagination. Physicians in practice routinely use therapies and techniques that were unknown during their training. Half of everything physicians do today for patients was unknown in 1950. Progress is so rapid that one physician can no longer know everything there is to know. Specialization becomes ever more important to maximize the benefits of emerging technology. Yet, with that specialization comes the specter of the technician handling only small portions of care, thus frequently having only a fleeting and superficial relationship with patients. This adds to the impetus for primary care: people want to have a "homebase" from which to learn about their care and the necessity for specialized care. There is an inherent conflict between wanting intimacy and technical prowess.

Society, however, has to come to grips with its discoveries and decide if it is willing to accept the social and economic consequences of medical progress. This will be the great dilemma for the future as the possibilities increase and the resources to support them seem increasingly circumscribed. Without much question, as we look to the future, health care as broadly defined could take up every resource society provides, yet is it clear there are other imperatives in society that cannot be ignored, such as education and the national infrastructure.

Here, then, is the rub. What should be done in health care, who should do it, and to whom should it be done? There are no easy answers, but certainly some obvious challenges. How those challenges are addressed will make all the difference in how well society is able to capitalize on modern medical miracles. Increasingly, physicians will be frustrated knowing they can do so much more, that there is so much more to learn, and all the while resources are inadequate, and people refuse to face the prospects of "applied medicine", meaning that not everyone can have everything.

Looking to the future, which is nearly upon us, several issues will become crucial. Among them are: How is technological progress translated into human progress? How are the knotty ethical issues resulting from technical progress to be decided and by whom? How are resources to be allocated? What are one's own responsibilities to maintain health? And how does the community reestablish a sense of shared responsibility? There are no easy answers, but answers must be found or the entire medical complex will implode, leaving people to fend for themselves in a frenzy of competition and fingerpointing. For this to happen would squander the progress of a century.

Technology is mindless, seeking only to solve a problem or fill a vacuum without consideration of consequences. Those producing the technology, therefore, have the responsibility to apply that technology wisely. The overall record thus far leaves much to be desired. Driven by public expectations, the contemporary philosophy seems to be if a procedure is available, do it, and if a medication is available, give it. Doing nothing is unthinkable. Perhaps the time has come to coolly assess the probability of a successful outcome with real benefit to the patient rather than prolongation of life at any cost. While without question some treatments will be limited under this plan, this should not be considered rationing. Instead it will be the wise application of current knowledge. Progress need not be stifled, but only those things that need to be done—with a reasonable expectation of success—should be done. Quality of life should become important, and those technologies that enhance that quality should take precedence.

Technological developments are now stretching the boundaries of medical ethics. Issues never conceived of previously are now the subjects of daily discussions. The capabilities of genetic testing, for example, assure there will be no shortage of ethical dilemmas. Preemployment screening, general screening of a population at risk, consideration of aborting genetically damaged children, and expensive genetic therapy will test the mettle of ethicists and society alike. For the first time, it will be necessary to weigh the individual's need versus that of society. There are no simple answers, but boundaries will have to be established. This is not the role of the medical profession alone. Society cannot ask the physician to become a double agent when dealing with patients and limited resources. The prospect that economic factors may be more influential than medical decisions is a frightening one. Before long progress and resources will require thoughtful analysis testing the very fabric of society.

The success of medical progress requires ever more resources to realize the benefits of that progress. Medical care is labor intensive and by definition a service industry does not lend itself to the efficiencies that can be achieved in industry. As yet, there has been no rational debate as to how these resources should be husbanded, or indeed what resources should be made available. If everyone is to share in the benefits of this progress there must be a determined a fundamental level of health care to which everyone should have access. Clearly, this will require that some things now taken for granted may not be generally available under whatever financing method may ultimately be adopted, leaving as discretionary those things not covered. There are those who say this creates a two tiered medical system, and it does. A basic fact remains, however, the rich will always get more than the poor and in a democracy people cannot be told how to spend their wealth. Priorities will have to be established and agreed upon by society, for again the physician cannot be a double agent.

Perhaps the greatest impediment to streamlining our health care system and its costs is society's reluctance or inability to recognize their personal contribution to health care expenditures which need not occur. Mayhem on the highways, a stubborn drug problem, reluctance to deal rationally with the AIDS epidemic, failure to provide basic inner city services, continuing crime, and increasing interpersonal violence, among other problems are all within our ability to control. Sadly, there is much talk and little action. As the elderly population grows relying on the younger members of the family for support, elder abuse is not unusual. Destructive life styles such as overeating, drinking too much, smoking, and failing to exercise contribute to a population of decreasing personal health. The only method to deal with these non-productive activities is to find a way to make people responsible for the consequences of their actions. Education and exhortation will only go so far, and it will not be until a penalty is extracted that people will pay attention. More than anything else, individual responsibility for one's health will make the greatest contribution to stabilizing health care expenditures.

Finally, one cannot ignore the breakdown of the family and slackening values as a source of real concern. No longer is caring for one's neighbor or relative seen as a laudable activity. If it becomes everyone for themself our society will certainly pay the price. It may take a generation to turn all this around, and re-education needs to begin at the lowest levels of school by teachers who see their job as more than conducting classes.

Meanwhile, physicians stand confused and anxious over the mixed messages they are receiving. Having produced the finest research facilities, the highest quality of medical care, and the greatest technology the world has ever seen, they cannot understand why seemingly they alone must suffer the consequences of their success. They are told they are too greedy, too impersonal, too technical, and too wasteful. Rules and regulations grow at an ever increasing rate. The business of medicine is making the practice of medicine a nightmare. For-profit organizations are entering the medical landscape not so much for improving health as for providing dividends to their investors. New forms of practice, for example, health maintenance organizations bring physicians together in groups. While effecting economies of scale, the physician's identity fades into that of the group. Clinical decision making is increasingly limited by those unfamiliar with the vagaries of health care. Funds for research and education are less plentiful. All of this is happening at a time when physicians can do more for people than ever before. Equally true, more harm can be done equally fast with the misapplication of technology adding to the need for excellence, and continuing education, now so much a part of a physician's professional life. Physicians have responded as best they know how, but have been all too docile in responding to the pressures put upon them. They fail to respond in a unified strong voice eschewing parochialism while protecting patients from becoming pawns in the "reformation" of our health care system. Some doctors are despairing, leaving the profession or accepting secure paying jobs within the profession letting someone else worry about the problems. A demoralized medical profession is not in the best interests of anyone, especially patients. While these are disturbing trends, most physicians remember why they went into medicine in the first place. Ask them and they will respond it was because of the opportunity to perform meaningful service and to use the marvelous tools of technology to heal the sick and help the helpless. One only has to look beyond a physician's clinical life and see the level of community service, the varied outside interests and the non-medical successes of physicians to realize the brightest and the best are still being attracted to medical careers. The opportunities are limitless for those willing to seize them, and fortunately many do. From the technological perspective, the golden age of medicine really lies ahead.

The essence of professionalism is competence, collegiality, and compassion. Medical gains come from a long tradition of education, research and sharing of information. One person's puzzle may be another solution. The emphasis on competence and business to the exclusion of collegiality and compassion do not serve our citizenry well. Medicine is a lonely calling. So many immediate decisions have to be made under sometimes very adverse circumstances with inadequate information and with no way to get the additional essential information. Worse yet, physicians have to suffer the consequences of these decisions and there is not a physician alive that does not agonize over their failures wondering what they might have done differently. The responsibility for a human life is awesome and one not lightly accepted. Contrary to the cynic's views, physicians do care, and care passionately about their patients and their profession. One need only read the episodes in this book to realize the rich contributions that physicians bring to their profession and society. These examples are not rare. The American Medical Profession is a national treasure not to be squandered.

Physicians should hold their heads high, sustained by the knowledge they chose their profession because they wanted to, and that choice was motivated by a desire to advance knowledge, share that knowledge with others, and to serve those in need. Doctors must become increasingly aggressive in protecting their profession, their science and their patients. Patients should be confident that when they consult a physician they will receive the best that physician has to offer.

Mark Twain once wrote: "It haunts my sleeping and waking, other things leave me, but it abides." This is the glory of physicians. They have a proud heritage which they should preserve. Their profession is indeed a divine mistress not to be denied.

James S. Todd, M.D.
Chicago

Acknowledgments

First, I want to thank the many physicians, patients, and others who shared their personal stories with me. Their stories are the heart and soul of this book.

My publisher enthusiastically supported the idea of a realistic look at the world of medicine and at the many compassionate doctors who try to make a life-saving difference for their patients, often against great odds. The staff of Bonus Books did a masterful job of pulling everything together into a finished book.

AMA's Tom Sharpe and Wayne Hoppe have smoothly handled the many administrative details required for the organization's support of this book.

Finally, the chief executive officer of the AMA, James S. Todd, M.D., has not only supported this project but has also contributed a powerful foreword that should be required reading for anyone interested in the future of American medical care.

Introduction

As an AMA staff journalist, I have attended numerous conferences and conventions in which the medical topic of the hour has been debated for hour after hour by concerned physicians and other experts. Often, though, my mind would wander. Important as these topics are, ranging over the years from the quest for cost-containment to today's battle over health care "reform," the rhetoric soon proved wearisome and my thoughts turned to other questions:

What is it like, I wondered, to be a brain surgeon? A heart surgeon? A ghetto doctor? A cardiac-rehab specialist? An AIDS doctor? To be caught up in mankind's strongest emotions of life and death, sickness and health?

Those thoughts led to this book, which is an inside look at the real world of medicine. What I found are compassionate and highly skilled doctors trying to help and heal sick and quietly courageous patients, often against great odds. These real-life medical stories take many forms.

By scrubbing with surgeons and witnessing brain operations, coronary artery bypasses, and heart transplants, I have been able to describe first-hand the dramas of life and death that play out every day in the OR.

Interviews with physicians—and their patients—in the gritty inner-city neighborhoods of Chicago and Washington, D.C., reveal the health dangers created by black-on-black violence, poverty, and the uniquely sad problems of the sick homeless; and, yet, they also reveal how physicians and patients alike continue to hope and heal.

Visits to lung surgeons and cardiologists—and their patients—explain the health dangers we inflict on ourselves by smoking, overeating, under-exercising, enduring stress, failing to control high blood pressure and high cholesterol, and pursuing other bad habits; and, yet, they also report the good news of how many of us have been able to change destructive lifestyles and regain our health.

Candid conversations with AIDS doctors—and their patients—confront the epidemic in unsparing words and report not only the sobering disappointments in the search for a cure but also the individual stories of enormous compassion and courage.

An exploration of the world of epidemiology and public health—the agencies charged with safeguarding the nation's health—offers the inspiring stories of how an epidemic of disease among pregnant women was traced to tainted cabbage and stopped in its tracks; and how an epidemic of childhood deaths was largely prevented by one physician's crusade to enact legislation to require kiddie seat belts.

Not all these stories are about doctors. There is an interview with a doctor's wife, who candidly discusses the gains and pains of a medical marriage. There is the story of an adventurous couple—a nurse and her physician husband—who dared once too often when they tried to climb a Himalayan peak. A profile of an Omaha businessman who has used showbiz pizzazz and his own millions to fight the "fatting" of America and to educate the nation about the dangers of poor diets and high cholesterol—a combination that had caused his own near-fatal heart attack.

Fittingly, this book ends with a section on tomorrow's medicine—DNA, genetic therapies, and the dream of eventually curing cancer.

From rare exclusive interviews with legendary Nobelists James Dewey Watson and Francis Crick—the discoverers of the double helix structure of DNA, the stuff of genes and heredity—and from visits to the best and brightest of today's genetic researchers—the people who are building on Watson and Crick's seminal find in a historic search to map all human genes and to find the genes that cause specific diseases, there emerges a story of new hope:

Medicine may soon be able to identify patients at increased genetic risk for everything from alcoholism to skin cancer and to provide life-saving advance warnings. Beyond that, it may someday be possible to isolate the genes that cause specific diseases, like diabetes, and to treat the patient not with insulin but by replacing the defective gene. And to isolate the genes that cause specific cancers, like breast and colon cancer, and to design improved therapies, even cures, by preventing the cancerous transformation of these defective genes. That's the dream.

Tomorrow's medicine, like today's, is built upon a long tradition of education, research, and the sharing of ever-expanding knowledge. One of the stories in this book, about two young doctors who hit the beaches of France as part of the Allied invasion of Hitler's Europe on D-Day, June 6, 1944, notes that they carried with them small vials of penicillin, then an unknown drug. Today, penicillin and its many cousins, the so-called "wonder drugs," are old hat. Medicine marches on.

That's why Americans can by and large be very confident when they visit their doctors, an event that happens four million times every day. This book is a small slice of that real world of medicine.

Dennis L. Breo
Chicago

DRAMA IN THE OR

In Good Hands

Brain surgeon and laser pioneer Leonard Cerullo, M.D., operates the old-fashioned way—from the heart

She had never felt any unusual pain, as over the years the tumor deep within her skull had grown and grown. The brain, devoid of sensation and immune to pain, had accommodated the intrusive growth for as long as it could, sending out only minor symptoms: headaches, occasional unsteadiness, ringing of the ears and difficulty hearing in one ear.

The latest symptom, however, had been scary—double vision. Her passion in life is doing needlepoint, and now she found it impossible. Her family physician in Downstate Illinois had sent her to a nearby neurologist, who discovered the large tumor at the base of her skull. The brain had run out of accommodation. Additional growth would choke off the vital brain stem and cerebellum. The neurologist referred her to the neurosurgeon who is perhaps the best in the world at laser neurosurgery and the removal of brain tumors—Northwestern Memorial Hospital's Dr. Leonard J. Cerullo.

On Easter Sunday the patient, Margaret Wilson [a

pseudonym], 54, checked into Northwestern's Passavant Pavilion for preoperative examinations. Cerullo [pronounced "suh-RULL-oh"] was returning that evening from Venice, where he had chaired the annual meeting of the Laser Association of Neurosurgeons International. The 41-year-old surgeon had been out of the country—and out of the operating room—for four days now, and for him this is an eternity.

Monday night an anxious Margaret Wilson and her husband and sons await the surgeon's arrival.

"We're all in this together," Cerullo tells the family. "This is a very large tumor in a very dangerous location, and the surgery I will be doing is very serious business. I think that your tumor is benign, but it is in a very malignant location. I'm going to be operating in the posterior fossa, the cavity in the back part of the skull that contains the cerebellum, brain stem and cranial nerves 5 through 12. There are two kinds of risks: The general risks of anesthesia and undergoing any type of surgery and the specific risks of operating this deep in the brain. The possible side effects of this type of brain surgery include loss of hearing, loss of balance and coordination, eye problems, inability to taste, paralysis of the face, paralysis of one side of your body and death."

Margaret Wilson, a grandmother, says, "Well, I mustn't lose my coordination. I've got my needlepointing to do." With a smile, the surgeon says, "This is serious business, but I am optimistic. We can offer you the best of care and the benefit of doing much of the surgery with the laser. I believe that you can come out of this greatly improved." Then, patting her head, he adds, "I will see you tomorrow."

Cerullo will later explain: "This can be a very lonely calling. With patients, I hold back nothing. I give them all of me—body, brain and heart. I look them directly in the eye when I tell them about the risks, but I offer them hope because *I* am hopeful.

"My philosophy on procedures this difficult breaks down into three principles: If the patient wakes up doing the same as before, I am happy; if the patient comes out of surgery doing better, I am ecstatic; and if the patient wakes up for the worse, I am devastated. Totally, utterly devastated. My self-esteem is shot, and I feel as if I should have never been born. Certainly the patient would have been better off if he had never seen me.

"But fortunately, the bad cases are rare. I believe that Margaret Wilson is going to wake up okay."

Cerullo is optimistic because in the past 10 to 15 years there has been a technological revolution in neurosurgery, the medical field that specializes in disorders of the brain, spinal cord and nervous system. His career has coincided with the advent of new ways to look inside the brain, including computerized axial tomography [CAT] scans and magnetic resonance imaging [MRI], and new tools for operating within the brain, including the operating microscope, the bipolar coagulator, intraoperative ultrasonography, monitoring of brain functioning and, the latest tool, the laser. A neurosurgeon trained in the 1950s would be lost in today's operating room, which is why Cerullo spends much of the little free time he has conducting workshops for his colleagues on laser neurosurgery.

From 1930-1970 there was essentially nothing new in neurosurgery. During Cerullo's relatively brief practice, the field has been dramatically changed. "Today," he says, "we can offer much better results. When I started my training at Northwestern in 1970, I hated to go near the neurosurgical ward. The patients were often comatose or paralyzed. Today many are making full recoveries."

A superspecialist who concentrates on brain tumors, Cerullo has grown up in neurosurgery's "era of gentleness." He explains, "It may sound crazy, but it's only recently that we've realized that gentleness counts when you're working within the brain. And nothing is gentler than the laser."

A visionary, he feels that today's striking advances are crude compared to what is to come. He looks forward to the day when "lasers will make surgery obsolete. The emerging revolution in laser imaging and surgery is going to put the traditional surgeon out of business. Tomorrow's brain surgeon will be sitting in front of a computer monitor pushing buttons."

At the same time, he cautions that we are only "in the Stone Age" of understanding nature's unique creation, the human brain. The brain, which has evolved over 500 million years, is the size of a grapefruit, the weight of a head of cabbage, the shape of a cauliflower and one of the miracles of the universe. There are perhaps 100 billion neurons, or nerve cells, in the brain, and in a single human brain the number of possible interconnections between these cells has been estimated to be *greater than the number of atoms in the universe*.

It is this feat of engineering that allows Cerullo not only to perform brain surgery [a "left-brain" or task-oriented activity] but also to appreciate it and discuss it [a "right-brain" or contemplative activity]. He says, "To think that the brain evolved from a single cell and that today it can direct laser beams aimed at destroying tumors one cell at a time, well, it makes one a believer. The brain has evolved a little bit here and a little bit there over millions of years and, if anything, is certainly not unidirectional. It's always in a state of dynamic equilibrium, perhaps even dynamic tension. With all we know, the brain remains a black box."

Meanwhile, however, he will be lying awake this night, "rehearsing" the Margaret Wilson case. "On difficult cases," he explains, "I want everything to be perfect—the positioning of the head, the drapings, the incision. At night I will go over in my mind the angle at which I want to approach the tumor, the tools I will use, the surprises for which I have to be prepared."

His mornings never vary. At 6:05 a.m. an alarm goes off in his head. Dressing quickly in the dark so as not to disturb his wife, Cheryl, he throws on a shirt and suit and slips out of his large house in suburban River Forest. His socks are stuffed in his pocket and a tie thrown over his shoulder ["I never put on a tie until I'm through with surgery and about to visit with patients"]. Often he forgets the socks and tie, but no matter; his office at 676 N. St. Clair St., in the shadow of the Northwestern University Medical School complex, is well stocked with both. He wheels the Cadillac El Dorado convertible with license plates "CERULLO" onto the Eisenhower Expressway and heads toward the city. Either he will be listening to classical music or there will be total silence, as he listens to his thoughts. Most mornings he has no memory of making the drive.

By 6:30 he is in the office, sipping tea, dictating medical records and studying patient charts. At 6:50 he heads down the hall to take a shower. "I get my ideas at two times in the day," he says, "driving to work and showering at work." By 7:15 he is again seated at the large antique oak desk that dominates his office. Behind him is a wall covered with plaques attesting to the 15 years of college, medical school and residency required of a neurosurgeon. In front of him is a panoramic view of the medical school and the lakefront. He looks amazingly happy and relaxed as he sips a final mug of tea. At 7:22 it's, "Let's go. I'm anxious to get started."

With military precision and speed-walking tempo, the surgeon marches out of his office and proceeds one block to Northwestern's Olson Pavilion. It is 7:30, and it is time to check on Margaret Wilson.

Built in 1980, Operating Room 12, on the sixth floor of the Olson Pavilion, is equipped for state-of-the-art surgery. For Cerullo the OR is a stage, where daily he must put on high-stakes performances.

The pace, however, will be painstakingly slow. By 7:30 Margaret Wilson is already deeply sedated by general anesthesia. Her long black hair has been partially sheared to expose a 7-inch-square section of scalp at the back of her head. Two young neurosurgeons-in-training are methodically preparing her for surgery, while at the far end of the room Cerullo studies the X-rays. The patient is placed in a semisitting position, head upright, on the $50,000 operating table, and a three-point headholder, looking like ice tongs, is screwed onto her skull. Cerullo will be approaching the tumor from the right side, so her head is rotated 20 degrees to the right.

"Once the head is draped," Cerullo explains, "you lose all your landmarks. That's why this positioning is critical. The headholder looks gruesome, but it keeps her head immobilized and it will leave no scars." Neurosurgery requires a lot of hardware, so a $5,000 Budde halo retractor—resembling a circular serving tray—will be attached to the headholder, so that the retractors and other surgical "appliances" are readily at hand.

It is shaping up as a very difficult case. The tumor, located between the cerebellum and the brain stem, shows up on the X-rays within the cerebellopontine angle, the area at the back of the head through which pass cranial nerves 5 through 12. It is an area that Dr. Harvey Cushing, the father of modern neurosurgery, called "the gloomy corner of neurosurgery," referring to the devastating results that typically accompanied these surgeries during his era in the 1920s. As recently as 1970, when Cerullo began his neurosurgical training at Northwestern Memorial, the procedure to be performed on Margaret Wilson carried with it a better than 50-50 chance of significant loss of function following surgery.

Cerullo is studying three sets of X-rays: angiograms, which use an injection of dye to display the brain's arterial system; CAT scans, which show a cross-sectional view of brain-tissue density, distinguishing among tissue, fluid, fat and bone; and magnetic resonance imaging, which uses pulsing magnetic waves to measure water content and to present a cross-sectional view of the various brain structures.

The three sophisticated imaging techniques all show the same thing: a tumor the size of a baseball. On the CAT and MRI scans, the tumor shows up as a black ball; on the angiogram as a circular area that has displaced the surrounding blood vessels. The high-tech pictures, however, can tell the surgeon no more, not whether the tumor is benign or malignant, whether it is cystic [fluid-filled] or hard, or whether it is separate and self-contained or entwined with the delicate surrounding tissues. To answer these questions the surgeon must look for himself.

Every year there are 10,500 new cases of brain tumors in the U.S., and no two are exactly alike; each requires subtle differences in surgical technique. Half will be "primary" malignant tumors of the brain, and 20 percent will be metastatic, representing the spread of cancer from elsewhere in the body. Both present slim chances of cure. Of the 30 percent that are benign, one of every five will grow back, despite the best of care. The brain surgeon faces long odds.

Cerullo is guessing: "It's a large acoustic neuroma, which is a benign tumor originating from the sheath surrounding the eighth nerve [which controls hearing and balance]." He adds, "Think of it as a pear embedded in Jell-O. We're going to try to remove the pear without disrupting the Jell-O."

Meanwhile, the neurosurgical residents are scrubbing and painting Margaret Wilson's scalp with two coats of iodine antiseptic. Before the incision is made, a third protective layer, a plastic sheet impregnated with iodine, will be placed over her head, which is then draped. The coatings of iodine give the back of her scalp a surreal orange-yellow glow.

Two anesthesiologists are monitoring $100,000 in equipment that will warn them of any potentially fatal changes in body functioning, including an air embolism [or clot] that could move to the heart from the brain and shut off the heartbeat, an increased risk because her head is higher than her heart. Throughout the operation the primary noise will be the reassuring "whoosh . . . whoosh . . . whoosh" of the heart monitor, whose sound mimics the normal heartbeat. If the sound should turn to a gurgle, there will be alarms, bells, action. Two other technicians are monitoring a $40,000 machine that measures the electrical impulses of the brain. Should the wavy lines fall out of pattern, there also will be alarms, bells, action.

For hour after hour the patient will be in a twilight zone, somewhere between a deep sleep and a cessation of being, and the monitoring equipment is there to make sure her vital signs stay active. The patient looks very vulnerable: A tube inserted in her throat helps her breathe through a ventilator; her eyes are taped shut; a catheter helps her pass urine; Ace bandages are wrapped around her legs to prevent blood from accumulating.

Taking a sterile marking pen, chief resident Dr. Herb Engelhard traces a vertical line down the back of Margaret Wilson's scalp. Cerullo adjusts the line just a hair. The resident asks for the scalpel and begins the initial incision. The operation is under way. Another essential tool to Engelhard is his tape player. He asks for "something by Crosby, Stills and Nash."

The first step, cutting through one-quarter inch of scalp and muscle to expose the bone below, is time-consuming. The muscle must be stripped laboriously from the bone with an electric Bovie knife, invented in 1928 by Cushing's partner, W.T. Bovie. It is a procedure that is usually accomplished very methodically, in about 30 minutes. Today it presents an emergency.

Cerullo, dressed in surgical greens has been playing genial host, explaining to a group of medical students exactly what is going on in his OR. Adriana Holly, a fourth-year student who is considering a career in neurosurgery, has been admiring the textbook "elegance" of the incision. Suddenly, Engelhard nudges Holly to get the attention of Cerullo. Her voice comes softly but with a question: "Dr. Cerullo?"

The neurosurgeon turns around and sees that his resident is splattered with bright red blood. The opening of the scalp has been just enough to tilt a delicate balance of pressure and to rupture a stretched blood vessel. This bleeding is precisely the kind of unavoidable circumstance of which neurosurgeons must live in fear, and now it has happened.

For Cerullo this is the start of the case. "In the OR," he has said, "the surgeon sets the mood, and in my OR I want that mood to be one of calmness, confidence—and cooperation." He calmly tells the resident, "Here, Herb, you keep your finger in the dike. I've got to get ready for surgery."

Engelhard shuts off the bleeding by pressing the vessel between his finger and the skullbone. Meanwhile, Cerullo has gone to a sink in the hallway to begin scrubbing his hands with iodine, the traditional 8½-minute routine that both sterilizes the surgeon's hands and calms his mind. From inside OR 12, assistant neurosurgical resident Dr. Barry Pollack looks out at the brain surgeon, who is pumping his head back and forth as he vigorously rubs his hands together. "Cerullo," Pollack observes, "he does everything intensely. Look at the way he scrubs!" The surgeon will later explain, "What I'm doing out there is praying. I'm thanking God for my gift and I'm asking that everything will go well for the patient."

At 8:30 Cerullo steps in and tries to narrow or salvage the blood vessel. It is not to be, and as the surgeon struggles, a stream of blood shoots to the back wall, splattering Cerullo from his operating glasses to his surgical clogs. A scrub nurse appears nauseated.

For 10 minutes he will attempt to repair the vessel, but the tissue has given way. Instead, the vessel is sealed off with a series of metal clips. A bloodstained Cerullo leaves the OR to change into new surgical gowns, putting Engelhard back in charge of the preparatory steps. The blood vessel has been sacrificed, but in this case the surgeon is not concerned. "The brain, unlike the spinal cord," he explains, "has many redundancies, and this patient has enough collateral circulation to compensate without adverse effect for the loss of one vessel."

Meanwhile, Engelhard is beginning the second step of the operation, a two-stage procedure to remove a section of skullbone. For the first stage the normal tool is a $10,000 Smith-Peterson power drill that quickly powers through the one-quarter inch of bone and automatically stops short of hitting the less-resistant brain membranes below. However, this day, the power drill, one of two, is out of commission, and the other is being used next door in OR 8.

The resident will instead use a hand drill to slowly carve out "burr holes" in the bone. "This is great for the triceps," he observes, adding, "This part of the operation is carpentry and hasn't changed much in thousands of years, except for the advances in anesthesiology and monitoring."

[Thousands of years ago the Incas used sharp-edged metal instruments to cut open the skulls of people who were behaving strangely. These apparently cruel "trephinations" actually cured some people who were suffering from hemorrhages of the brain's membranes. By opening the skull, the primitive "surgeons" allowed the fluid to drain out, relieving the dangerous pressure. The miracle, as evidenced by analysis of recovered skulls, is that the patients did not die from infection. Interestingly, a study done decades ago found that 10 percent of all U.S. patients hospitalized with mental illness suffered from such untreated hemorrhages. Knowingly or otherwise, the ancient Incas—and Egyptians—were on to something.]

Engelhard continues his drilling, sealing the burr holes in Margaret Wilson's skull with bone wax, first used to prevent bleeding in

1892 by Britain's Sir Victor Horsley, a pioneer in neurosurgery. In the second stage of removing the bone, Engelhard will use a $20,000 Midas-Rex rotating saw to cut along a line from burr hole to burr hole, making possible the removal of a section of bone approximately two inches square. The bone is stored in saline solution until the end of the operation, when it is sutured back into place with nylon wire. Now a window of brain has been exposed, and only the membranes, a series of three outer envelopes covering the brain and formally known as the "meninges," stand between the surgeon and his target.

It is 9:15 when Dr. Engelhard takes a small pair of surgical scissors and, working with headlight and magnifying glasses, gently begins to peel back the dura mater [Latin for "hard mother"—the three brain meninges are collectively known in Latin as "mothers of the brain"] from the brain's other two layers—the arachnoid, named for its spider-weblike appearance, and the pia mater ["faithful or tender mother"], which adheres directly to the brain itself. Because the two bottom meninges are transparent, the stripping back of the dura will expose the brain itself. Upon this exposure, the right hemisphere of the cerebellum or "little brain" will be dramatically visible. Located beneath the larger cerebral hemisphere, it controls fine-motor skills.

The naked cerebellum is an awesome sight: The wondrous organ pulsates with life, quivering with each beat of the heart.

"Now that the stuff Herb would like to do is about to begin," assistant resident Pollack quips, "Dr. Cerullo will step in and do the challenging stuff." At 9:30 Cerullo sits down to the task at hand and begins what will become a marathon day. The music is changed to a classical recital by the Stuttgart Chamber Orchestra, but it may as well not be playing. For 10 hours Cerullo will be a solitary craftsman, intensely engaged in a battle of wills—his against the tumor's. Time stands still; there is nothing but the target.

The target is easy to see, and it is easy to see what had caused the bleeding. Margaret Wilson's tumor is everywhere—protruding from the cerebellum as an angry red-gray mass. Metal retractors costing $5,000 are used to gently push aside the cerebellum and allow the surgeon to work on the tumor.

The challenge will be to remove the entire tumor, "which has the consistency of carrot-cake," without hitting the cerebellum or the [out-of-sight] brain stem, the primitive "reptilian" brain that controls automatic functions like breathing and heartbeat, or any of the delicate nerves and vessels supplying these life-sustaining organs. The tumor must be teased out and removed from the cranial nerves with which it is entwined—cranial nerve 5 [controlling facial sensation], 6 [eye movement], 7 [eye movement and taste], 8 [balance and hearing] and 9, 10, 11 and 12 [swallowing, taste and the involuntary muscles of the heart, stomach, chest and intestines].

The surgeon will be dealing with fractions of a millimeter; the slightest slip can be disastrous. And now that he can see the enemy, he has the answers that the space-age imaging techniques could not give him: The tumor appears to be benign [only a biopsy can confirm this diagnosis], but it is indeed in a very dangerous location. It is not cystic [which would make things easier because when lanced, the tumor's fluid would wash away and the remaining tissue could be peeled away] but of a maddening consistency that defies a clean removal. It is not separate and self-contained [which would minimize risk to surrounding tissue] but has entwined and indented and insinuated itself with all the normal tissues.

For this case Cerullo needs the surgical tool that he himself has in the past seven years helped pioneer—the laser.

The laser sits beside him, looking humble enough—a mere console, one side linked to two ordinary pressurized tanks of carbon dioxide [CO_2] and nitrogen, the other side equipped with an arm articulated into seven segments and looking like a dentist's drill. But inside that console there works a miracle first conceptualized 75 years ago by the brain of Albert Einstein, who dreamed of "light amplification by the stimulated emission of radiation," a theory that today is wondrous reality, known by its acronym, laser.

Inside the console are two separate laser tubes—a carbon dioxide laser and a helium-neon laser. The CO_2 laser, a wavelength in the invisible range, is the "scalpel of light" that will do the cutting or, actually, the vaporizing; the helium-neon laser, which is visible and is similar to "pointers" used by lecturers, is focused to be coincident with the CO_2 laser. Its twinkling red pilot light guides the surgeon.

As the CO_2 atoms are stimulated by electrical energy, the electron revolving around the atom's nucleus of one proton and one neutron spins into outer orbit, traveling faster and faster. Then the excited electron is stimulated with a second and identical jolt of electrical energy. This second jolt stimulates the electron to give up its energy, emitted as a photon of light, and to return to a resting state. This process is multiplied many millions of times, the resulting photons being harnessed in the CO_2 laser tube and released as an amplified beam of light that is columnated [the light is in the shape of a column and has a direction], coherent [the waves are synchronous, existing in the same time and space] and monochromatic [one color on the electromagnetic spectrum]. The intense laser energy is then directed into the articulated arm, which has a series of seven mirrors arranged at 45-degree angles to reflect the beam. The arm delivers the unfocused beam to either a hand control, which looks like a fountain pen, or to a "joystick" bolted to the operating microscope. These controls enable the surgeon to focus the beam into a precise cutting tool. The CO_2 laser is brighter than sunlight, capable of zapping through steel and is easily absorbed by water. Given that the brain is 80 percent water, the CO_2 laser has become the laser of choice.

Northwestern Memorial's Cooper Lasersonic 870 CO_2 laser costs $120,000 and is the workhorse of Cerullo's practice. It is backed up by a $100,000 Molectron Nd:YAG laser [an acronym for neodymium, yttrium, aluminum, garnet], which is particularly useful in coagulating blood during small-vessel work. So new is the technology that a manufacturer's representative for the Nd:YAG is standing by should a question about the machine's operation or a malfunction arise.

In using the laser on Margaret Wilson's tumor, the neurosurgeon will also use the ceiling-mounted operating microscope, itself a device that came of age in the 1970s. The surgeon's entire work on Margaret Wilson's brain will be done within the confines of a ¾-inch-square surgical "window." But the $90,000 scope magnifies the view 25 times and presents it in three dimensions. Overhead, a TV camera shows the surgical opening, but it is little more than shadow and light compared to the magnified 3-D view the surgeon sees through his eyepieces. The scope's focus and all its other controls are built into a $50,000 operating chair, but, unfortunately, the focus on this scope is not working. Cerullo calls for a new chair, and within seconds nurses have wheeled in one that works.

The surgeon settles into his chair and moves up to the scope eyepieces. In his hand he holds the scope's joystick, resembling the controls used on airplanes and video games. He activates the laser with a foot pedal.

As Cerullo guides the beam with the joystick, his own brain must play tricks with reality. The CO_2 laser is invisible, but the helium-neon pilot laser indicates where the CO_2 laser is striking. But there is absolutely no tactile feedback, usually the surgeon's guide: Cerullo must imagine from what he sees exactly what the laser is doing.

Cerullo's brain is orchestrating four different notes on the laser: Controls on the console select laser wattage—1 to 80—and continuous or pulsing modes; the foot pedal controls the duration of the beam; a micromanipulator on one side of the joystick can focus the laser beam to target areas of tissue as small as 1/50th the thickness of a human hair—fine enough to vaporize one cell at a time; and a micromanipulator on the other side of the joystick adjusts the laser's impact zone, changing from a target of a few cells to a much wider area. The surgeon "unconsciously" works the various controls to get the effect his mind tells him is right. "With laser, what you see is what you get," he explains, "but it's a lot like programming a robot to shake hands. Too much and you'd break someone's hand; too little and the person would never feel it."

On the overhead TV, an observer can follow the movement of the pilot light, but it is difficult to understand what is happening. Tissue is being changed, but there is an eerie, other-worldly quality to it. One does not see the usual picture of tissue being manipulated—pulled and tugged and often traumatized.

Every time Cerullo presses the foot pedal and aims the laser beam, a cell—or many cells—of Margaret Wilson's tumor heat up past the boiling point and explode into gray vapor. Like magic, the tumor literally is disappearing. Because the CO_2 laser is easily absorbed by water, there is little danger of its being deflected onto normal tissue. And because it coagulates the tiny blood vessels it passes through, there is little risk of bleeding. The healing light can coagulate, vaporize and weld.

But the surgeon still cannot afford a false move. The laser can, if misdirected, just as easily burn through vital tissue or even, with devastating effect, strike through to the brain stem.

Laser neurosurgery is not a magic wand. The surgeon must be skillful and intensely vigilant. In Margaret Wilson's case, this vigilance will extend for hours, through three shifts of nurses, two shifts of anesthesiologists, two shifts of brain-monitoring technicians and two shifts of neurosurgical residents.

Cerullo alone will remain, glued to his operating scope [later he will apply a salve to the rub burns beneath his eyes]. For hour after hour he will battle the tumor with the tools of his trade—the CO_2 laser, the nonstick bipolar coagulator [refined at Northwestern to cauterize and control bleeding] and the suction aspirator. Alternately, he will burn off tumor, coagulate the tiny normal blood vessels nearby and suck up the blood, smoke and tissue. He later will tell Margaret Wilson that brain surgery requires some of the same attention to detail and concentration as needlepoint.

Some neurosurgeons criticize the use of laser because it offers no tactile feedback, chars the tissue [making it hard to tell tumor from normal tissue] and is slow—very, very slow.

Cerullo regards slowness as a virtue. "Gentleness counts," he says, "because all that pulling and tugging traumatizes normal tissue. Sure, there are other tools that can remove tumors more quickly, but that's not the touchstone. The touchstone is how long the patient will live afterward without adverse effect. I have an aunt who has been paralyzed for 40 years. She had a brain tumor and was operated on by one of the leading surgeons in the country. He used the accepted technique of the time—removal of the tumor with the index finger. The index finger! That's why I'm in this business, to try to get better results every time I operate."

A biopsy sample has been sent to pathology, and now a nurse's voice rasps over the intercom: "The sample is too charred and too small for definitive diagnosis. Can you send a larger sample?"

Cerullo takes another bite of the tumor. A half hour later the pathology report is returned: "Sample appears consistent with a tumor originating from the sheathing of the nerves."

The news is a boost: Margaret Wilson's tumor has been diagnosed as benign. Cerullo continues "burning and burning and burning." Engelhard observes that the tumor is "massive, simply massive." Cerullo is operating on laser power as high as 30 watts; the normal is 5 to 10.

At one delicate point the surgeon asks his anesthesiologist to adjust the mechanical ventilator [which breathes for the patient] "from a rhythm of 5 large breaths to 20 small ones." He explains, "The brain is pulsating too fast, and if the target moves too fast, it can be as disastrous as misdirecting the laser." As the ventilation rate is changed, the surgeon checks the brain-function monitor. "An advantage of the laser," he says, "is that you can monitor brain waves. The old tools knocked out the electrical signal required for brain monitoring."

During one brief respite, Cerullo observes that Latin was his favorite subject in high school and that it comes in handy in understanding the brain. "The limbic region," he explains, "governs the survival emotions of fight, flight, feeding and sexual desire. One area of this region is shaped like an arch; it's called the "fornix," which comes from the Latin word for arch or vault. In ancient Rome the ladies of the night lived in underground dwellings with vaulted ceilings. The Romans associated the vaults with passion and this part of the brain with passion."

At 4 p.m. the surgeon "hits the wall." The most intricate part of the surgery, unfortunately, comes toward the end of the day, when mental and physical fatigue cry out for relief. The 6-foot-2-inch Cerullo, who has been on a diet [dropping from 240 to 190 pounds within months], has eaten neither breakfast nor lunch. "Everybody's metabolism is different," he explains, "and I find that I get most fatigued when I have a heavy meal weighing down on me." But by 4 p.m. he is becoming irritable. He is both fatigued and mesmerized. He calls upon an unlikely tool—a saying of the late football coach Vince Lombardi: "Lombardi said, 'When the going gets tough, the tough get going,' and that's helpful to me." So is a glass of orange juice, which is brought to him by a nurse.

The surgeon must will himself through the final hours. "By 4 p.m.," he will later explain, "I could clearly identify all of the eight cranial nerves, as well as the brain stem and cerebellum, and I knew that I hadn't hurt her. One option was to close her up and leave the remaining tumor for the next morning, when I would be fresh. But I would hate to have my head opened up and have the surgeon quit before he'd gotten all the tumor. When I get to where I have to quit on an operation, I'll know it's time to quit. I want to get it all."

By 7 p.m. his goal is accomplished, but his prayers are still unanswered. "The best time for me," he says, "is when I'm on top of a challenging operation and everything appears to be going well. I'm all pumped up and I'm pushing both my personal limits and the limits of my equipment. The worst time is immediately after we close the skull. There's a limbo period before the patient wakes up, a gray zone of maybe 30 minutes when everything is out of your control. You've done your best, but the patient may still wake up devastated. The bad cases are all similar. There's unexpected bleeding or swelling or something else over which you have no control—maybe a blood vessel will spasm, or a nerve will be stretched too far and the opening of the head will have tipped the balance, or the patient will have a heart attack on the table, or an air embolism will block the flow of blood, or there will be a later infection and the brain will swell, or there will be an accident from the anesthesia. It only happens maybe once a year, but it's a terrible, lonely feeling."

For 12 hours some 23 medical professionals [all but the surgeon have a back-up] have worked on Margaret Wilson with $1 million worth of equipment; this one operation has cost $25,000, and yet for 30 minutes the outcome is still in doubt.

But this night the prayers will be answered. Margaret Wilson wakes up and though still groggy looks slowly around her. Cerullo gives her a few hand signals, and she is able upon command to move her eyes, arms and legs. He helps her off the operating table and "slides" her to a nearby gurney, which will wheel her to intensive care. "Move over here," the physician says. "You're going to be fine." Margaret Wilson whispers, "Thank you, doctor."

Cerullo is ecstatic: "A patient cannot do any better than that. In difficulty, this procedure is a '10,' and she came out of it with everything intact. She looks groggy now, but she's cured, normal. Maybe a month from now, she'll have a slight headache or two and need some aspirin. That's it, though. Ten, 15 years ago, when I began my training in neurosurgery, a case like this very likely would have caused loss of hearing or difficulty in swallowing or facial numbness or paralysis. Today she's home free. She'll never know what almost hit her, and in no time she'll be back to her needlepointing."

The surgeon doesn't "celebrate" happy results like this, but he is clearly on a high. "Good results are to be expected," he says, "so I try not to get too excited. It's the bad cases that stir me up."

Typically, after Margaret Wilson's case, he would have unwound with his partner, neurosurgeon J. Thomas Brown, over a beer or two at Tiff's, the corner cafe across from his office. But on this night he is late for a celebration of Brown's 42d birthday.

All afternoon outpatients had been stacking up in Cerullo's waiting room as he kept instructing the surgical nurse to inform his office that he would be delayed, first an hour, then another, then a third—until finally he had the appointments rescheduled. The party, too, is pretty much over by the time Cerullo arrives, stylishly dressed in a light-gray glen-plaid suit, pink foulard tie and braces ["Until a few years ago I never owned a suit. So now my wife buys all my clothes"]. He and his partner take a few minutes to dissect their days.

Tom Brown is one of the few people who understands.

Earlier that day Cerullo's wife had left with their three young daughters for a visit back East. The departure seemed an opportune time to have tradesmen refinish the dining-room floor. So Cerullo's house is off limits for a few days.

This prevents him from indulging in his only real relaxation—cooking at home. Typically, he will unwind after a long day in the OR by whipping up a special pasta for his wife. Weekends—unless emergencies arise—are reserved for his family; the brain surgeon, dressed in his favorite jeans and cowboy boots, will broil steaks in the back yard. "The only drawback to my work," he says, "is the time it takes from my family."

This night he will adjourn to the nearby Barclay Hotel for dinner. He will go to sleep after alternately reading Elmore Leonard's "Glitz" ["for escapism"] and Christopher Marlowe's Elizabethan poetry ["for perspective"]. The next day's surgical schedule is "light," but he will awaken in the middle of the night to brainstorm on Thursday's case, which is another suspected acoustic neuroma, one that could, perhaps, also last 12 hours or more.

Time is . . .
Too slow for those who wait,
Too swift for those who fear,
Too long for those who grieve,
Too short for those who rejoice
But for those who love, time is eternity.

—Henry Van Dyke

Cerullo majored in English literature in college, specializing in the Elizabethan poets. He became a brain surgeon in a quirky, roundabout way, but once involved in the profession, he has had an unwavering devotion to improving it, to getting better medical results.

The above verses by the American clergyman and poet are inscribed on the inside cover of an unlikely volume—"Operative Neurosurgery," a textbook published in 1968 that includes detailed instructional drawings on removing hard brain tumors with the index finger. Cheryl Cerullo, a former nurse, understands her husband's drive for perfection; in 1973, shortly after their marriage, she knowingly inscribed the poem on the how-to manual.

He grew up in Hazleton, Pa., the middle child of a large tri-generation Italian family. There were 11 Cerullos living in adjoining houses, including his parents, an older sister, a younger brother, his grandmother and grandfather, three spinster aunts and a great-uncle. His mother had seven sisters and one brother, his father four brothers and six sisters. He grew up "comfortable," but Hazleton, a coal town near Scranton, has since fallen on hard times, a result of the decline of the anthracite mines. Today the leading source of income in the town is Social Security.

"I was spoiled in one sense," he recalls. "I never had a baby-sitter who was not a member of the family and I never had to eat a peanut-butter-and-jelly sandwich. We were a very close and very loving family. In a way, though, I never felt truly American. My father's parents barely spoke English. At Thanksgiving and Christmas we never had turkey; we ate ravioli."

His parents had met at the Hazleton General Hospital emergency room. "Mother was an ER nurse, and Father brought in a friend for treatment. That's how their romance started."

The future Dr. Cerullo developed a love of learning and a love of reading, but he has no idea of his inspiration. "I don't think my father ever read a book in his life, and my mother was not much of a reader, either. Actually, the educated one in the family was one of my aunts, who was a nursing educator.

"We were never pushed to make good grades, but we were expected to work hard. That's because my father worked hard to build up businesses, first in electrical supplies and later in household appliances. I guess the message I got was, 'Whatever you do, work hard and do it right!'" His sister, Carol, has been married for 25 years, has six kids and "still acts as a foster mother for children who are waiting to be adopted. She has two foster kids in her home right now and is anxious to take a third. She just loves children." His brother, John, "is the bright one in the family. He has a Ph.D. in history, teaches at the University of New Hampshire and does film criticism for a Boston radio station."

Leonard Cerullo was a late bloomer. In high school he made good grades, was elected class president and starred in class plays. His favorite subject was Latin; he quit football "because I was too slow." He never thought of being a doctor: "I hated the smell of carbolic acid, and the hospitals of those days reeked of it." Also, there was the matter of his invalid aunt, the one who became paralyzed after her brain tumor was removed with a finger. She later had to be institutionalized.

He enrolled at Georgetown University for no better reason than that his cousin ["the other bright one"] was studying chemistry there and told him that all the boys "dressed in elegant navy blazers." He explains, "I just thought that sounded very cool—a navy blazer—so I applied to Georgetown." He also knew that it was a Jesuit school and "at that time I was thinking of maybe going into the priesthood." He adds, "Georgetown is the only college to which I applied. If they hadn't accepted me, I'd probably still be working for my father in appliances."

At Georgetown he became lovesick over the girl he'd left behind in Hazleton; the popular former class president became a recluse, taking refuge in Elizabethan poetry and lifting weights—"both solitary pursuits." He snapped out of it in time to earn a 3.2 grade-point average and to begin thinking about medical school.

He explains, "I had forgotten about the priesthood—in fact, I almost forgot about religion for a while there—and I began taking pre-med courses. The flip reason I give for wanting to be a doctor is that the students in the white lab coats seemed to get all the girls. The real reason, I suspect, is that I wanted to be independent, to be my own man.

"I've always seemed to be in the right place at the right time, and in 1966, when I graduated from Georgetown, the medical schools were looking for the well-rounded student, not the nerd. With my major in poetry and minor in philosophy, plus some last-minute pre-med courses, I was able to get into Thomas Jefferson Medical School [in Philadelphia]."

That summer, however, as a college graduation gift, his parents offered him a new car or summer school in Japan. He studied Japanese literature that summer and returned in the fall to Hazleton to find all his medical-school books waiting. "After a summer of studying literature," he says, "the medical texts seemed alien to me. I was sure I had made a mistake, but I decided to give it a try, anyway."

He was sure he would never be a surgeon, though, "because I hated the blood and guts. I decided I wanted to study the mind, not the matter, so I chose to specialize in psychiatry. Unfortunately, the psychiatrist who was my faculty adviser abandoned his wife to run off with a secretary, and somehow this didn't strike me as responsible behavior.

"Then, by mistake, I got into neurosurgery. Since I had given up on psychiatry, I figured that neurology was my next best bet, so I chose as my new faculty adviser a physician who I thought was a neurologist. He turned out to be a neurosurgeon and one of the most important role models in my life. Dr. Robert K. Jones was everything I admired—cooperative, gentle, intellectual, quiet, reserved. He was also a terrific neurosurgeon. Despite my Jesuit training in logic, I made an illogical but lucky assumption: I extrapolated from the man to the specialty. I figured that if Dr. Jones was this terrific, then all neurosurgeons must be terrific. In point of fact, many of the neurosurgeons of that period were arrogant, overbearing—and often stupid. They all had big egos and would scream and throw things. But I had worked in the lab with Dr. Jones and I was hooked.

"I don't know what he saw in me. I guess I was a *tabula rasa*—a blank tablet upon which he could inscribe his plan. At the beginning I didn't even know how to knot a suture. Dr. Jones said, 'Here, tie this.' I replied, 'I don't know how.' He said, 'Tsk, tsk, Cerullo. [William] Halsted [a famous American surgeon] would turn over in his grave.' I began practicing tying knots at night and became pretty good at it. Dr. Jones decided that if I were to become a neurosurgeon, I must study under Paul Bucy [since-retired but then regarded as one of the world's premier neurosurgeons] at Northwestern.

"In 1970 I picked up my M.D. and headed for Chicago." His luck was still holding. "One of the big divides in life," he says, "is going from being a medical student to being a real doctor. Suddenly nurses—and others—begin to treat you as a desirable product."

Balding since age 16, the young Dr. Cerullo grew a mustache ["it seemed cool"] and moved into Northwestern's new living quarters for interns—the remodeled Carriage House hotel. "I had been told that interns lived in hovels and existed on dog food," the physician recalls, "and here I was living with maid service on the Gold Coast!"

He returned briefly to Philadelphia to rejoin Dr. Jones and to study general surgery for one year at Lankenau Hospital. He also met nurse Cheryl Weir and persuaded her to become his wife. Returning to Northwestern in 1972, he spent the next five years learning to become a neurosurgeon, taking side trips to Paris to study skull-base surgery and to New York City to study neurosurgical imaging techniques.

The specialty "was just beginning to change from crudity to gentleness when I was in training," he says. "My wife has only seen me operate once, and that was in 1973. Once was enough because it was pretty gross. Cheryl was a nurse then at Northwestern, and one day I was scheduled to do a procedure. She thought she'd drop by to see me perform some 'delicate neurosurgery.' Well, the patient had fallen into a coma and slipped under a radiator. His entire scalp tissue had been destroyed, and I had to remove the entire outer table of his skull [leaving intact the bone marrow and inner table]. My tools were a hammer and chisel, and it took almost all day. The operation was a lot like chiseling a marble sculpture. Today we'd use a high-speed drill and be done in an hour or two. The man survived, but Cheryl was not impressed, and she's never been back."

Having long since given up the hammer and chisel, Cerullo today is at the peak of his surgical powers, hoping to be able "to hold the edge for at least another 10 years." He got interested in lasers out of necessity ["I knew there had to be a better way"]. Now he wants to hold on as long as possible but fears, "General surgeons can do gall bladders until they're 80, but I don't see myself keeping this up past 55. Brain surgery requires tremendous emotional, mental and physical stamina and involves the highest degree of risk of any medical procedure."

In short, being a brain surgeon is an awesome responsibility, and in many of the cases success is impossible.

Engelhard notes, "In neurosurgery you have to work long, long hours under intense pressure. The residents [there are 12 at Northwestern, training under 7 neurosurgeons at Children's Memorial, the Veteran's Administration, Evanston and Northwestern Memorial hospitals] are on call 24 hours a day, 7 days a week. I typically work 12 to 16 hours a day, 7 days a week. I'm in my sixth year of training since receiving the M.D. and I make $25,000."

Engelhard adds, "Many women get their idea of doctors from the soap operas, and when it gets down to the nitty-gritty, they can't take it and they cut out. It takes a special woman to stay with a neurosurgeon.

"And in my case there won't be a lot of money in the near future. After my residency, I want to do research into the cause of brain tumors—I suspect that environmental carcinogens are a key factor—but we really know very little. We spend a fortune on high-tech treatment and almost nothing on basic research. I'm having trouble finding even modest funding." He adds, "We see a lot of sadness in the OR, but that's what much of medicine is about—disease and dying. Once you accept that, you can get on with it. Actually, surgery is the most curative of all the medical specialties."

In Cerullo's case the payoff is well into six figures a year, but he notes, "When I completed my seven-year residency in 1977, I joined the Northwestern faculty at only $40,000 a year. That figure went up only about $10,000 a year until I went into private practice in 1981 [he was acting chairman of the division of neurosurgery at NU from 1984 until April]." He believes he earns his money.

A major stress is the occasional bad result, like the one he suffered just a few weeks before Easter. "This lady had a tumor similar to Margaret Wilson's. We had just opened the arachnoid membrane when there was a terrible hemorrhage elsewhere in the brain. Immediately we had to redirect the scope and everything else to try to identify where the damage was coming from.

"It's a lot like digging for a body after an avalanche. I'm digging and digging with the bipolar and the suction, but the brain is bleeding and swelling, and the digging is devastating the brain stem. I finally stopped the bleeding, and I removed the tumor, but after we closed, she had a bout of swelling. That did her in. I had to tell the family—this was a Hispanic woman, and there were 16 relatives in the room—that my patient's brain waves were flat.

"I hope that that's my bad case for 1986 and 1987. One thing I've never learned is how to cope with a bad result. I take it very personally. I guess I just let it take its piece of me. Let it take its piece and try to muster the courage to go on. The next morning I'll be a little gun-shy and I'll have to proceed very cautiously to rebuild my confidence.

"Over the years I've had a good dozen cases that have taken their piece. Usually I go off by myself and cry. Cheryl and I never discuss surgery at home, but when I've had a bad case, she knows. People think that the brain surgeon is some kind of strange beast, but we're very human. Just like anybody else, I have up days and down days, marvelous times with my wife and arguments with my wife."

He adds, "No one loves their neurosurgeon. People love their family physician or their pediatrician or their gynecologist, but nobody loves the neurosurgeon. If we cure them, they go away, and we never hear from them again. And if we don't cure them, we hear about it in unpleasant ways."

Another major stress is the possibility of a lawsuit, merited or otherwise. The threat of a malpractice verdict hangs over the heads of high-risk surgeons like smog hangs over Los Angeles. Cerullo believes that actual medical malpractice is rare; he attributes the problem "to the fact that people do not want to believe that accidents *do* happen. Or, even if they believe it is an accident, they want someone to pay for it."

He has been sued four times, about the norm for surgeons in high-risk specialties, and he pays $86,000 a year for partial protection. "One guy was bleeding to death on the table," he says, "and I brought him back. I left a sponge inside this man's back, but, hell, I would have left a kitchen sink! I couldn't stop the bleeding. Later I removed the sponge, and he's doing fine, but he sued anyway. In a second case, I performed a spinal-cord procedure to try to arrest a woman's relentless progress toward quadraplegia. Unfortunately, the procedure could not help and actually accelerated the progress. It was a risk that had to be taken, but she sued anyway. In the other two cases, the patients sued everybody connected with their cases.

"One of these suits is asking more in damages than I have in insurance. In theory, the patient could attack my personal property if I'm found negligent. So I would not only lose the case, I would also lose my house and my car and my swimming pool. Sure, when you hit the wall at 4 p.m. on a difficult case, these kinds of thoughts are in the back of your head. Not only, 'Will I lose the patient?' but, 'Will I lose my house?' That's why I've transferred my assets to my wife. But that's emasculating, and I'm not sure it would stand up anyway. [All four cases are pending.]

"But you have to override these kind of fears. You have to continue to do what you do best. The only things that can stop you are laziness and fear of failure.

"My entire purpose in life is tied up in brain surgery. I've never been out of surgery for more than 13 days, and the last time I went that long I felt I had to cut short a Caribbean vacation to get back to the OR. When I'm on vacation, I take a stack of books up to my knees. I guess I'm not good with free time, and the best way I can release the tension that builds up is to get back into surgery."

Having the Elizabethan man as his ideal, Cerullo still worries that "I am well-read but I am not well-rounded. A photographer looking for photos around the house asked me if I rake the leaves, if I putter in the garden, if I fix up the house. I had to answer 'no' to everything. I just don't have the time. Even with the pool, I don't swim; I just jump in and splash around for a while."

His one other relaxation is acting. This summer Cerullo for the second time will star in a play about Ernest Hemingway presented by Oak Park's Synergy Players. Hemingway is one of his heroes. He says, "All that talk about Hemingway being a bully and a drunkard. He was a very sensitive man with very deep feelings; otherwise he never could have written the way he did." In talking about Hemingway, Cerullo is also describing himself. Occasionally, he muses about "going to law school or opening a restaurant when I'm too old for this." But then again, he says, "I'm not so sure that I'll ever be able to leave surgery."

In early April there were at least three other patients who can be grateful that Cerullo continues to operate:

- A woman experiencing double vision was discovered to have a benign tumor wrapping around her carotid artery and optic and third nerves, putting her at high risk of stroke and blindness. After five hours in OR 12, she was cured. The CO_2 laser had vaporized the tumor, the size of a large marble, without damaging the nerves or artery. "She and her husband have invited me over for dinner," an exultant Cerullo reports.

- A middle-aged La Salle Street executive was terrified when told he had an acoustic neuroma the size of a large plum. The patient was suffering from loss of taste and severe nausea and vomiting [which had caused him to lose 20 pounds] and loss of balance, coordination and hearing. He was admitted to the medical ward, given a CAT scan that revealed the tumor and scheduled for surgery. The night before, Cerullo recalls, "He was terrified, as was his wife." The surgeon was braced for an all-day procedure with the laser, one that conceivably would have to be done over two days, requiring the patient's skull to be opened and closed twice. Instead, upon surgical examination, the tumor was found to be almost entirely cystic, and the laser was not needed. Cerullo burst the cystic tissues with conventional cutting tools, and by noon the case was successfully closed. Cerullo concludes, "His hearing has returned. He'll be able to walk normally, and he'll be able to regain that weight—if he wants to." The grateful patient recently returned to give a talk about his surgical experience to Cerullo's medical students, who normally spend their time "memorizing a telephone book every other week."

• An elderly man who was having trouble walking because of pressure on the spinal cord bounced back after a two-hour cervical laminectomy accomplished with the freehand CO_2 laser [in which the surgeon does not require the operating microscope; the laser is aimed by a device that looks like a fountain pen]. Cerullo says that in general the laser "makes possible 'dry surgery,' with much less bleeding, and this is an important factor today because of the fear of AIDS [for the patient from transfusions, and for the surgical team from a patient's infected blood]." The laser quickly made the incision down to the spinal cord, where other cutting tools were used to remove the bony spurs causing the problem.

After the drama of brain surgery, Cerullo's outpatient visiting hours seem tame. There are two patients with broken necks, and both are healing fine with braces. One, a young man who broke his neck skiing, has made a remarkable recovery and is now concerned that the doctor won't vouch that he needed to take an ambulance from Madison, Wis., to Chicago. Otherwise, the insurance won't pay. "Of course, I'll approve it," the physician says. "What did they expect you to do, walk?" The next patient, a woman, is fully recovered from a severely sprained back and now wants to take a vacation—skiing! Cerullo says, "Well, I can only advise, but why not the beach?"

A male patient, who appears healthy as a bull, is concerned about "a deficit in his little finger." The doctor thinks that the complaint of numbness is of little consequence. The man persists. Cerullo counters, "Well, we can admit you, put you in traction for a week and try heat and massage . . ." The man agrees to "give it a little more time." The next patient, a single woman who has just turned 40, literally has a "pain in the neck," which she ascribes to "carrying in one hand a $20 bag of groceries once a week for seven years from the supermarket to my apartment." The physician thinks that more likely the problem is a vicious cycle of emotional stress and muscle tension, the resulting wear and tear upon the spinal cartilage and pain—all accompanied by an incipient midlife crisis. He does admit *her* for a week of traction. "If you don't break the cycle now," he tells her, "you may end up needing surgery, and I'd like to avoid that." A psychiatric consultation is also scheduled.

An elderly lady with severe trigeminal neuralgia, an excruciating pain that shoots through the face, is dubious about taking the cure—surgery to deaden the facial nerve. This is her third visit. "It's your decision," he says. "You have to feel comfortable with it." She demurs, "Well, it feels okay now, but yesterday . . ." Knowing that the pain is akin to being electrocuted—several times a day—he asks her how she can stand it. "I can't," she concedes. The surgery, a routine procedure, is scheduled. The next patient, a workman's compensation case, has already had surgery for trigeminal neuralgia and is on partial disability for facial numbness. Claiming that his pain remains despite the heavy use of pain-killers, the man insists he needs another operation and a higher classification of disability. Cerullo routinely orders a medication check, which reveals that traces of the eight pills the patient claims to have taken this very day are not to be found in his blood. "These workman's comp cases," the physician exclaims, "they're very unrewarding."

The next patient, however, will galvanize his attention. The man, 52, "has never been sick a day in my life. Never even take aspirin, Doc. I just played four sets of tennis yesterday." He is there because that morning he awoke with blinding headaches, the kind medication cannot relieve. His wife is with him. Cerullo slaps the large plastic CAT scans [from a neurological exam that morning] against the lightboard and points to a dark mass in the middle. "This," he says, "is a tumor, and it has to come out. The crescendo nature of your headaches and the fact that they are posturally related—worse when you lie down—lead me to believe that your case is unstable. We need to move quickly. I'm recommending surgery—tonight or tomorrow."

It is 5 p.m., and the patient is stunned by the significance of the physician's words and the suddenness of his own crisis. He hesitates, "Well, this is a big decision. I need a second opinion." The doctor replies, "You don't have time. You need to be in intensive care. One more straw and you can go into seizure, fall into a coma and die." The man concedes that he did feel a little funny playing tennis and had, unusually, lost all four sets. His wife tugs at his sleeve. "Honey, you're going into the hospital." Their previous medical concern, her planned hysterectomy, is put on hold. Cerullo explains that the tumor appears benign and that the chances of full recovery are excellent. The next morning at 7:30, less than two days after playing four sets of tennis, a very lucky man is wheeled into brain surgery. He will come out again able to play tennis—winning tennis.

In reflecting on his job, Cerullo observes, "You've only seen a slice of neurosurgery. You haven't seen any vascular disorders. Or aneurysms. Or serious spinal-cord cases. Or malignant tumors. Or trauma, though last weekend I was called to the OR to treat a man who had fallen down an elevator shaft. We opened his skull, and his brain spilled out from the swelling. There was nothing to be done."

Operating almost every day he is in town, Cerullo will in a year perform 400 to 500 surgeries [2 or 3 on some days]. Two-thirds of these operations involve tumors, the overwhelming majority in the brain, and half of these brain-tumor cases will be treated with the laser. More than half of such cases come from out of state, as his reputation is widespread. By now he has operated on almost 1,000 brain tumors, "and each one is different." Of the nation's 500,000 physicians, only 2,800 are brain surgeons [fewer than 100 are in the Chicago area]; a population of at least 100,000 is required to justify one general neurosurgeon. However, a neurosurgeon who specializes only in tumors, as Cerullo would like to do, needs a population base of at least 7 million, the entire Chicago metropolitan area.

He strongly believes that neurosurgeons "should super-specialize. My specialty is operating with the laser on deep brain tumors, and I would like to do nothing but that. It would be fine with me if some other brain surgeon did all the aneurysms in the country. The operations are so difficult that you have to specialize."

Prepaid health plans, with their emphasis on cost-control are a special aggravation. "An ophthalmologist friend of mine," he says, "examined a woman who was losing her vision. He suggested a CAT scan. Her health maintenance organization [HMO] wouldn't allow it because if the scan is negative, the HMO loses money on her case. A year later, she comes back, and her vision is even worse. The ophthalmologist insists that she have the CAT scan, even offers to pay for it himself. She waits another six months before finally paying for her own CAT scan. It shows a tumor pressing on the optic nerve, and by now much of her loss of vision is irreversible. I think that this kind of penny-wise and pound-foolish reasoning is obscene. Let's say that there's a patient in California with an acoustic neuroma and he's referred to me by another physician. Well, chances are that if he's in an HMO, he's going to have to see Joe Blow across the street for the operation. He's not going to have an option to look for a superspecialist."

Cerullo thinks that the medical super-specialist of the future will be an expert in lasers and physics, as well as in medicine. So-called "superlasers" will revolutionize medicine, he predicts.

Ecclesia abhorret a sanguine.
["The Church is opposed to the letting of blood."]
—The Edict of 1163

During the Middle Ages, in the shadow of the Church's disapproval, surgery was taken up as a trade by unschooled practitioners, often barbers or others of low rank. As recently as the turn of this century, the results of brain surgery were so alarmingly bad and the mortality rates so high [much in excess of 50 percent] that most surgeons had given up on intracranial operations. Less than 80 a year were performed in 1900. The dying specialty was rescued by Dr. Harvey Cushing, who in the 1920s used meticulous techniques and electrocautery to reduce bleeding and bring mortality rates down to an acceptable risk. The widespread use of bone wax and refinements in X-rays also helped, and in 1931 the nation's neurosurgeons formed the Harvey Cushing Society [since renamed the American Association of Neurological Surgeons, which is headquartered in Park Ridge].

By the turn of this century, Cerullo believes, "The modern OR will be fully automated, and the brain surgeon, like an airline pilot, will be sitting at an instrument panel, programming a computerized laser attack upon diseased tissues."

His hope springs from the same research breakthrough that has brought us President Reagan's "Star Wars" defense initiative, namely the "free-electron laser" or FEL.

This experimental laser was invented by California physicist John Madey, who dreamed up the idea that free electrons—those not bound to a specific atom—could be fired from a particle accelerator and forced to "wiggle" through a variable series of magnets to create an infinite variety of powerful laser beams. The idea came to him, naturally, while taking a shower. The military has been authorized \$20 billion over the next five years to use the new laser technology to pinpoint enemy targets. For medicine less than 1 percent of the \$20-billion total, some \$40 million, has been authorized to target diseased tissue at six leading medical centers: Northwestern, Harvard University, the University of California at Berkeley, Stanford University, the University of Utah and the University of the Uniformed Military Services in Bethesda, Md. Cerullo directs the Northwestern program through Chicago's Midwest Bio-Laser Institute.

Currently there are only eight lasers with clinical usefulness in medicine. There are five whose wavelengths are in the visible spectrum—argon, krypton, helium-neon, gold-copper vapors and the argon-pumped dye. The other three are invisible—CO_2, Nd:YAG and excimer.

Using the FEL, researchers can search for laser wavelengths across the entire electromagnetic spectrum. Because there is a different wavelength along the spectrum at every nanometer [one-billionth of a meter], there is, in theory, an infinite number of new laser wavelengths that may have clinical significance.

"Practially speaking," Cerullo says, "the technology right now is wishful thinking. But I believe that in the next 10 to 15 years we will be able to find many new laser wavelengths that will fight disease. The surgeon is limited only by his imagination. First, we have to find the new wavelengths; then we have to find which ones have clinical usefulness.

"The new lasers will improve both imaging and therapeutic techniques. Some wavelengths will make parts of the human body as transparent as a goldfish. Some wavelengths will be able to melt away tumors. Right now our X-rays, including the CAT scans, are very primitive, a medley of different wavelengths. The CAT scan is like a sledgehammer compared to a single beam of laser light that may be able to X-ray parts of the body. The difference between a CAT scan and the new laser imaging will be like the difference between a standard photo taken in room light and a 3-dimensional hologram, which is made of pure light from lasers.

"In terms of therapy, we believe that it may be possible to find wavelengths that are specifically targeted to the cellular subparticles where disease originates. The problem with cancer is that once a cell begins to grow crazily, it cannot shut itself off; the new lasers, pulsing at billionths of a second, may be able to turn the cancerous cells off. And genetically engineered chemicals that are attracted to cancer or other diseased cells could be tagged with laser-sensitive toxins. By shining laser light throughout the body, the toxins would be turned on to kill the disease while sparing healthy cells. We may have different wavelengths to treat different diseases."

Conceding that he is a romantic racing ahead of the scientific rubric of his time, Cerullo muses: "I firmly believe that by the year 2000 we will be able to melt away an acoustic neuroma like the one Margaret Wilson had without opening the skull. The patient will be an outpatient, with fiber-optic imaging lasers attached to her head like hair curlers, and the physician will sit at a computer console, pushing buttons to direct lasers to silently pass through the skull and melt away the tumor. When this happens, the surgeon had better have a more delicate mind than hands! Here's my dream: Wouldn't it be ironic if, just as we study the skulls left by the Incas, many decades from now our survivors will look at skulls like those of Margaret Wilson and marvel at how primitive brain surgery was in 1986!"

Intensive Caring

Renée Hartz, M.D., who grew up as the daughter of a Michigan miner, is now saving lives as a top heart surgeon

She is a mover and doer, always on the go, but sitting in her office this day in the Northwestern Memorial Hospital complex, Dr. Renée Hartz is lost in thought as she ponders a question:

How did she, one of seven children of a poor miner and a waitress in a dying mining town in Michigan's Upper Peninsula, find happiness as one of the outstanding heart surgeons in the United States?

"Oh, at one time I might have been happy as a hairdresser or ski bum," she muses, "but I guess I always knew there was something more out there, a whole new world. But the problem was, you see, I never thought I was particularly bright." Nevertheless, Hartz, who is 42 but asks, "Can't you please say I'm around 39?" used her native talents and remarkable persistence to transform herself from a waitress into the *only* woman heart surgeon in the nation who has academic tenure at a major university medical center.

She was born Renée Semo, the second oldest of

Rita and Rudy Semo's five daughters and two sons. The grandparents were immigrants from the Czechoslovakia-Yugoslavia border and Poland, and she was raised to work hard. "I think I've always been driven," she says with a sigh. She ranked 7th of 200 students in her graduating class at the public school in Ironwood, Mich., population 10,000, but thought that "the bright kids were the ones who finished 1-2-3."

She left Ironwood to attend college at Western Michigan in Kalamazoo for no better reason than that a former boyfriend was there. For that matter, she had earlier transferred out of Ironwood's Catholic high school because a priest threatened to expel her for holding hands with her steady boyfriend on the school's campus. "The environment was stifling," she recalls. "I mean, I bought this beautiful strapless prom dress, and the school made me sew sleeves on it!" At Western Michigan, she acquired a degree in biology, graduating magna cum laude, but still might have returned to the Upper Peninsula had not her older sister, Rita, been living in Aurora and had not a college boyfriend relocated to Chicago. The day her life changed is a vivid memory:

"I had been living with my sister in Aurora and trying without success to get a job as a lab technician at Argonne National Laboratory [in Lemont]. One day, reading the ads, I saw that the Northwestern Medical School needed lab technicians. I drove into Chicago from Aurora and got lost going the wrong way on Lake Shore Drive, but the minute I got untracked and found the Northwestern [downtown] campus, I fell in love. It was a gorgeous day in July with the sailboats out on the lake, and I was hooked. I was hired as a technician to work on a research project involving the immune system, and I was fascinated. Through the school's bulletin board, I found a female roommate, and we moved into an apartment in New Town, which was then the trendy area. I'll never forget the day I moved in—July 14, 1969, the day our astronauts walked on the Moon! I had great expectations."

It is nearly 20 years later, and she is jolted from her reverie by her beeper. A patient has just been taken to the hospital's "cath lab" for an emergency angioplasty, a procedure to unclog arteries that supply the heart with oxygen. A balloon-tipped catheter, or tube, is threaded through a blood vessel in the arm or groin and directed to the area of blockage. The balloon is then inflated so the blockage is squeezed against the artery wall, enlarging the opening and restoring the life-sustaining flow of blood. It is a fast and painless alternative to open-heart surgery, but it does not always work.

The operating-room nurse has a hunch it won't work in this case—the nurses, Hartz says, have great instincts about these things—and she is calling to alert Hartz that her services may be required. The surgeon had hoped to spend the afternoon in her lab working on research into the use of "cold" lasers to open clogged vessels, but now her adrenaline is rising. Bustling about the office, she says: "I don't have enough time in the day to do everything I want. I've published 35 to 40 scientific papers on my research into lasers and on the implantation of automatic cardiac defibrillators to reverse potentially fatal irregular fast heartbeats, but it seems that I'm always behind. At my age, a truly accomplished researcher would have published at least 70 to 75. But I have to admit—I'm happy as a clam in the OR."

Slender, shining, smiling, Hartz cannot mask the obvious fact that she is having a ball. Her office is small and cramped, dominated by diplomas, plaques, books, journals and boxes of slides. A photo of Tyler, however, the oldest of her two sons, and a large poster of a windsurfer attest to two other passions. "I know there is life beyond the hospital walls," she says, "and I would die if anyone thought I were one-dimensional. People have called me a workaholic—and I *am* in cycles, especially at surgery—but I have a great time with my life. I can stay in the OR forever if the opportunity and challenge are great enough, but I also love to be with my sons and stay in shape and ski and windsurf and be with my friends and have a social life, too. I work hard at whatever I'm doing, but I'm not a workaholic."

She has spent the last 20 years at Northwestern—as medical student, surgical resident and the last seven as attending heart surgeon—and she knows its hallways and people by heart. At 42, she is nearing the peak of her surgical powers, and the thrill is simply explained:

"I was a junior resident in 1976, still undecided about my medical specialty, when we received an emergency call. A 19-year-old secretary had collapsed from a clot in her lungs and was wheeled into the intensive-care unit by paramedics. Our surgical team, headed by Dr. John Sanders, was waiting—fully gloved and gowned. Dr. Sanders, who was then new to Northwestern, made a snap decision to operate the minute he saw her."

Within 15 minutes, Hartz says, the patient was on the heart-lung machine to restore her heart function and the doctors had cracked her chest and were opening her pulmonary artery to remove the clot. "Dr. Sanders never lost a minute, and the operation restored her blood flow," Hartz recalls. "Eight days later, she went home—cured. Without any tests or hesitation, he had, with only his knowledge and his hands and his skills and the abilities of the modern surgical team, saved a life. I had found my calling."

The beeper sounds again. The patient *does* need heart surgery, and Hartz's team is standing by. She snaps to attention, commanding, "Let's go." Dressed in high heels, a stylish skirt and her gray doctor's coat, she leaves a reporter trailing behind as she marches full tilt from her office at one end of the medical center to the 4th-floor heart-surgery suite at the Olson Pavilion at the other. Knowingly using both basement corridors and rooftop walkways to save time, she strides into battle. "I still run down stairs," she says, "but I take the elevators to go up. A few years ago, I was driving in a rush from my home to the hospital, and another car almost broadsided me. When I got to the hospital, the patient was already dead. Now, I figure, take it easy. . . ." Her path takes her down a corridor lined with the stodgy photos of all the previous chiefs of surgery at Northwestern and with the plaques honoring all the hospital's outstanding surgical-training residents. All the photos are male, and all the plaques are engraved to men, except for the 1978 plaque honoring Dr. Renée Hartz "for *his* outstanding empathy, skill, and understanding of patients and dedication to their care." She smiles and says, "Oh, yes, I've always meant to draw an arrow off to the side and write 'her'!"

In the cath lab, the patient is fighting for her life. Marian Hyllon, 70, collapsed sometime this morning with a heart attack. She was rushed to the cath lab for an angioplasty after being admitted to the emergency room in profound shock, with a systolic blood pressure—that is, with the heart beating, as opposed to resting—of only 60-70; normal is 120. All angioplasties require surgical backup, and the operating-room suite is right across the hall.

The patient has been in the cath lab for about 90 minutes, and Hartz is impatient. The angiogram shows a total blockage of a portion of the left circumflex, one of the three major arteries that supply blood and oxygen to the heart. The three life-sustaining arteries and their many branches girdle the heart like a crown, or "corona," which accounts for the term coronary disease. Hartz looks at the angiogram and quickly concludes: "She's dying. She's had a huge heart attack and is still in shock. In cases like this, we have only six hours—maximum—to restore the blood flow to the heart muscle, and we don't know what time this morning her heart attack started. It's a huge 'OM,' a total blockage of the obtuse marginal branch of the left circumflex artery."

It is now 1 p.m., and the tension in the cath lab is mounting. The admitting cardiologist, Dr. Gary Martin, watches anxiously as the invasive cardiologist, Dr. Barry Kramer, feverishly works to keep the artery open. Using a small balloon at the tip of the catheter that has been threaded from an incision in the patient's groin to the circumflex artery, he has been able to open the artery several times and raise her blood pressure, but—ominously—the artery keeps closing, and the blood pressure keeps dropping severely. A long, narrow balloon has also been threaded through an artery in her groin up to the aorta, the great artery that sits atop the heart and distributes blood to the rest of the body. This balloon is rapidly inflated and deflated in synchrony with the heartbeat. It is connected to a complex, computerized console that precisely regulates these inflations and deflations so that they improve the performance of the heart and the circulation.

In addition to her earlier heart attack, or blockage of blood to the heart, Mrs. Hyllon has, while being worked on in the cath lab, also suffered one cardiac arrest, or a total cessation of heart function. Electrodes were strapped to her chest and her heart shocked back into beating by electric paddles, but now it looks as if she might arrest again.

Hartz has made her decision and changes into scrubs for surgery. Her team has been patiently waiting for longer than they would like, but the angioplasty team is equivocating. Dr. Kramer wants to continue his rescue attempt. The surgeon will have to impose her will.

"These dilemmas happen every day," she explains. "Dr. Kramer is a very aggressive angioplasterer, and most angioplasterers are frustrated surgeons. But it appears from the angiogram that this is a fresh clot and is not going to stay open. It's like a sponge—you stick something in it, and it keeps closing around it. If she arrests again, her chances even with surgery are minimal. I try to do for every patient exactly what I would do for my own father, and this patient needs surgery. I wish she had been in the OR two hours ago! And, once I've made up my mind, I lean on the other doctors pretty hard."

She confers with Dr. Martin, who has the ultimate responsibility to make the emergency clinical decision, and he opts for surgery. Hyllon's daughter, Grace Kaats, 50, who is in the surgical waiting room, is called to sign a consent form for open-heart surgery. Without surgery, Doctors Martin and Hartz explain, her mother's chances are zero; with the operation, 50-50. The daughter is still in a daze from her mother's sudden collapse, and she looks anxiously at the woman surgeon. "I'm Renée Hartz, your surgeon" she says. "Our team has successfully performed this type of surgery many times." She doesn't mean to be cocky, only to offer hope to the distraught daughter. Hartz appears very confident. The daughter signs.

Hartz stands at the cath-lab door, demanding that the patient be transferred to the operating room. "Hell, Renée, why don't you just bring the bed in here and take her out!" Kramer exclaims. "An excellent idea," Hartz rejoins, and the operating-room table is wheeled in to claim the patient. Later, Hartz explains, "In these high-stress situations, you have to be able to read people. I've worked with Barry for years, and I know that he is in agreement with me that she needs surgery. It's just that he's frustrated that the angioplasty failed."

The clock is ticking, and Hyllon's vital signs have virtually stopped. Her life now depends upon the kind of sophisticated all-out heart surgery that is best provided by university medical centers, such as Chicago's Northwestern Memorial Hospital and others in the Chicago area.

Hartz first orders the injection of a huge jolt of epinephrine. The drug attaches to receptors on the heart muscle and summons the body to muster its last reserves of energy in an all-out effort to restore heart function and blood pressure. Because the patient's condition is so desperate, the surgeon decides to put her on heart-lung "bypass" before the chest is opened. She uses the guide wires previously inserted in the groin for the angioplasty to connect the tubings of the heart-lung machine. Within five minutes, Hyllon is on full bypass, with the heart-lung machine taking over for her own failing heart, which can now be isolated and protected during surgery, and lungs.

Once the patient is on bypass, Hartz observes, "The surgeon can say, 'Whew!' We've got some breathing room." Hyllon is quickly draped and prepped, and within minutes her breastbone, or sternum, is cracked with a sternal saw, and the surgical team is looking at her heart. "This was one of the worst I've ever seen," Hartz recalls. "It looked dead—dilated with blood and not beating, more like a balloon than a pump. Her outlook seemed terrible."

The rescue effort, however, will continue for five hours. The surgeon from the Upper Peninsula likes her OR kept cold, and the temperature is 62, prompting a few shivers and complaints. "I mean," says Hartz, "with all our gowns and masks and caps, it's easy to stay warm." Normally, Hartz likes music in the OR, preferring the Rolling Stones or Talking Heads, but this case is too dicey. There is too much tension in the OR to listen to the driving beat of rock groups.

Hartz places a clamp on the aorta, effectively isolating the heart. She also uses small tubes to drain the excess blood from the swollen organ. Next, to protect the heart from further damage she directs the heart-lung machine perfusionist, a nonphysician, to divert some of the patient's blood from the machine, cool it, mix it with potassium and other additives, and direct this solution through the arteries back to the heart muscle. This use of the patient's own blood is called "blood cardioplegia," and it serves to slow the heart's metabolism. In Hyllon's case, it was supplemented by topical cardioplegia, an "ice-slush" mixture. The workload on the patient's heart is now minimal.

Because time is critical, the surgeon has time only to bypass the severely occluded (blocked) obtuse marginal branch of the left circumflex artery and not a second, smaller blockage on the right coronary artery. An assistant harvests a saphenous vein from the lower right leg, which can be spared because the body develops alternate pathways to return blood from the legs to the heart. The surgeon pulls down her jeweler's loupes, which provide a magnification of 2½, and swiftly and surely begins to sew one end of the vein to the aorta and the other to the obtuse marginal artery beyond the blockage on the back of the heart. This bypass graft now provides an alternate route to supply blood to the heart muscle. She later jokes, "The women get by with loupes of 2½; the men always need 3½, since they have weaker eyes."

All kidding aside, the surgeon's work is far from over. Working with extreme caution and meticulousness, Hartz slowly weans the patient off of the heart-lung machine. A warm cardioplegia solution is then used to gently nudge the patient's heart back into beating on its own. Remarkably, the patient has survived the surgery; miraculously, Hartz observes, it appears that she has lost none of her heart muscle. She will need intravenous drugs for her heart and a mechanical respirator to breathe as she is wheeled out of the OR and into the cardiac surgical intensive-care unit (CSICU) down the hall, but she is still living. It is 6 p.m., and Hartz and nine other medical professionals have worked for seven hours to save this one life. The cost? Maybe $30,000, but Hartz says: "I don't care what it costs. There's an incredible rush when a patient in this bad a shape pulls through."

Hartz wants to savor the momentary triumph because she knows only too well that patients can be lost suddenly in the OR—even when the risk appears low—or with agonizing slowness during post-operation complications. "Heart surgeons, more than most," she says, "have to make that long walk to the waiting room to tell relatives that their loved ones didn't make it. It's an unbelievable downer, and you mercilessly question your performance, often concluding that the patient would have been better off without surgery or, perhaps, even with a different surgeon."

Hyllon is hardly out of the woods. The hours of profound and prolonged shock she suffered have deprived her brain of oxygen, and the medical staff must now worry about irreversible damage. The buildup of fluid in the lungs during her heart failure has caused a breathing problem, requiring a respirator and a subsequent tracheotomy (placement of a breathing tube into her throat).

During the next 10 days, the patient becomes depressed and fails to make any purposeful movements or responses. The medical staff begins to despair of her brain recovery, as does her daughter, who insists that she and her mother had previously discussed that under no conditions was she to be kept alive by machines and tubes. On the 11th post-op day, a priest is summoned to administer last rites. Ironically, Hyllon chooses this moment to make the sign of the cross and wave to her daughter, the first purposeful movements she has made since her heart attack. It is decided not to remove the respirator.

One month later, Hartz and a visitor go to see mother and daughter in the patient's recovery room. Hyllon is sporting a new hairdo and makeup to accommodate a photographer. "Why, she even brushed her teeth today!" the daughter exclaims. The mother tightly clasps her daughter's hand, and a nurse attests that if it weren't for the tracheotomy that is still in place, Hyllon's mouthings would be coming out as grateful words. The breathing tube is scheduled to come out in days, and Hyllon will speak again. The brain damage was reversible.

Hartz thinks that following rehabilitation Hyllon will make a full recovery. She will soon be taken off the antidepressants. A recent addition to her medical chart is this notation from a neurologist: "Miraculous recovery!" It follows by only weeks a notation by a psychiatrist: "Hopelessly gone." The daughter who agreed to the desperate operation now has the luxury of more prosaic worries. The mother and daughter live together in Bridgeview, and it is a long drive to Northwestern's lakefront hospital. The daughter worries, "How can I park my car at the rates being charged by the garage across the street?"

She adds, "I can't say enough about Dr. Hartz and the people at Northwestern. They've given my mother back to me. She's always been full of pep—really, she acted younger than I did. . . ."

Hartz's beeper sounds again. It's time to report for another operation, one that will go late into the night.

The real beauty of Renée Hartz, her friends and colleagues say, is that she is both a special person and a regular person. No wonder—she has always been too busy to put on airs. Her mother, one of 13 children, raised her brood of seven to be self-reliant and hardworking. Hartz, who started working as a waitress at age 14, says, "I worked as a waitress during both college and the summer before medical school, and I feel that one reason I can quickly size up patients is the insight I acquired during all the years I spent waiting on people.

During college, when her father was out of work, she used to send her student-loan checks back to Ironwood to help her family. She made up for it by working as a waitress at the nearby Holiday Inn. "I guess I've always been the Santa Claus in my family," she says. "My father was a 'no-collar' laborer, and the mines in Ironwood were drying up. We were very poor."

Her fortunes began to change when she became a lab technician at Northwestern. "I was working with both physicians and patients," she recalls, "and I loved it. Within three months I applied for medical school. My roommate was a psychiatric social worker, and she pushed me to apply."

Hartz was accepted to the Northwestern University Medical School in December, 1969, for admittance the following fall. She hung the acceptance letter on her Christmas tree. "I had also been accepted at other medical schools," she says, "and I almost went to the University of Michigan, but I decided that Chicago was home." She paid her way through the four years of medical school through a combination of work at the hospital's lab, student loans, a small scholarship and money she had saved from waitress work.

In 1972 she married Wilson Hartz III, a medical student at Northwestern who is now a general surgeon practicing at Northwestern Memorial Hospital and whose father is also a Northwestern physician. The couple divorced in 1986 and now alternate custody of their two children—Tyler, 10, and Colin, 6. In 1974 Hartz acquired her M.D. degree and promptly began a seven-year surgical residency.

"Medical school was pure drudgery during the first two years," she recalls, "but the minute I hit the patient wards during my junior year, I was in heaven. It was obvious that I was a doer. I wanted to do the spinal taps and the suturing myself, and I was a very aggressive student. I actually got to do surgery as a medical student. My first operation was modest—a circumcision on a 40-year-old man—but I loved it. The next week, I did a hernia, which qualified as a real operation. I loved everything during my clinical rotations except psychiatry—you don't "do" anything—and gynecology—it just wasn't appealing to me. But my true love was heart surgery.

She now does about 200 open-heart procedures a year, as well as other operations. She works about 70 hours a week and is paid "barely six figures"—about a fourth of what she could make in private practice doing less-complicated heart surgery. She says the money is not that important.

"I keep a doll on my bedroom dresser at home," she says. "It is one of the few mementoes I have from my life in Ironwood, but I keep it to remind me from where I came."

Hartz lives on the city's Near Northwest Side in a three-story, four-bedroom stucco house built in the Old Chicago style of 1907. She gutted the kitchen and rehabbed it with enough modern cabinets and appliances to enable her to throw gourmet dinner parties when she can find the time. She remodeled her old master bathroom into a modern showplace gleaming with white tile and a two-pedestal sink. Another indulgence is a big brass bed in the master bedroom.

She turned the large basement into a recreation room for her sons, featuring a 7-foot G.I. Joe aircraft carrier, nets for floor hockey and a 25-inch television (one of four in the house) set up for video games. Her children are firmly fixed in the computer generation, and Tyler has his own Apple IIGS student computer for education and graphics, while Mom uses a Zenith laptop model.

The home is cheerful and neat throughout, except for the mess in the basement, which she explains as "toys, toys, toys." The downstairs living room features a stereo and large speakers for Hartz's favorite music: oldies from the '60s and heavy rock.

Her key to being a single mother, she says, "is my live-in housekeeper, Julia Casas, who's been with me for 10 years. She's always with the kids, living either at my house or my ex-husband's, who lives nearby. She's the continuity, and I trust her with the kids." Hartz still talks to her ex-husband almost every day and says the two are very proud of their cooperation in raising their sons. "I married the wrong man for me," she says, "but, in many ways, we're better friends now than when we married." She likes to bowl with her sons, go to movies ("we see everything"), and read children's stories to Colin. Tyler, she says, "is a readaholic, when he's not playing games." She adds: "Sure, I spoil my kids—that's life—but I made a very calculated decision to raise my sons as city kids, not suburban kids. I have them play hockey at the McFetridge Center with the sons of working-class policemen and truck drivers and not at some swank suburban rink. I send them to private schools because I think that education is very important, but I want them to know the real world, too."

As a medical student and resident, Hartz had no female role models, but today she is a role model for medical students and residents of both sexes. Her training at Northwestern coincided with the golden era of improvements in heart surgery. Dr. Lawrence Michaelis, chief of cardiothoracic surgery at Northwestern Memorial Hospital and the Northwestern University Medical School, says, "When Renée achieved certification by the American Board of Thoracic Surgery, she was only the 13th woman in the entire country to achieve this distinction."

There are 4,500 board-certified cardiothoracic surgeons in the U.S., and only 43 are women. Hartz says: "My proudest accomplishment to date is that I am an associate professor of heart surgery—with tenure—at the Northwestern University Medical School. This means that I do research and teaching, as well as surgery. It means that I am an academic surgeon, part of a great university team. In five to seven years, I'll fulfill the requirements to become a full professor. The real reason I stay at Northwestern is that because of our technology and our team approach we can offer patients the best heart surgery possible. What I need to do for a patient is always possible, and, somehow, we always seem to get it done."

Now firmly established "as one of the boys," Hartz says she had to surmount subtle sexism during her training. "There was an attitude," she recalls, "as if nobody expected me to be good. It was never overt, and it was never sexual—I would never put myself in a position where I would be subject to sexual harassment—but there was a bias. In 1978, when I returned to my residency after having my first baby, I temporarily felt very depressed and very pressured. I started to blame myself, as if I were not good enough. But I realized that no one is perfect, and I made myself talk to the people who I thought were being unfair. In hindsight I can see that during all my rotations through the different medical specialties, I would be a wreck for the first week because I did not feel in control of this new field. But it passed as soon as I took control. It took me a while to convince myself that I really was a very good surgeon, but once I did, I never looked back. And, of course, toward the end of my residency, the other surgeons accepted me as a peer, and the sexism evaporated. Oh, one old doctor insisted on calling me 'honey,' but he calls everybody 'honey.'"

Colleague John Sanders, a superb heart surgeon and one blessed with unfailing amiability under pressure, says: "Renée will do me if I ever need heart surgery. She's that good." Similarly, Dr. Jay Alexander, the cardiologist who successfully treated Mike Ditka with drugs, observes: "I refer a lot of surgical patients to Northwestern and Renée, and it's highly possible that if Ditka had required surgery, Renée would have done it. Certainly, she can do me if my turn ever comes. She projects a real air of confidence."

Dr. Pat Pappas, a seventh-year surgical resident at Children's Memorial Hospital, is also a former Northwestern Outstanding Surgical

Resident of the Year and knows well the pressures of surgical training. "Renée has always been a role model for me. She's unique. First, she's a woman heart surgeon, and there aren't too many of these; second, she's an outstanding heart surgeon who is technically gifted and has real compassion for her patients, and there aren't too many of these, either; third, she is a terrific mother for her two sons and manages to balance a heavy surgical schedule with being a single mother, and I really respect that; and, fourth, she's simply a good person."

Cardiac anesthesiologist Dr. Carolyn Brent, who is married to longtime Michigan Avenue bookseller Stuart Brent, adds: "I've known Renée since she was a 'little girl,' and it's been exciting to see her blossom into an outstanding surgeon." Another cardiac anesthesiologist, Dr. Peter Lichtenthal, who has worked hundreds of cases in Hartz's OR, adds: "We regulars sometimes call her 'Stella' from the play 'A Streetcar Named Desire.' You know, she's our Polish Queen. In the OR, she's just one of the guys, so to speak, and the atmosphere is always very relaxed."

Deaths from heart and blood-vessel disease have dropped 24 percent over the last decade, but it remains the nation's biggest killer, taking a life every 32 seconds, according to the American Heart Association. The decline in death rates is attributed to a combination of healthier living habits and improved medical treatments.

Dr. Sanders puts things in perspective. "When I started my training back in the 1960s, heart surgery carried a 30- to 50-percent mortality rate—and that included all the otherwise-healthy middle-aged people who came in for elective procedures. Thanks to improvements in imaging the heart muscle and vessels, in surgical techniques and in methods to protect the heart during surgery, we've been able to reduce our overall mortality to 4 to 6 percent, and this includes taking all comers who walk in the door, including patients who are very old and very sick and have multiple ailments. The mortality rate for middle-aged men and women who have elective surgery is only a fraction of 1 percent." As for the future, Dr. Michaelis predicts, "The era of the brilliant, charismatic, maverick surgeon is over. He—and they all were male—is being replaced by the team philosophy, though the surgeon will always be the quarterback. . . ."

Hartz thinks her research may help redefine how heart surgery is practiced in the future. Her work on cold lasers, which do not generate as much destructive heat as the normal variety, may eventually help unclog arteries without the need for opening the chest and without causing the long-term development of dangerous arterial swellings, or aneurysms, as do the "hot" lasers.

She has also helped pioneer the surgical implantation of the automatic implantable cardiac defibrillator to prevent a fast irregular beating of the heart, called arrhythmia, and sudden cardiac death.

The first page of the Northwestern house staff manual for cardiothoracic surgery notes, "These guidelines are not laws. . . . *There is no substitute for common sense.*" All who know her say Hartz is blessed with abundant common sense, fortified by extensive experience. There are no jokes about female hormones and "estrogen storms" when this woman takes command of the OR. And, most mornings, when her bathroom alarm clock rings at 6 a.m., she is off for the OR. "I'm unlike most surgeons in that I hate early morning," she says. "That's why I keep the alarm in the bathroom—if I had it next to the bed, I'd be tempted to shut it off. Once I'm up, though, I'm ready to go full speed."

For which many Chicago patients are grateful—prominent attorney Thomas Foran, for example. Foran, 65, was a Navy fighter pilot during World War II, a football player at Holy Cross, a former U.S. Attorney for Illinois who helped try the Chicago Seven and an unsuccessful candidate for governor of Illinois in 1972. Now he's a big-income criminal-trial attorney, with opulent offices in the Loop and a large home in Lake Forest. Three years ago, while performing a cross-examination, he had a massive heart attack and, fortuitously, crossed paths with Hartz.

"I thought I was a goner," Foran says. "You know the feeling you got in the pit of your stomach when you were a kid and somebody jumped out from behind the door and scared you—well, that's how I felt. The pain was murderous, and it felt as if an elephant were sitting on my chest. My arms went numb, and I was almost in too much pain to talk, which is cruel and unusual punishment for an attorney. Well, the ambulance rushed me to the Northwestern emergency room, and Dr. [Barry] Kramer performed angioplasty, which relieved the pain a little. But I demanded to see a priest. I thought that I was going to meet my Maker. Then I sort of passed out, and the next thing I recall I was looking up at this knockout babe—Renée Hartz. I thought that I'd gone to heaven. She said,

'I'm Renée Hartz, and I'm going to be your surgeon.' I'm a real male chauvinist pig, and I asked, 'Are you any good?' She said, 'I'm the best'—and I believed it. I'm used to bossing people around myself, and I could tell that she had the respect of everyone around her. She's not only a beautiful woman, she looks intelligent, and she has strong, capable hands. I said: 'Well, then, hurry up. I have a cross-examination to finish.' She told me, 'You're going to be all right—you sound like a keeper.'"

(Hartz explains, "It's not so much that I think I am the best surgeon as it is that I say this when I can tell the patient needs to hear it. . . . And I know that I am a very good surgeon, and I've earned the right to say so.")

Foran had what surgeons call a "widowmaker," a total blockage of the left main coronary artery. Hartz and her team repaired it and two other diseased arteries. Within eight days, Foran was out of the hospital. That fall he tried a major criminal case in Miami. Today he feels better than ever. He says: "This woman is special. She's not just a doctor, she's a physician. . . . Whatever honor I can give this woman, I will. I owe her."

Hartz recalls only one time when she lost her composure in the OR—the time her mother came to Northwestern for bypass of five diseased arteries. She explains: "Doctors Michaelis and Sanders were doing my mother's surgery, but a case came up in the other OR, and the surgeon needed an assistant. I scrubbed and jumped in to help, because I didn't want anyone diverted from my mother's case. Well, I just couldn't do it. I was worrying about my mother, and I lost it. My hands actually began to shake—which is something that never happens. I left the OR and went back to where I belonged—the waiting room!" Rita Semo sailed through just dandy.

Her parents are enormously proud of her, Hartz says, "but they really cannot relate to my life as a surgeon in a big-city medical center. The one who understands is my older sister, Rita." Hartz's two brothers are carpenters, another sister is an ex-nun and recent new wife and mother living in Aurora, and the two younger sisters still live in Ironwood.

Rita Semo Wickham, 44, is also an achiever. She married a serviceman at age 17 and settled down in Aurora, where she and her husband have raised four children. Along the way, she acquired her high school diploma by mail and earned bachelor and master's degrees in nursing. Today she is an academic nurse at Chicago's Rush-Presbyterian-St. Luke's Medical Center, caring for cancer patients and pursuing her Ph.D. in nursing. She travels about the country lecturing on modern nursing care. She says: "What impresses me most about Renée is the way she makes time for her kids. She juggles her schedule so she almost always makes her kids' hockey games and school plays. When she's not in surgery, she's with them."

On a recent night at a lounge near the hospital, Hartz gathers with her sister, Rita, her two closest friends, Camille Tracer of Chicago and Debbie Johnson of Wilmette, and former patient Foran. The talk soon turns from surgery to fashions and men. Hartz, a flashy dresser—but a bargain shopper—has, postdivorce, dated mostly doctors, including artificial-heart inventor Dr. Robert Jarvik, but she also has dated and been linked in the gossip columns with then Bears quarterback Mike Tomczak. "He's just a good friend," she says.

"At this point in my life, my children and my surgery take up most of my time, but I hope to find the right man and marry again. My social life is very important to me, but I don't have time to just date around."

The three friends are planning to open a Chicago clothing store, specializing in leisure and sports clothes for women, perhaps to be called Hartz' Desire. Hartz, dressed this evening in hot pink ("my favorite color") slacks and turtleneck set off by silver tennis shoes and a bulky white sweater appliquéd with fuchsia flowers, looks the part. She works out in a "no-nonsense" gym to stay in shape.

Tracer, who is married to a psychiatrist, interrupts. "I am very happy that Renée is part of my life," she says, "but it is hard to be her friend. That's because she's a perfectionist, and she does everything well. I mean, she's beautiful, a terrific skier, a gourmet cook, a champion windsurfer and a supernice friend. But what amazes me is what a regular person she is. We met because our children both attended the same Chicago school. The first time I called her on the phone, she was retiling her bathroom floor. I thought, 'Here's this hotshot surgeon, and she's busy retiling her bathroom!' At parties, she used to say only, 'I work in a hospital.' Eventually she worked herself up to admitting, 'I'm a physician.' Now she says, 'I'm a heart surgeon.'

"And she used to get up at 3 a.m. to drive to Oshkosh, Wis., to be first in line for the 7 a.m. opening of a factory outlet selling children's designer clothes at bargain prices! I think that what she really wants is a bright, accomplished man, but one with dirt under his fingernails, a little bit of grit. A lot of men are intimidated by the mystique of her being a surgeon, but Renée is really a regular person with the down-to-earth values typical of someone raised in a lower middle-class family. One local real estate mogul sent his chauffeured Rolls-Royce to pick her up for a date. She was appalled; she'd rather be out bowling!"

"Sometimes I think that men want to go out with me because of the status image of dating a surgeon," Hartz says. "That turns me off. I want a man who is accomplished in his own work and who is secure. And he must be ambitious. I cannot stand a man who because he is excessively good-looking thinks that he can be lazy about his personality. And he must make me laugh!"

Hartz explains: "There are sacrifices you have to make to do what I do. Sometimes I would like to chop my hair short, dye it a different color and stay up all night dancing. I have the energy to do it, but I won't do anything that reflects poorly upon my credibility as a physician."

Debbie Johnson, who is divorced from a surgeon who trained at the same time Hartz did, has the last word. "Renée has a wonderful heart," she says. "I have tons and tons of memories about our times together. She's a doctor, but when her own kids get sick, she almost gets hysterical and gets on the phone asking *me* for advice. When she was pregnant with Tyler, she became convinced that she had miscarried, which was silly. She was doing surgery right up until she delivered. One of our good friends is a nurse who used to ride to the hospital with Renée. During the drive, she told me, the talk was all girl stuff. The minute Renée walked in the door, however, a gleam came to her eye, and she became a general, ready for battle.

"The two of us and Renée's two children recently vacationed at a Club Med in Mexico. She enjoys me because I am fun. The men were all over her, using the usual lines and asking, 'What do you do?' When she explained that she was a heart surgeon, they looked doubtful—for about five seconds. I mean, she can have it all. Here's this terrific heart surgeon walking in a bikini along the beach with her two sons and turning heads. And she's my best friend. It's enough to warm your heart."

A Gift for Lauren Aggen

The Christmas Day tale of an infant, a heart defect, and one family's ordeal

"There's something wrong." Disturbing words almost always, but perhaps never more disturbing than when spoken by a pediatrician to a mother shortly after a birth—then "There's something wrong" is a heart-wrenching substitute for "Everything's fine, and you can take the baby home tomorrow." For a suburban couple, those staggering three words, coming as they did three days before Christmas, triggered a year-long emotional roller-coaster ride, a bumpy journey yet one that has filled them with a sense of wonder as their daughter, the youngest recipient of a heart transplant in the Chicago area, continues her struggle to live a normal life.

It had started so routinely—if, in fact, there is anything routine about the miracle of birth.

Janet Aggen, 39, had worked until the week before the birth at her two jobs, as a speech therapist for the Elgin school district and for an Elgin home for emotionally disturbed children. The day before the birth, her husband, Dave, also 39, arose as usual at 5 a.m. to drive to Elmhurst, where he teaches math at York High School. Shortly after he arrived at their Algonquin home that evening, Janet went into labor, and soon they were on their way to Good Shepherd Hospital in Barrington. Pre-birth screening tests, including the sophisticated ultrasound fetal monitor, already had assured the Aggens that their second child was to be a girl and that she would be healthy.

And so it first appeared. Lauren Ann Aggen was born at 3:45 a.m. on Dec. 22, 1989—7 pounds, 3 ounces. The happy mother was told that her little girl appeared pink, boisterous—and healthy. Christmas, no doubt, would be doubly rosy this year.

Buoyed by this knowledge, the proud father left the hospital hours after his daughter's birth to share the good news with their 7-year-old son, also named Dave, and to call friends and relatives. It was while performing the traditional fatherhood rituals that he received the fateful call from his wife, the call that relayed those three disturbing words and set into motion a period of handwringing and soul-searching over a decision that could affect four people for decades to come.

The "something" that was "wrong" was the baby's breathing: Lauren Ann Aggen, so healthy at birth, was suddenly turning blue from a lack of oxygen. Rushing back to the hospital, her father learned that the Good Shepherd medical team had detected a heart murmur and diagnosed the problem as a heart defect.

"At first, our pediatrician told us: 'Don't worry. It's not that serious; it's not something requiring a heart transplant,'" Janet recalls. "I distinctly remember thinking and telling a friend at my bedside: 'A heart transplant, so soon after birth? How can that be—such an extreme thing?'"

But, indeed, the blessed event had become a tragic event: The Aggens' baby was dying. Unable to breathe for herself, the newborn was immediately placed on artificial respiration, with several nurses and a respiratory therapist taking turns over the next seven hours to force oxygen into Lauren's lungs by way of an air bag connected to a tube in her windpipe. She would remain on artificial respiration for the next 18 harrowing days. The new baby's bedroom, which had been wallpapered in a warm pink, would lie empty for a long time.

Meanwhile, the sorely pressed doctors at Good Shepherd had quickly decided that morning to transfer young Lauren to Children's Memorial Hospital in Chicago. But here, too, complications trampled all over the normally routine. The Chicago hospital's ambulance-helicopter had been assigned downstate, and it wasn't until 5 p.m. that the emergency chopper and its trauma team finally arrived to transport the Aggen infant for the 12-minute ride to Children's.

An hour or so later, the shaken parents received a phone call—heart surgeons at the Chicago hospital wanted to meet immediately with the father. The couple, though, decided to confront the crisis together, and Janet Aggen, just 14 hours after giving birth, checked herself out of Good Shepherd Hospital to make the long trek to Children's Memorial.

It was bitterly cold—12 below—and the weather, like the bad news, had hit the Aggens "right between the eyes," Janet says. "We thought we were going to see our daughter die." Husband Dave adds, "I was in no shape to drive, so we rode down to Children's in the van of our pastor, the Rev. Gary Miller of the Congregational Church of Algonquin." With them was their son.

At Children's, the news was most troubling. Lauren was suffering from a severe form of hypoplastic left heart syndrome, or HLHS, a uniformly fatal birth defect in which the heart's main pumping chamber, the left ventricle, is malformed and cannot pump enough blood to supply the body with life-sustaining oxygen. The only hope: a new heart.

Lauren was otherwise healthy. The ultrasound had missed the baby's catastrophic birth defect because, unlike most cases of HLHS, all four chambers of her heart were fully developed. Sadly, however, the aortic valve of the heart was completely sealed, and the left ventricle, in trying to pump against this immovable resistance, had become scarred and weakened, a development that had escaped detection because Janet Aggen's heart was able to supply all the fetus' needs until birth.

HLHS is the same defect that six years ago prompted California surgeon Leonard Bailey to transplant a baboon heart to replace the failing human heart of an infant who became known to the world as Baby Fae. Bailey attempted the extraordinary animal graft because—at the time—there were no infant human hearts available for transplant. Baby Fae died after 20 days, but the publicity over the bold experiment at Loma Linda University Medical Center spurred a surge in the donation of infant human hearts.

As a result, Bailey was able to transplant his first human heart into a baby in 1985, and his success has slowly encouraged other medical centers to do the same. Today Loma Linda and Children's Memorial in Chicago are the leading centers in the world for infant-heart transplantation. Still the technique remains in its own infancy; less than 100 heart transplants for infants under 1 year have been done throughout the world, 56 of them at Loma Linda and nine at Children's. The procedure is important because HLHS, which occurs for unknown reasons in about one of every 5,000 births, is fatal to 500 to 600 babies a year—unless the baby undergoes a transplant.

Thus, the choice given to Dave and Janet Aggen on the night of Dec. 22, 1989, was as overwhelmingly simple as it was momentous: You can put your baby on a waiting list for a heart transplant or let nature take its course—and you have to decide by morning. The medical team at Children's—pediatric surgeons Constantine Mavroudis and Carl Backer and cardiologist Vincent Zales—emphasized that both choices would be right, depending on many factors, both tangible and intangible.

"We were in a daze on the night of Dec. 22," Janet Aggen remembers. "It was an awesome decision we were being asked to make." After the Rev. Miller baptized the endangered infant, the beleaguered parents went home to wrestle with their consciences.

"We were numb, really, from being exhausted and from the stress of the day and the tremendous amount of information we were being forced to digest in such a short period of time," Janet says. "Adding to our confusion was the uncertainty over whether a heart would be available and whether our insurance policies would pay for a transplant."

The Aggens had to grapple with questions like these:

Could they afford it? The cost—about $15,000 alone for procurement of the new heart, $30,000 for implantation surgery, $2,000 a day for intensive care, plus doctor's fees—would add up to about $120,000. Would they have to sell their house and car? Could they handle the lifetime regimen of drugs Lauren would require at a cost of $1,000 a month to prevent the body's rejection of a heart it knows not to be its own? Was it fair to spend this much money on one life at a time when so many people have to go without basic medical care? Was the risk and sacrifice fair to them and their young son? Could they handle the stress? Would a heart be found in time?

"Our No. 1 question was what would be the quality of our daughter's life, a question for which nobody has an answer," Janet says. "The longest-surviving infant with a heart transplant has lived for only five years. I asked the people at Children's how Lauren would do in school, and nobody could tell me."

The Aggens' decisive moment came the next morning as they again made the long drive from the northwest suburbs to the city. Dave Aggen turned to his wife and said: "Let's face it; if something happened to Dave, we would do everything we could to save his life. I think that the same thing should apply to Lauren." The parents had decided, in Dave's words, "that no matter what, we were never going to look back. We are parents, and we are going to do what parents do—take care of our kids." The Aggens had made a leap into faith.

When they reached the hospital, however, they almost changed their minds. Little Lauren looked still and lifeless—she was receiving life-sustaining drugs to keep her damaged heart beating, she was connected to a ventilator that breathed for her and she was surrounded by machines and tubes that were meant to mimic the conditions of the womb and conserve her energy. "We both cried," Janet says, "but we stuck to our decision."

Still, the doctors had given the baby only three days to live. The pounding of the ventilator and her own poor circulation were destroying her kidneys. Would she be able to survive the average waiting time—21 days—to find a donor heart?

Although 100 babies die every day in the U.S. from either trauma, respiratory problems or infections, it is hard to find a donor heart: Most parents and physicians remain reluctant, because of the emotions involved and other factors, to donate the heart of an infant who has suddenly died. As cardiologist Zales notes: "Five babies die every day in Chicago, and yet, because of a failure to educate Chicago physicians about the value of heart transplants, we have had to fly all over the country to find donor hearts. Three infants have died on our waiting list."

The last baby to be given a transplant at Children's had waited 38 days before a donor heart was found in Philadelphia. "I prayed only for the strength of getting through our ordeal," Janet Aggen remembers, "because I knew that for Lauren to get a new heart, another mother's heart must first be broken."

In this time of anguish and uncertainty, the Aggens turned for support to their family and friends, who responded with prayers and hospital bedside vigils. On Christmas Eve day, Janet Aggen was taken to the Good Shepherd Hospital emergency room to be treated for bronchitis. The next morning, though gloved, gowned, and masked, she could not hug her young daughter for fear of infecting her.

Lauren Aggen was expected to die on Christmas Day, but somehow she endured, as her parents, brother and well-wishers sang Christmas carols in her brightly decorated intensive-care room. "As tough as things were, we had a very, very pleasant time," Dave says.

By Dec. 29, however, one week after her birth, Lauren appeared at the end. The physicians expected her to die within 12 hours and were about to take her off the waiting list; the Aggens were beginning to discuss funeral plans. But at about 6 p.m., as they prepared to make the long drive home, a nurse interrupted them with the first hopeful words they had heard since the ordeal began: "Stick around a while longer," she said. "We may have a donor heart."

The Children's Memorial medical team was about to get a fighting chance to save the baby's life.

Bold surgical programs are usually led by bold surgeons, and Dr. Mavroudis, one of only 200 pediatric heart surgeons in the country, fits the mold. The challenge of performing heart transplants on infants and children was one of the main reasons the 44-year-old physician accepted the position of chief of cardiothoracic surgery at Children's last fall, replacing the retiring pediatric heart surgeon, Farouk Idriss. On May 13, 1988, Dr. Idriss had performed Children's first heart transplant into Sharell Arnold, then an 18-month-old girl dying from cardiomyopathy, or swelling of the heart muscle, and today a thriving 4-year-old.

Thus far, the Children's team has done heart transplants on 22 children, and 17 survive. This includes nine infants under 1 year of age, of whom seven survive. These young patients and their courageous families are supported by the entire Children's Hospital team, including financial planners, social workers and nurses.

Lauren Aggen is the seventh surviving infant, but it was not an easy process.

Dr. Mavroudis was in the north suburbs returning some Christmas gifts when he received the alert from Backer, who is prepared to fly across the country whenever necessary to "harvest" the tiny hearts of deceased infants. "When we find a donor heart for one of these kids," Mavroudis says, "we drop everything and go for it."

As Mavroudis drove down to Children's to prepare his surgical team and the Aggen infant for surgery, Backer and Becky Carlisle, Children's organ-procurement coordinator, were busy talking to the medical staff at Breckinridge Hospital in Austin, Tex. A 2-month-old boy was brain dead from Sudden Infant Death Syndrome, but his vital organs were being kept alive by artificial means, and his heart had been listed on "UNOS," or the United Network for Organ Sharing.

The race and sex of a donor have no bearing on a successful transplant, Backer says. "What is important," he stresses, "is to determine that the donor heart is a good heart, that it is free of viruses and that it is blood- and size-matched to the recipient."

These factors checked out, and at 10 p.m. on Dec. 29, Backer, Carlisle, a surgical resident and an OR nurse left by ambulance for Midway Airport, where they boarded a Lear jet for the three-hour flight to Austin.

"It had been bitterly cold in Chicago," Backer recalls, "and the weather in Texas was spectacular—warm and muggy. A white Lincoln limousine was waiting for us at the airport, and I remember thinking, 'Boy, these Texans do it right.'"

Once at the hospital, Backer and his team required about 90 minutes to remove the infant's tiny heart and to preserve it in a plastic bag containing a slush mixture of vital chemicals, ice and saline. The precious cargo was placed in a small blue-and-white Igloo cooler filled with ice, very similar to a beer cooler in appearance but so dramatically different in content.

Backer kept a tight grip on the cooler. Many of these procedures involve multiple teams acquiring multiple organs, and it would be unspeakably tragic to leave with the wrong organ. In another practical procedure, he had arranged for a guide to escort the team out of the hospital. "It's easy to get lost in a strange hospital," he says, "and lose valuable time."

The "ischemia time," or the time elapsed between the taking of a heart from a donor and its implantation into a recipient, refers to the time the heart is without nourishing oxygen. The outer limit is about four hours, and for this reason the flight to Austin was about as far as the Children's team could go to find a heart.

When Backer and his team reached the Austin runway, their jet's engines were up and running, and the plane was immediately given medical clearance for takeoff.

Approximately three hours later, at about 5 a.m., the team reached Chicago, where, once again, complications arose, this time in the form of an ice storm.

"We couldn't land at Midway," Backer says, "and if the ceiling had been a few hundred feet lower at O'Hare, we would have been diverted to Indianapolis or Milwaukee, and the mission would have failed. When we stepped off the plane, it was like a ice-skating rink, and I almost fell. I told our ambulance driver to 'take it easy' on the expressway."

Meanwhile, Mavroudis had decided to bring Lauren Aggen down to the second-floor operating room hours earlier than usual. "She was so sick," he says, "that I was afraid we would lose her on the elevator ride from [floor] 8 down to 2. Her blood pressure was very low and almost dropped out on the elevator, but I got her on the heart-lung machine just in time."

Lauren Aggen would require about a pint of blood to replace what was lost during the opening of her chest, and several of the Aggens' friends whose A-positive blood matched that of Lauren's had on the previous evening rushed from a church party to the hospital to donate what was needed.

Now, as dawn was about to break, the Aggens, surrounded by family and friends, about 15 in all, looked out from the second-floor waiting room at the hospital's Christmas lights and saw the ambulance pull up and Backer emerge with the vital cooler.

"I'll never forget," Dave Aggen says, "that when Dr. Backer and the others ran in with the new heart, the entire OR team gave a loud cheer."

By 7 a.m., exactly 12 hours after the drama began, Lauren Aggen's new heart was in place and beating strongly. The tiny muscle implanted into her chest during a one-hour procedure was reddish-brown in color, measured 1 inch in circumference and 1½ inches long, and weighed only 1.2 ounces—about the weight of a first-class mailing envelope. The new heart kicked in immediately to perform its life-saving role.

"When I first saw her hours after the implant, she was beat up and bruised and puffy and looking like a big red balloon, but it didn't matter," mother Janet says. "I could tell that the heart was working and that she was returning to pink."

There followed 30 days of slow hospital recuperation, and the Aggens treasure their copy of Lauren's hospital chart. It was three days after the transplant before Janet Aggen was able to see her daughter "finally wiggle a toe."

Among the key chart entries:

Dec. 30, 1989—Transplant. (Beside this, Janet Aggen drew in red ink three tiny hearts in the shape of smiling faces.)

Jan. 3, 1990. Chest tube removed . . . central line [for intravenous feeding] removed.

Jan. 9. Extubated [removed] from the ventilator. (Notation by the happy mother: "YEAH!")

Jan. 12. Echocardiogram shows normal left ventricular function and better right ventricular function.

Jan. 17. Breast feeding begins!

Jan. 19. Echo shows normal function!!

Jan. 22. Removed from intensive care and transferred to 6 West.

Jan. 24. All oxygen support discontinued; tolerates room air.

Jan. 27. 24-hour nursing care provided by Mom/Dad.

The entries end on Jan. 29.

The next day, the Aggens finally brought their daughter home, where they were met with a gratifying outpouring of community love and support. Balloons and a big banner on the family garage proclaimed: "Welcome home, Lauren Ann. You're gorgeous!"

Then the real work began.

"The medical procedures are dramatic, but these are simply mechanical things," says Children's social worker Kiyo Yoshimura. "What impresses me most is the courage it takes for a family to make this kind of decision and to live with it."

In the last two years, five families have decided not to seek a heart transplant for their dying babies.

"You don't just put a new heart in these kids, pat them on the head, send them home and wish them a happy life," says Dr. Zales, the cardiologist in charge of the medical followup. "What we've done with Lauren Aggen and the others is trade a fatal condition for a serious chronic condition that will require lifelong management. This never goes away, and these kids are always vulnerable."

Placing the voluminous chart of a heart-transplant patient next to the records of a "simple" open-heart surgical case, he continues:

"We believe that what we're doing is right and that in five years or so we'll be proven right. We're learning new things every day from our first class of 17 surviving transplant patients. In the meantime, we hope that some bright researcher out there will figure out the immune system and tell us how to prevent the patient from rejecting the new heart. Right now, all we can do is try to fine-tune our drugs to regulate and suppress the immune system in a way that prevents rejection of the transplanted heart but at the same time protects the patient against infections.

"The next modest step will be an improvement in our drugs to prevent rejection. The next *giant* step will come if we can coat the transplanted heart with a miracle substance so that the body does not recognize it as alien and we can thus achieve true tolerance of the transplanted organ, not just immunosuppression of the body's defense against an invader. If this happens, the new heart will be forgettable and truly a miracle treatment."

In the meantime, though, treating her daughter/patient has turned life upside down for Janet Aggen. Now on leave from her teaching positions, she does all her grocery shopping, for example, at about 11 p.m. "I have to make sure to get to the deli and meat counters before they close, but the Dominick's and Jewel stay open until midnight out here, so it's a perfect time to shop—no crowds. Plus I get back in time to do Lauren's 'vitals' and medications at midnight. I have to wake her up to do the blood-pressure reading, but she can usually sleep through the rest. By now she must think that all kids have their vital signs taken three times a day and need seven different medicines at seven different times a day."

The routine seems to work. Last October Lauren Aggen passed an important milestone: Her first heart biopsy was, in Zale's words, "as clean as a whistle—absolutely no sign of rejection." The biopsy is the "gold standard" to detect what could be a fatal rejection, and infant patients must be at least 6 months old or weigh at least 15 pounds before being subjected to the crucial test. At 9 months old, Lauren was 26 inches long and weighed exactly 15 pounds; both measurements are well below the average for her age, a condition explained by the three anti-rejection drugs she has been taking.

The biopsy offered good news, but at a price. The veins in Lauren's legs are so scarred from her previous ordeal that Zales had to use the jugular vein to thread a catheter to her heart. (The leg veins will eventually recover.) The jugular procedure necessitated the use of anesthesia and a ventilator, and she was kept overnight as a precaution. The cost: $6,000.

Lauren now makes monthly clinic visits to Children's to have her blood drawn, her heart evaluated by echocardiogram and her drug dosages adjusted. She will need a biopsy every three months for the next 18 months. Since leaving the hospital last Jan. 30, she has been back for checkups 25 times, and her mother calls the hospital almost daily for advice. Still, Lauren Aggen has never been readmitted to the hospital for infection or rejection, a fact Zales calls "remarkable. Her progress so far is as good as we can hope."

On a recent golden Saturday morning in late October, the Aggens entertained a writer and photographer at their Algonquin home before taking son Dave and baby Lauren out with another heart-transplant family—Annette and Steve Frerichs'—for an afternoon of apple-picking in Wisconsin. "We're very selective about where we go," Janet says, "but we take Lauren out as often as possible."

Dave and Janet Aggen, married for 17 years, both grew up in Chicago and met at Elmhurst College. They confide that they had not planned to have their second child. As they reminisce, their son comes in from the yard and displays a prized possession—a Ryne Sandberg autographed bat bought for him as part of a benefit auction that the Algonquin Jaycees sponsored to help defray Lauren's medical expenses.

Those expenses have now reached $255,000, but thanks to community benefit funds and the belated decision by Dave Aggen's insurance company to reimburse at least some of the expenses as "investigational therapy," the cost has not yet been a strain upon the family's finances. In discussing finances, Janet says: "We would not want cost alone to deter any family from considering this option. At first, the uncertainty of our insurance coverage added to our anxiety, but everything seems to be working out and, even if it weren't, the uncertainty would be outweighed by the wonder of seeing Lauren grow and develop and make baby talk and play pattycake."

Cost liabilities can vary widely in such circumstances. Fully one-third of the child transplant cases so far have involved inner-city children whose expenses have been paid by Medicaid. In the Aggens' case, though, the insurance situation was touch and go, and even today, most of the bills remain "in process."

The financial planners at Children's explained that Janet's school-district insurance provided a policy with a $500,000 cap, a limit she was astonished to learn might be low for what would eventually be needed. "I was told that if we'd belonged to an HMO, with its coverage limitations, we would have been ushered out the door," she says. As it turned out, though, her insurance will pay for much of the initial hospitalization and actual transplant.

The rest, it now appears, will be paid by her husband's insurance through a separate self-insured school-district fund. The insurer initially branded the transplant as "experimental" and refused to pay, but the entire school district went to bat for the Aggens, and using documentation provided by Children's hospital, compiled enough of a case to have the insurer reverse its decision and term the treatment investigational for this one case. "When the secretary called to say the insurer had reversed its position and was going to pay, she was crying," Janet says. "She told me she was 'going out on her lunch hour to buy a gift for Lauren.'" Among other things, the reversal of position means that Janet will not have to go back to work just for insurance coverage.

Janet adds: "My first OB bill is still being processed, but once we made the decision to go, we were committed to pay as best we can. At least we were told that we would not have to sell our house." Dave concludes: "We have been very fortunate. The day we returned from the hospital with Lauren, there was a note from the church slipped under our door. It read: 'You've made the right decision. Don't worry about the cost, because, if necessary, we'll raise every penny you need.'"

(Adult transplants, though costly, are now fairly common; infant heart transplants, however, have lagged in acceptance and reimbursements.)

In the meantime, at 8 o'clock on this Saturday morning, Janet takes out her blood-pressure cuff to take Lauren's reading, the result to determine whether she will need three doses this day of Captopril, a drug to lower her blood pressure, which is elevated by the anti-rejection drugs. Mom will also measure her daughter's heart rate, respiratory rate and temperature, a routine she will repeat at 4 p.m. and midnight.

Cyclosporine, to guard against rejection, will be given at 8 a.m., 4 p.m. and midnight. Zales notes that if the drug is not taken for as brief a period of time as two days, Lauren will surely and swiftly die from a massive rejection of her new heart.

Another drug, Nystatin will be given at 9 a.m., 3 p.m. and 9 p.m. to prevent oral thrush, a fungus that thrives under conditions of immunosuppression and that gives the tongue a cheesy coating.

Depending upon the results of her monthly tests, she also receives the anti-rejection drug, Imuran, on Mondays and Thursdays. A third anti-rejection drug, Prednisone, was recently discontinued, which should enable Lauren to grow more rapidly.

There are also thrice-daily doses of baby aspirin, to thin the blood; the antibiotic Bactrim, to guard against infections; and a vitamin.

The routine comes easily now, and these medications are administered with a tiny oral syringe that Lauren regularly tries to spit out. Later, sitting on the living-room floor next to Alexandra Frerichs, a baby who received a heart transplant only weeks before the Aggen infant, Lauren swipes at a balloon and makes happy baby talk. For all the world, these two unique babies look absolutely normal. But, as Janet reminds, "The only difference between us and any family with two young children is that I can't return to work—yet. I need to be with my daughter.

"Everyone remarks at how wonderful a baby Lauren is, and I tell them they're right. Then I add, 'Sure, she changes her own diapers, washes her own bottles, takes her own medicines. . . .'

"This experience has really changed our son too. He's been with us every step of the way, and he's been very supportive. When we first told him that Lauren had a new heart, his reaction was, 'Great. Now when are you going to bring her home?' He knows his sister's drug routine so well that he reminds me, 'Now don't forget to give Lauren such and such.'

"Still, it's been pretty hard on him. Recently, he was told he would need an X-ray for a sinus condition, and afterward, I found him crying in his room. When I asked him what was the matter, he replied, 'Are you telling me everything, or are you keeping something from me?' After seeing what his sister has been through, he's a little afraid of the doctor's office. Fortunately, we've been able to reassure him that what happened to Lauren is a once-in-a-lifetime thing."

Is the transplant worth it?

Dave Aggen says emphatically: "You see the proof right in front of you, playing on the floor. Every night when I put her to bed and she snuggles up against my chest, I can't believe that we ever had any doubts." Janet Aggen simply looks at her daughter and smiles in agreement.

Mom excuses herself to breast-feed her daughter, after which it is time for the baby to nap in the pink-wallpapered bedroom. Lauren Aggen loves music, especially lullabies and, appropriately enough, Christmas carols.

The feeding completed, Janet Aggen, busy mother and medical technician, turns on the music, kisses her daughter on the forehead and watches as she, now apparently out of danger, drifts off to sleep.

The gift for Lauren Aggen was being shared by all.

GHETTO DOCTORS

Picking Up the Pieces

Psychiatrist Carl Bell, M.D., is a man with a mission—stopping the epidemic of black-on-black violence

An explosion of noise welcomes Dr. Carl Compton Bell, a psychiatrist, to the weekday Bible class for the children of Chicago's Messiah-St. Bartholomew Church on the South Side. The rector, Rev. Darryl F. James, hushes the children and introduces his guest as a "fighter for the future of the black community."

The bespectacled Bell, 39, is dressed in his habit: sandals; blue jeans from Sears; one of his baseball caps, this one featuring the Chinese characters for *yin* and *yang*, or balance; and a full beard that masks a boyish face. His white T-shirt proclaims his cause: "Stop black-on-black murder." Vaulting onto a stage in the church's basement, he begins to scrawl some grim numbers on a chalkboard, the sad facts of a pattern of violence among blacks that has made black-on-black murder a silent epidemic.

"I'm here today to talk to you children about the leading cause of death among black males between 15 and 34," he begins. "The cause is murder, and I can see that there are at least 25 or 30 of you boys out there.

Well, if something is not done to change things, one of every 21 of you will be murdered before you're 34." The children titter. One boy whispers to his friend, "I know it won't be me."

The psychiatrist asks his class, "Now, why are all these black men being murdered?" The answers come from around the room, from boys and girls: "Robbers" . . . "the devil" . . . "drugs" . . . "gangs" . . . "jail escapers" . . . "thieves" . . . "bad people."

He cuts them short.

"All y'all wrong," Bell says. "The answer is 'us' and 'guns.' Black men are being murdered with guns by their families and friends. That's what happens in three of every four black-on-black murders." He asks the children, ages 7 to 11, "Now, how many of you know about guns?" Again, the answers come from across the room: A girl: "I found bullets in my house." A boy: "My grandmother found my cousin carrying a gun." A girl: "My daddy keeps a gun in the closet." A boy: "My uncle has a gun hidden under his bed." A girl: "My auntie carries a gun in her purse."

He asks, "Now, why do we need all these guns?" The answer comes back as a roar: "Protection!"

"All y'all wrong again," Bell explains. "You are a fool if you have a loaded gun in your home to protect yourself from a burglar. That gun is 118 times more likely to kill a family member or a friend than a burglar. These burglars are not dumb. They come when you're gone. And more people are shot with their own guns by burglars than the other way around. That's the fact.

"Do you know what a 'myth' is? That's something people may believe in even though it's not the fact. I like to talk about three myths: First, the myth that young black men are murdered by the police or by gangs. The fact is that they usually are murdered by family or friends. Second, the myth that black women are raped by strangers. The fact is that they usually are raped by family or friends. Third, the myth that black men and women are robbed by experts, who know exactly what they're doing. The fact is that usually they are robbed by family or friends."

He continues, "Who can tell me how [singer] Marvin Gaye was killed?" A girl answers, "His daddy killed him with a gun." Bell asks, "Who knows how [Chicago high school basketball star] Ben Wilson was killed?" A boy answers, "A friend killed him with a gun." Bell says, "Yes, and if those guns had not been loaded, if those arguments had taken place without a loaded gun nearby, Marvin

Gaye would still be singing, and Ben Wilson would still be making baskets.

"But we're talking about more than guns. Murder is just the tip of the iceberg. For every murder, there are 100 other acts of black-on-black violence—sexual molestations, rapes, robberies and physical assaults. And do you know what sends more black mothers to the hospital emergency room than all the auto accidents, muggings and rapes combined? Husbands, that's who. We have got to teach black people to stop beating each other to pieces right in their own living rooms."

The children are growing quiet. Bell presses his point: "Now, we all have a right to defend ourselves, but if you go beyond self-defense to murder, you're going to end up in jail. There are very few things that are worth going to jail for. Let's take insults." He asks one of the adults in the room to say something "bad about me," and the response comes back: "You're a bow-legged, bad-looking baboon." The psychiatrist asks softly, "What?" The insult is repeated, but with less force. Again, he says, "I'm sorry, but I didn't catch what you said." This time, the insulter cannot repeat the words without laughing.

Bell explains: "Let me tell you a true story. I was at this party, and on the way back to my group of friends I stepped on what I thought was a chair leg. It turned out to be the toe of a man with a gun. He said, 'Hey, man, you stepped on MY TOE!' I could see that he had a gun, and I could see that he had been drinking. I said, 'I'm sorry, I didn't hear what you said.' He repeated, 'You stepped on my toe.' Well, as he was talking, a lady walked in between us. I said, 'I'm sorry about this, but the lady distracted me. Would you mind repeating what you said?' He replied, 'Aw, shoot, man, forget it.' These violent impulses only last a moment or so, and they usually can be turned aside if you can engage the person's mind with humor or thought. But if I'd said, 'Yeah, what are you gonna do about it?' we might have had a different ending."

In his spare time, Bell teaches martial arts. He tells the children: "Now, sometimes you're going to have to defend yourself. Father James, come on up here. Let's pretend Father James has a knife and he's a mad killer." The children laugh loudly as their pastor, in clerical collar, comes onstage and stabs a rolled-up newspaper toward the physician's chest. In one swift movement, Bell deflects the weapon and flips the pastor head over heels and [gently] onto his back, with the make-believe knife now against the offender's throat.

He explains: "I've got him, and he knows I've got him and I know I've got him. He's helpless, and I've got a knife at his throat. But if I stab him, I go to jail because I've gone beyond self-defense and I've become a murderer. You can protect yourself only to the limits of self-defense. I've defended myself, but I don't have to kill the man to make the point."

As the shaken pastor attempts to regain his composure, Bell adds: "Let's have some applause for Father James. I promised him I wouldn't hurt him because he's sorta my boss [the clergyman is a board member of the Community Mental Health Council, which Bell supervises as executive director]." The class is in an uproar, but Father James restores order by noting that his guest now has a gift for everyone:

A T-shirt just like Dr. Bell's.

The psychiatrist likes to conclude his talks to community groups by handing out the T-shirts, and he always does it at his own expense or with the cost of the shirts being his honorarium. This day there are not enough right sizes for one and all, and at least one little girl ends up with an extra-large T-shirt that comes down almost to her ankles. But she wears it proudly as she comes over and tells him, "I've seen you on TV." And Father James asks him about the three-hour call-in show he will be hosting this evening on WVON. His guest, Mayor Harold Washington, will also receive a T-shirt.

With the children, Bell, himself a child of the ghetto, is preaching primary prevention. He knows from his own surveys that by age 11 four of every five black children will have witnessed a beating, stabbing or shooting, and as a "community psychiatrist," he wants them to know that there is a better way.

Unfortunately, however, the many patients who come to see him and his staff at the Community Mental Health Council will be treated after the fact as sad examples of crime and victimization who now require what he calls secondary and tertiary prevention. Many are emotionally disturbed, and Bell wonders whether they might be emotionally ill because they were victimized, rather than the other way around. Or a little of both. "Whatever," he says, "it is a sad situation." In a study on which he is collaborating, among mentally healthy blacks who walk in for routine medical care, one of every six women has been raped and two of every five men beaten or robbed. Often the occurrences are considered to be so routine that the victims find it unusual that anyone would ask. Bell is picking up the pieces.

He explains: "Once a piece of china is cracked, it will never be the same again. However, you can glue it back together and keep it in service. Many of the people who come to see us are like that. They've been broken by the violence that is so common in the black community, but we can help them rebuild their lives."

Bell, a former street kid and gang member who transformed himself from your "typical juvenile jerk" into a physician, decided to commit his own time and the resources of the mental-health center he runs to fighting black-on-black violence "because I was tired of picking up the pieces."

He graduated from the predominantly black Meharry Medical College in Nashville in 1971 and decided to pursue psychiatry "because I want to explore life's mysteries." After a three-year psychiatric residency with Chicago's Illinois Psychiatric Institute, he served two years as a medical officer with the U.S. Navy Reserve at Great Lakes. From 1976–78 he juggled three assignments as staff psychiatrist to the Chicago Board of Education, Chicago Board of Mental Health and the Community Mental Health Council. From there he became associate director of the department of behavioral medicine at Jackson Park Hospital, where he established a psychiatric emergency service. In 1982 he returned to the mental-health center as medical director, and this past July he was named executive director, supervising a $2 million annual budget and a staff of 85 who care for 2,000 patients a year.

The center itself was founded in 1975 when a group of concerned citizens from South Shore and Chatham opened a modest day-care facility, with only 10 staff members, at 7818 S. Stony Island Ave. Over the years the center expanded, moving, finally, to its current location, 8704 S. Constance Ave. Bell aims to turn the center "into a major force to stamp out mental illness on the South Side and to stop black-on-black violence."

He adds: "Growing up in the ghetto, I was always aware of the gangs and the violence, but my interest in fighting black-on-black murders really started in 1979, when I was serving on a task force convened by the Office of the Cook County Public Defender.

"I was doing psychiatric evaluations of young black men and women who had committed murders, usually of other young black men and women, and I was struck by the familiar pattern. The murders were almost always crimes of passion, usually between families and friends. One day a colleague, Alan Goldberg, said: 'What's going on here? Something should be done to stop this.' The seed was planted."

Two conferences on violent behavior at the National Institute of Mental Health solidified his resolve. In 1986, as the chairman of the National Medical Association's (NMA) psychiatry section, he recommended both to NMA (the major organization for black physicians) and to the American Psychiatric Association that physicians should routinely screen their black patients for violent feelings, as a means of addressing black homicides as a public-health problem. "The two go hand in hand," he explains. "Today's victim of crime will be tomorrow's perpetrator unless we can intervene." The appeal made the front page of the New York Times, and Bell's cherished privacy was replaced by speeches to law-enforcement agencies, by appearances before community groups and by media interviews on a topic that has drawn criticism from colleagues who feel that it will put the black community in a poor light. He plans to push on.

Though he is single-minded about his crusade, Bell is a man of many contradictions. He describes himself as "very traditional" in male-female, physician-patient and teacher-student relationships, but he is also proud "to be a little peculiar," notably in his clothes and hobbies.

For his installation as executive director of the mental-health center, he did relent enough to wear a T-shirt with a doctor's coat and stethoscope stenciled on the front "because I promised Father James [who made the announcement] that my attire would be appropriate." He wears the white doctor's coat hanging in his office "only when it's cold," but he is quick to note: "No patient has ever been in doubt that I'm the doctor. I have a way about me that says, 'I'm in charge, and I know what I'm doing.'"

A man who devours psychiatric and scientific texts and who is very proud of the numerous scientific papers he has published on the causes and effects of black violence, he likes to relax by reading comic books and garbage novels. A dynamo at work, he spends his weekends "either in bed or soaking in the bath," unless, of course, he's writing a paper or out of town giving a speech. His wife, Dr.

Dora Dixie Bell, claims that her husband has taught her "the fine art of hanging out."

A fitness fan, he can stand neither to swim ("too boring") nor run ("it bangs up my feet") but instead enjoys judo and karate ("they involve the mind as well as the body and are essentially nonviolent") and scuba diving ("it's a completely mysterious world beneath the sea").

He needs his diversions because the work at the center can be very grim, and to enjoy it a therapist must be able to see the trees for the forest and to take consolation in the small triumphs among the many sorrows. Consider the case of Cecilia.

She will tell a bitter story of fear and loathing, but, nevertheless, Bell emphasizes, hers is a success story. "To fully understand what we have been able to accomplish with Cecilia," he says, "you would have had to have seen her when she first came to us, and you don't have this before-and-after view.

"Do you know how a dead spider looks when it gets all balled up? Well, that was Cecilia. She was shriveled up and ready to die. She was extremely depressed and could not look anyone in the eye, especially men."

Cecilia (a pseudonym), 48, sits in a small consultation room and stares sadly at the falling rain. A pretty woman, she is brightly dressed in a green floral-patterned dress, with matching earrings and shoes. "I have seven children," she begins, "but I raised eight. Whenever it rains, I think of Edith out there all alone in the cemetery, lying in the cold and rain. But, me, no way can I make myself go near that place. It hurts too much.

"It was the day they buried Martin Luther King Jr. in 1968 that I moved away from my husband. I moved away with eight babies, but I've always been a doer, and I took care of my babies, working in restaurants and catering and working for the archdiocese and doing some sales on the side. I never smoked or drank, and I taught my children to try to be with the church people. But I wanted the children to see their father, and I made it easy for him to do this.

"I still can't believe it, but Edith was raped by her father. Oh, I didn't know it at the time, but when she was 17, he raped her. He was mad at me, and he thought that the best way to get back at me was to rape our daughter. I later found out that right under my nose he had been trying to turn all the kids onto drugs, handing out reefers as Christmas presents. He'd turned Edith onto marijuana and cocaine, and then he raped her. I remember when she started working at the bank how she began to talk in a high-pitched voice and how she was always snifflin' and carryin' on, and I told my boys, 'There's something wrong with Edith.' They said, 'No, Momma, she's just growin' up,' but a mother always knows her child.

"For about seven years Edith was bouncing in and out of hospitals, and I used to think it was because of the drugs. She was 21 before I found out that she had been raped by her father. He'd kept her quiet by giving her drugs and by convincing her that I was just jealous—that I'd gotten old and fat and that he'd left me because I didn't want any more babies—as if eight were not enough."

Edith became a prostitute as well as an addict and moved out of state with her pimp. After a brief, drug-free return home, she returned to her pimp, leaving a son with Cecilia.

"It was Thanksgiving month, 1984, on a Monday, when I last talked to Edith. To this day I get nervous when I hear from all my kids on the same day because that's how it was this Monday. I talked to Edith and I talked to my other seven, and we all were real happy because Edith seemed to be doing so much better.

"The next morning about 11 I got a call from a woman on the West Side, one of Edith's girlfriends. Well, they found this girl's name in Edith's Bible, and now she was telling me that Edith had been killed, that Michael [her pimp] had stabbed her to death.

"That's about all I remember, though they tell me that I did some bizarre things. That night they found me out in the street, walking in the rain in my nightgown without any undies on, cars stopping and horns blasting. I don't remember any of it. I don't remember even going to the funeral. I never saw the body—the boys wouldn't let me because she'd been so brutally stabbed. A few days later I was looking for my favorite red blanket, and my oldest daughter reminded me, 'Momma, you took it to the cemetery and placed it on Edith's grave to keep out the cold and the rain.' I guess I did. Edith had a red dress on the night she was killed. She was only 24.

"This really affected my thinking, and when I first came here [to the center] in January, 1985, I was a real mess. I'd never seen this Michael—only a photo—and he's a spitting image of Dr. Bell. The first time I saw Dr. Bell I couldn't stand to look at him. I'd slide down in my chair and close my eyes so I wouldn't have to see him. My daughter, Ann, tells me that once I walked into Dr. Bell's office with a blackjack in my purse. No, it wasn't for defense. I intended to do to him what had been done to my daughter.

"Over the years, I've been able to work my way through some of this. Every morning I begin my day by saying, 'Lord, I thank you for helping me through this, and I am going to write down the day when I can first quit grieving for Edith.' Well, I have yet to see that day, but I am coping.

"Edith's son was so traumatized that he had to be hospitalized right after the murder. He's 10 now, and he's making it, too.

"I am a Catholic, and whenever I hear of anyone who's going through what we went through, [my grandson] and I volunteer to go talk with them. If you ain't been there, you can't understand, and we've both been there."

Bell says, "She's only halfway home, but the very fact that she can even be interviewed is absolutely amazing, compared to the way she was. What we're able to give her is only tertiary prevention, but she is much, much better."

"Larry," 36, volunteered for counseling after it was reported to the Illinois Department of Children and Family Services (DCFS) that on several occasions he had sexually molested his 12-year-old daughter, although he had stopped short of raping her, thanks to the alcohol and cocaine that rendered him temporarily impotent.

Larry is short and wiry, and his sad eyes are hidden behind sunglasses. He has just finished a day shift at the post office. While he talks, his two sons, ages 9 and 11, play outside the door.

"There were 12 of us in my family," he begins, "and I never knew my daddy. My mother started having kids when she was 14, and she had 12 by four different men. By the time she was 20 I guess she'd had five kids already. Oh, I know which man was my father, but he wasn't the type who'd recognize me as his son. How'd I feel? That's a good question. I guess I've been cold about it ever since I was a little kid, what with living in the slums and playing in the garbage and never having any decent clothes and always seeing the men beat up on my mother.

"Oh, it had a powerful effect on me, and I guess it made me pretty hostile. I can remember when I was 6 and one of the men just beat and beat my mother. That beating must have gone on for an hour, and I can still see it in my mind. And there was nothing I could do at age 6. I'd just look at his muscles, and it was like looking up at a tree trunk. Later, when I got older, me and my brothers would use sticks and stones and bottles and jump some of these men when they beat my mother. Now, most of these beatings were a drunk-type situation, and if the man were drunk enough, we could usually stop him. By the time he slept off the drunk, we were in school.

"But it had a powerful effect on me. I can remember walking to school one day with holes in my shoes and pants and promising myself that if I ever had children I would be the father to them that I never had. And because of the way I was raised, I never beat up on women. To this day, if I hear that one of my sisters is being beaten, I'll rush right over and tell the man to leave her alone. And to argue with me outside—away from the kids.

"Now, the first woman I married . . . was no good, and after our two children were born, she ran off with my best friend. Well, I had a gun, and I thought about killing her—him, too—I mean she was my wife and he was my best friend, but I thought, 'No, what good will that do?'

"I got my two kids back, but the oldest boy was a diabetic and had to go into foster care. What he needed was a square meal every day, and my wife was never the type to cook. Later, my daughter went into foster care for a while, too.

"I took up with another woman, and we had my two youngest boys. And I got my daughter back, too. But this woman started running around on me, too. I'd come home and find out that she'd left the kids with the neighbors. And my daughter told me that other men would be calling when I was gone. I guess she got into drugs and, maybe, prostituting. She left, too.

"Now this thing with my daughter started when I was on drugs. I was working nights at the main post office, and most of us were on speed and cocaine to stay alert.

"It cost about $50 for one-half gram of coke, and that might give you a buzz for only three or four hours. I was spending all my money on drugs. They were turning off the water, turning off the electricity because I couldn't pay my bills. I was never one to steal money, so I'd borrow, but by the time I got my check and paid off my creditors and bought some more drugs, there was nothing left to pay the bills.

"About this time I began messing with my daughter. It's something that only recently I have been able to look in the eye. I'd take some coke with my friends, and, boom, my next stop would be home because I couldn't function on the streets. And I'd usually have a few beers to chase the coke because it leaves a burning, dry taste in your mouth.

"And I guess when I got stoned, I'd go after my daughter. I don't remember it, but she'd always tell me the next day. She wasn't real angry at me, but she'd try to get me to understand. I guess I was feeling on her, and when she would tell me to stop I'd start to beg and plead with her. Thank God that I never actually had intercourse with her. She told me that these things only happened about four or five times, but sometimes I wonder if she only told me about the bad times.

"Finally, the guilt and hurt got to me, and I asked for help, but I was told that DCFS could help me only if my daughter were first placed in foster care. Then they said they would have to take my daughter. That really hurt. We thought of running off, my daughter and me, until the money ran out, but I decided I didn't want her to live on the run. Then, after they took her, I thought about getting a machine gun and shooting up the offices at DCFS for taking my daughter away and destroying her life. I was thinking crazy there for awhile.

"I came here [to the center] in January, 1987, and now I think I'm over the hump. I've been off drugs for six months, and I know that if my daughter were to come home now, she would not be in danger. I've been able to look at my own experiences and to understand the pattern I was repeating. My daughter's aching to come home, but I'm not ready yet. Me and the boys miss her greatly, but I want her to have more time and me to have more time. But she'll be coming back.

"In the meantime, I never have any time for myself because she's not here to take care of the boys the way she used to. When I leave here, I'll have to fix dinner for the boys, help them with their homework and spend time talking to them. By then, it's time to go to bed.

"I've been working since I was 9 years old, and I never have any time for myself. But that's okay. I'm all my kids have got."

Bell says: "We have had to alert the Department of Children and Family Services about his conduct, but I am confident that if he sticks with his therapy, there will be a happy outcome. He will be reunited with his family, neither he nor his daughter will have to worry again about the risk of incest and both will be better off."

Today Bell helps many patients like Cecilia and Larry to rebuild their lives, but a generation ago, in the days of the Mississippi Freedom Marches and the civil-rights struggle, he was a confused, frightened teenager who within the space of a few months had lost his mother, his natural father and his only brother. All that stood between him and despair was his stepfather and uncle and a dream that he was meant to be somebody.

In addition to being a community psychiatrist who practices "social medicine" and makes house calls to places like Messiah-St. Bartholomew Church, Bell also practices traditional psychiatry, administering medication and motivation to both the mentally ill—including those suffering from psychotic breaks—and the mentally normal—who, nevertheless, are worn down by the stress of living in an environment that often offers blacks high frustration and low opportunities. It is an environment that many blacks feel they cannot control. Often the men escape to alcohol, drugs, crime and prison, with a jail term often the equivalent of a finishing school; the women, usually left alone to rear the children, turn to despair.

Bell knows the ways of the ghetto, including among his credentials membership in the once-fearsome Blackstone Rangers. He tells his story in a slow, soft voice occasionally punctuated by an explosive laugh.

"There are two things that say it all about me," Carl Bell begins.

"First, my parents raised me to be free—to be independent and uncompromisable—and throughout my life when the tough times came, when things looked the worst, there would come from deep within me this music that I call the 'spiritual stuff.' I become real cool and convinced that, somehow, things are going to be okay. As a black man growing up in America, I never had the roots that, say, the Anglo-Saxons had or even the Irish and the Italians—the ability to look back at a culture and all its rituals. But I believe I had this innate spirituality, this inner music, that kept me going. I'm not attached to any particular church, but I believe in the Indian proverb—'What kind of god can this white man's god be if it is confined to the box of a church; the god we know is as big as the great outdoors.'

"Second, I've always been bright, but I used to think of myself as simply eccentric. When you're smarter than a lot of the people around you, they begin to treat you like you're peculiar, and you begin to think you're peculiar. When I was in high school, I was told that my IQ was 140—and that was when I learned IQ is important. At the time I thought 140 sounded low—there were higher scores, after all—but I began to realize that I was out of step with some of the things going on around me. For one thing, I've always had a sense of ethics, even though I always knew how to go with the flow. And I've always believed that exploring life's mysteries is the biggest adventure of all. But it wasn't until I got to medical school and a classmate told me, 'Bell, you're crazy,' a comment I'd heard many times before, that I had it explained to me differently. I'd been arguing with the chairman of obstetrics over whether or not a pregnant woman would have twins. I had examined the woman with my own hands, and I thought I had felt twins; the chairman thought otherwise and had X-rays to back him up. He asked me if I wanted to make a friendly wager, and since I had no money in those days, I said, 'Sure, I'll wager my grade, and why not let me deliver the woman?' Well, I delivered twins, and later, at lunch, the chairman told me and my friend: 'Bell, you're not crazy. You're just bold and arrogant.'"

Bell adds: "When I started to talk about black-on-black violence, some members of the black community got upset and said, 'Shh, shh, you're washing our dirty linen in public, and the whites will only say, "We told you so—blacks *are* violent."' Well, I asked them, 'Where do you think I get my facts? From the white health and police agencies, of course!' They already know what's going on. And, more important, violence is a problem of all the poor, whose lifestyles have never been properly studied. When you adjust for economics, the poor whites suffer as much from violence from family and friends as do the poor blacks. My wife is also a physician, doing a family-practice residency at Christ Evangelical Medical Center in Oak Lawn, a community with only 19 black families. She sees the same kind of child and spouse abuse and family beatings that I do. And, finally, violence, including auto accidents, has become the leading killer of *all* the nation's young people, due in part to a rising suicide rate that appears linked to a combination of alcohol and guns. I'm talking only about black violence because I'm a black psychiatrist treating black patients."

Recalling his own youth, he says: "I went through all the classes—poor, working class and middle class. My natural father, William Bell Jr., and my mother, Pearl Debnam Bell, were both masters-degree social workers working for adoption agencies, but my father left soon after I was born. I don't know why, but they've told me it was over a dispute over how I should be raised. My mother wanted me to be free, my father wanted me to have more discipline.

"From birth through age 7 I lived on the West Side at 1633 S. Spaulding Ave., where the Cobras were the big gang. My brother, William III, was seven years older and a gang leader.

"All the blacks lived together, and we all were poor. I can remember going without shoes and eating bread and molasses because a lot of the people were from the Deep South and that's what they'd eaten down there. It would take years for a hole in the street to be filled, and I can remember that one of my favorite pastimes at age 4 was to throw dirt into the street holes and wonder if I could ever fill it up.

"When I was 7 we moved to 51st Street and Ellis Avenue on the fringe of Hyde Park, and I went to Kozminski public grammar school. My mother had remarried Mattie Pratt, who was a house painter. The big gang was the Vandells, and my brother, Bill, was a big leader. He was my protector, and nobody would mess with me. By the time I was 10, I'd made three or four zip guns. Someone would buy a .22 rifle, cut the barrel down with a hacksaw into three or four parts, find something to serve as a wooden stock, fashion a hammer and trigger out of some metal and, presto, you had a zip gun. It might not kill, but it would hurt. I never used one, but I knew how to make one. I can remember a lot of my brother's friends, all sons of working-class parents. They're all dead now.

When I was about 11 or so, Bill joined the Army, and I detached from the gang.

"But when I started at Hyde Park Public High School in 1961, which had changed from a white school to a black school, I joined the Blackstone Rangers. It sounds strange, but you had to join the gang to get into the school. They 'recruited' you, and it could get pretty silly, with dues and passwords that changed every day. Someone would say 'apple,' and you had to answer 'banana.' For initiation, you'd have to box one of the older members. Well, I've always been a pretty good boxer and able to take care of myself, and I didn't have too much trouble. I thought of myself as being 'in' the gang but not 'of' the gang.

"As a psychiatrist, I can now see that gangs are in many ways just a means for adolescents to work out the issues they have to deal with during the teen years. You could probably replace street gangs with a better alternative, like the Boy Scouts.

"From 13 to 17 I was what we called a 'floater,' with friends in all the social classes. I could hang out with the Rangers or I could hang out with the working-class people around 47th Street or I could handle myself at a party in Chatham, which we called the 'gold-plated ghetto.'

"I always thought of myself as being pretty lucky. At home, my mother had a lot of black art and other cultural things that instilled black pride. I was allowed to be free, as long as I wasn't flunking out of school or getting high on drugs on hurting people or getting girls pregnant, and I wasn't doing any of these things.

"It used to be a big thing for a lot of the gang members to go down to the Loop and steal shirts from Brooks Brothers. They thought that having a shirt without a pocket would give them status. Psychiatrists call it 'compensatory grandiosity' for lack of self-esteem. Well, I wouldn't do it. I figured I could live without the status, but everyone said, 'Bell, you're strange.'

"Once I was walking my girl home from school, and this guy from another gang followed me with his buddies, grabbed my jacket and began jumping around, challenging me to a fight. I thought, 'This is cute!' knowing that he intended to have his buddies help him out. I tried to talk my way out of it, but suddenly he began to take his coat off, which of course, left him helpless with his arms tangled in his sleeves. I flipped him over my head and stood there a while, actually considering whether or not I should throw him in front of a bus. In fights, I had often knocked somebody down, but I had never been one to stomp somebody who was down. There was always a little voice inside me, saying, 'Don't do that!' Now I heard the same voice. I put him down and continued on. A few blocks later, he did it again. This time I picked him up and considered throwing him through a picture window before I thought, 'No way.' The third time the police came and broke things up.

"Now he might have pulled a knife or gun on me, but there was a certain ethic at work. To lose with your fists and to be forced to pull a gun is to lose face on the street. But had he done it or had his friends jumped me, my future medical career might have ended right there.

"The gangs were part social. I can remember collecting dues, hiring a band, renting a room at the Palmer House or Conrad

Hilton Hotel and throwing a party for 500 people or so from the South Side. We always did all right with the ladies. But there was a dark side, too. Once, I was accused of losing the Stones' 'execution gun.' This is a 38-caliber barrel hidden in what looks like a pen or a fancy chalk-writer. The penalty was to be shot in the leg, but I managed to talk myself out of it.

In grammar and high school I was pretty much of a jerk because that's what we all were. But I also had some things going for me. I had one teacher in grammar school, a Mrs. Hayes, who wouldn't accept excuses, and she made me learn math. And I was a good reader because I always read a lot of comic books, and the Marvel comic books had a lot of words that would send you to the dictionary—words like 'cacophony' and 'perilous circumstances.'

"I also had a sense of curiosity, but one of the biggest frustrations in growing up in the ghetto is that you can never find anything to make anything. I wanted to make a desk from orange crates, but I didn't have any nails. I would have to scrounge around for bent nails and then straighten them as best I could with a hammer. I never had a straight nail.

"I was pretty much a juvenile delinquent until I met Milton Benz, my high-school geometry teacher, who is black. Benz saved a lot of us. When I was 15 or so, I screwed up something in his class, and he embarrassed me by asking in front of everybody, 'Mr. Bell, are you going to use your brains or are you going to be a jerk for the rest of your life?' I was furious, and I decided to get him—but on his terms. From that day on, every time he failed to cross a 't' or dot an 'i' or explain a theorem proof properly, I jumped all over him.

"Suddenly I learned how to learn, and I was on my way. For the rest of high school, I went to class from 8 a.m. to 2, studied from 2 to 4 and made straight A's. From 4 to 9 I still hung out on the basketball court with the other guys, but I was beginning to get excited about learning."

He recalls: "I graduated from high school in January, 1965, and spent the next six months on my butt doing absolutely nothing. I decided to graduate from college within two years—starting that summer. I had been going to high school for eight hours a day, and I didn't see much sense in going to college for only three or four hours a day."

During his first semester, the roof fell in.

"First, my brother was killed," he recalls. "Bill had gone from the gangs to the Army to being a Chicago cop. That's the route for black males, then and now. There was a robbery one night, and Bill, who was off-duty and out of uniform, joined two uniformed white officers in chasing the robbers, who were black. After a chase Bill had trapped one of the robbers in a vestibule. Well, two other policemen had joined the chase, and they apparently weren't aware of who Bill was. When they saw him—a black man with a gun in his hand—they killed him. I was told that he had six bullets in the back.

"Within a few more months my mother died of kidney disease, and my natural father died of heart disease. Neither had received the kind of medical care they needed. My stepfather was still alive, but he spent most of his time either painting or drinking or both. That's what you did. There's a lot of step-parenting in the black community, and I loved my stepfather. In fact, on the few occasions that I saw my natural father and he would introduce himself as my father, I would say, 'No, you're not my father, that's my father over there.' But my stepfather wasn't as smart as I was, and I couldn't talk to him about my plans to graduate from college.

"I was very upset about what had happened, and I didn't know what to do. I was only 17, and you don't know anything at 17.

"I chose to stay in college, and I think that the reason I studied as hard as I did was negative—I wanted to prove that blacks are not academically inferior. For a while I lived in a small apartment at 60th Street and Dorchester Avenue that had so many roaches the kitchen had to be boarded up. Then my stepfather's brother, Bert Pratt [now dead], took me in."

By 1966 Bell had two years of college credit at Chicago City Colleges, and in June, 1967, he was graduated from the University of Illinois at Chicago with a major in biology and minors in calculus and chemistry. He decided to go to medical school "because I had majored in biology and it was either teach biology, work in ecology or become a doctor."

Bell wanted to attend the University of Illinois Medical School but wasn't accepted. He had been accepted at Meharry and was determined to work his way through.

He stayed four years in Nashville, working during the summers at the medical school as an extern in a dietary study. During that study, the physician-to-be learned that "half of the black children we saw at our clinic were deficient in vitamins A and C and were anemic." In the meantime, he was doing his own informal study—seeing how long he could go with as little food as possible.

I had to save my money to pay my tuition," he says, "so I budgeted only $1.50 per week for food. And I tried to squeeze a dime or so out of that so I could buy a pocket book once a week. You get very tired of reading nothing but biochemistry texts, and newspapers cost money. I didn't have a radio, and a TV was out of the question, so my only diversion was pocket books, and I loved the mysteries and garbage novels, which usually ran about 120 pages. I would ration my reading to 15 or 20 pages a day so that a book would last the full week. That was my entertainment. As for my food, once a week I would go down and buy seven cans of Chef Boy-ar-dee ravioli—it worked out to about 15 cents a can.

"I would get up in the morning and go to work, work eight hours and come home and eat one can of ravioli. When I tried to stretch my money even farther, I would go out and buy a bottle of ketchup. You heat up some hot water and pour in some ketchup and you have tomato soup.

"The absolutely low point came one day when I stood in a supermarket looking at a can of dog food. It actually looked edible, and it was cheaper than Chef Boy-ar-dee. I bought a can, took it home, opened it, put it on a plate and looked at it. But, no way!

"Shortly after that the chairman of the dietary study invited me to his home one night for a discussion *after* dinner. I was too proud to tell him of my financial difficulties, even though I was taking the school's Maalox samples to treat my hunger pains. At the end of the night he offered me a tomato from his garden to take home. Within three steps of leaving his house I had swallowed it nearly whole. A tomato has never tasted as good, before or since.

"During the school year I was in better shape because a friend traded me food in exchange for cooking and doing the dishes. Knowing him was a lifesaver, but my summers were very, very long."

It was during the medical-school summers that Bell also turned his back forever on "anything remotely illegal," explaining: "Some of my buddies came down from Chicago one summer and stayed at my apartment. They had guns and were living high on the hog and admitted to dealing drugs and cough syrup, but I figured, 'It's cool.' After all, I had grown up in that environment. And at 19 or 20, you're not really awake.

"One weekend I borrowed their car to go to a friend's wedding in Alabama. It was a 1968 Pontiac GTO, a very fast car that also had a broken speedometer. Driving back through the hills of Tennessee, I was stopped and told I had been doing 120 miles an hour. Well, I was used to junky cars that rattled at high speeds, and this car didn't make any noise at all, or so I told the patrolman, who took me into Pulaski, Tenn. In the town square there was a statue that read: 'Home of the Ku Klux Klan.' They took me to the county jail and stuck me in a cell with no ventilation and s— on the floor, explaining, 'Well, niggah boy, if you can't prove this car is yours we're gonna lock the cell door, and the last time it was shut, it took three days to get it open.' I was allowed one call, and I called my buddies back in Nashville:

"'David, will you please tell me the registration number on your car, so I can get out of this town?'

'Carl, the car was stolen in New York.'

"Well, my life sort of flashed before my eyes, but then the inner music washed over me. The sheriff relented and allowed me more calls, and the medical school finally contacted a Dr. Spockwell, a Meharry grad and black physician who was practicing in Pulaski. He came down to the jail with a roll of bills the size of an apple, saying, 'I understand you have one of my people in here.' I could have kissed him. The sheriff took the money and told me to get out. Dr. Spockwell was one of the few physicians in town, and he was allowed to take me to a local restaurant, where he bought me a malt.

"The day after I got back to Nashville the FBI knocked on my door. They had traced the registration papers for 24 stolen cars to a phone number in Alabama that had repeatedly been called from my apartment. I told my friends to get out and stay out.

"Before, I had always thought that if somebody broke a window and I were just standing around watching them, I hadn't done anything wrong. After Pulaski, Tenn., I knew differently."

In 1971 he became Dr. Carl Bell, a physician who decided to specialize in psychiatry because it "was the one subject I didn't understand." Some 16 years later Bell is running CMHC. The center has four major programs:

• Screening and medical assessment, including a 24-hour emergency hotline; special counseling for persons whose driver's licenses are revoked for drunken driving; and assistance in dealing with other agencies such as Social Security, public assistance and the Veterans Administration.

• Family systems for adults and children who have "nonsevere" emotional problems (without a history of psychiatric hospitalization, psychotic episodes or criminal activity), including individual, couple, family and group therapy; and a special emphasis on victims of violent crimes and incest.

• Outpatient services for adults with "severe" emotional problems (at high risk of requiring hospitalization or rehospitalization) in need of long-term treatment, including a special emphasis on the elderly.

• And the "milieu program" to provide day treatment and supervised residential and vocational services to the chronically and severely mentally ill who need to develop independent living skills to avoid rehospitalization.

Bell is especially proud of the CMHC's motto: "We dare to care." And just as he used to make things in the ghetto out of bent nails, he has published an outpouring of what he calls "bent-nail" research. He explains: "I don't have all the manpower, money and computers I need to do research according to the strict academic model. But we are doing basic hands-on research on black patients, and I believe that most of it is dead right." The pun is unfortunate, he acknowledges. Most of his findings have been published in the Journal of the National Medical Association, including papers on "Coma and the etiology of violence." "The prevalence of isolated sleep paralysis in black subjects" and "Preventing black-on-black homicides."

It is important work. He theorizes that panic disorders and sleep paralysis, often related to the social stress of growing up black, may be early markers of high blood pressure, the original "silent epidemic" in the black community, and that early intervention may help prevent it. In regard to black-on-black murders, he theorizes that in addition to the often-cited environmental factors (poor educational, job and housing opportunities) and psychological factors (self-hatred and low self-esteem), there may also be *acquired* biological factors, such as head injury and heavy alcohol use, both of which are much more common among poor people. The combination of all three, he proposes, leads to the frustration and impulsiveness that can cause violence.

This theory is not original with Bell. A decade ago Meharry Medical School psychologist Ruth Dennis contended that prolonged social stress causes deviant behavior among many young blacks: "Young black men don't fear jail. They want to be a part of it, otherwise they'll become conversational dropouts among their friends."

She added that black churches, organizations, schools and families are being "shattered" and concluded that blacks, like the American Indians, might be unable to merge into the larger American society.

She also put the problem into personal terms, noting that her daughter was dating a young black man who had once killed another young black man and who was suffering emotional ills. "He was sitting around with some friends," Dennis explained. "They'd all been drinking, he had a gun—and when someone said, 'Shoot him,' he pulled the trigger."

Bell's research on black victimization is striking. In total, 427 patients were screened, representing all the open cases at the CMHC in May, 1986. Of the 427 patients, 99 percent were black, 68.3 percent lived on $7,400 or less annually and 61 percent lived alone. Females made up 58 percent of the sample, and 20 percent were children under 18. The study shows:

• Women—One of every 3 [33 percent] had been raped, and another 1 of every 3 [32 percent] had been sexually molested short of rape; 2 of every 5 [40 percent] had been physically assaulted, and almost 1 in 2 [44 percent] had been robbed.

• Men—Some 41 percent reported they had been physically assaulted, and another 41 percent said they had been robbed; also, 10 percent had been sexually molested, and 4 percent had been raped.

• Children (under 18)—Physically assaulted, 37 percent; robbed, 13 percent; sexually molested, 11 percent; and raped, 6 percent.

The study also asked patients if they personally knew of anyone who had been similarly victimized, with similar results.

Bell's study—conducted with CMHC staffers Karen Taylor-Crawford, M.D., head of the council's family services division; Esther J. Jenkins, Ph.D., a research associate; and Deborah Chalmers—involves patients who are to some degree emotionally disturbed, both moderately and severely.

To supplement his data, Bell commissioned a similar study among a mentally normal population at the Near North Health Services Corp., operating out of the giant Cabrini-Green housing project. This study, coordinated by internist Dr. Carolyn Hildreth, involved healthy patients who came in for routine checkups and treatment. The results, while reduced, are also striking: One in six adults reported being raped, one in six molested, one in six assaulted and one in four robbed.

"Clearly, what we have here," says Bell, "is a pattern of victimization that is so common as to be almost a way of life." This routine victimization inevitably leads to murder, with 90 percent of murdered blacks the victims of other blacks, usually family or friends. "In 1983," Bell says, "blacks, who represent only 12 percent of the U.S. population, accounted for 43 percent of the nation's homicide victims." Or, "In Chicago, people in black police districts are 11 times more likely to be victims of violent crime." Or, "In 1981 more blacks lost their lives from black-on-black murder than the number of black men killed during the Vietnam War."

The Chicago Police Department reports that from 1980–85 there were 2,381 black-on-black murders, representing slightly more than half of all city homicides.

Bell is very much aware that there are faces behind the statistics and that many of these people are trying to rebuild their lives with the assistance of his mental-health center. Among them:

• "R.T.," a woman who endured 30 years of beatings from her alcoholic husband, only to rebel when he not only threatened to kill her with his pistol but also confided that he had been cheating on her with their former landlady. Threatened with being shot, she responded, "You should be ashamed of yourself—threatening to kill me after all I've done for you," whereupon her husband laid his gun down upon a bedside table and retreated to the bathroom. "I told you that if you ever double-crossed me, that would be the end of us," she said and shot him to death through the bathroom door. "R.T." was subsequently acquitted on grounds of insanity and released to

Bell's medical supervision. Today she still has trouble recalling what happened, but she says, "I'd never put up with the beatings again; 30 years is time enough to learn."

• "Maynard" describes himself as "light, bright and damn near white," to him an unfortunate condition of birth that—combined with a "bad attitude" and some bad luck—had almost done him in with his black brothers, who often referred to him as a "white boy." He wasn't completely accepted in the black world, and he had no interest in trying to pass as white, but living in the twilight zone almost drove him nuts: "For years I was treated with anti-psychotic medications, as if I were crazy. I had an explosive temper, and whenever I would feel tense, I would assault someone. Once he [Bell] began to treat me as if I were normal—instead of crazy—by prescribing Inderal [a medication usually prescribed for high blood pressure but that can also be used to control explosive tempers] and psychiatric therapy for my violent impulses, I began to think that I am normal. Today I am relieved to be off the anti-psychotics. I no longer feel like a guinea pig. And every day I give myself 'self-talks' on how to get along with people instead of arguing with them. I've learned that unfriendly people draw unfriendly circumstances, and I'm working on being friendly."

• Adrienne, a 28-year-old woman, has just finished a three-year prison term for stabbing her brother-in-law to death. She says that after hearing reports that her favorite sister was being beaten by her husband, she accompanied her grandmother, cousin and older sister on a trip to straighten things out. All she remembers is a discussion that turned to an argument that turned into a fight that led to "seeing my brother-in-law start to throw a stereo down upon my sister's head." There was a butcher knife lying on the coffee table, and Adrienne used it to stab her brother-in-law in the back. She is bitter because she believes that her sisters and cousin turned state's evidence against her and framed her—without accepting their responsibility in the murder—and because her family does not seem to care as deeply for her as she does for it. She has completed three years of college and is very bright, but her recovery, her therapist says, depends on her willingness to talk about her lingering bitterness toward her family's disinterest in her welfare. And her inability to care about herself as deeply as she cares about others.

Bell likes to tell the medical students who often tag along with him: "Some of these patients may be crazy, but that doesn't mean that they're stupid. I've learned a lot by treating crazy people."

On Tuesdays he maintains a "private practice" at Jackson Park Hospital, with which he has been affiliated since 1972. He sees a steady stream of longtime patients, many of whom are psychotics or schizophrenics stabilized on medication.

Many are beaten down, not only by the hammers pounding on their heads but also by the many other medical ills they endure because they cannot afford proper care. Often it enrages Bell.

"I had a lady come in here last week with what looked like a baseball-sized tumor growing out of her jaw. She wasn't talking to me about her jaw, she was talking about something else. I asked, 'What happened to your jaw?' She replied, 'Oh, that. Just a toothache.' Well, it was some toothache. She had a huge abscess that required immediate care, but she could not find a dentist who would accept Medicaid. I got on the phone and twisted some arms and finally got one dentist to agree to see her.

"I've always had a sense of responsibility for the people I treat. Many of them are so beaten down that they don't think that they deserve medical care. I tell them that they have to CARE [his voice rising] ABOUT THEMSELVES. And it's not just because they're poor blacks. I can go to Haiti and walk right past the beggars. That's because they're hustling. But some of my patients walk with their heads down and their faces all screwed up, and it really upsets me.

"Of course, they have their reasons. One of my patients is a grandmother who was looking forward to her 'golden years.' One day her son-in-law stabbed her daughter to death right in front of her and her grandson. Suddenly, her daughter's dead, her son-in-law is in jail and she's responsible for taking care of her grandson. Worse, the child, who is my patient's only link to her dead daughter, looks exactly like his father—the man who committed the murder. This elderly lady finds herself thinking about hurting this little boy, who is also suffering from extreme emotional trauma. Thank God, they've come in for help. I think that we're going to be able to save them."

At the mental-health center he also sees "about 30 patients a day," in between running group-therapy classes and overseeing administrative details. His salary is $75,000 a year, but he says, "When I go through my checkbook at the end of the year, I usually find that I've written more checks as donations than I've written to pay bills. I'm not driven by money."

Many of the patients at the center are also drug-stabilized psychotics or schizophrenics, coming in for regular shots of Prolixin or Thorazine. Most look sad and tired and glad to receive the medication that stops them from hearing voices and becoming lost in their own fog. It can be a sad business. "Do you still hear voices?" he asks one elderly lady. "Oh, no," she replies, "That stopped when you put me on that new medication." "Do you get confused?" "Sometimes." "What month is it?" "August, doctor." "Who's the mayor of Chicago?" A long pause. "Daley," she says.

Bell has a theory that many blacks suffering from alcoholic insanity and hallucinations are incorrectly diagnosed as schizophrenics. "Look around the black community," he says, "and you'll see liquor signs everywhere. A lot of black males start drinking when they're 13 or 14, and by 15 they're doing a pint a day. Well, if you do a pint a day for 10 years, you're going to destroy your mind, and when these young black men are found in the street walking around in a daze, they're sent off to a psychiatric hospital and diagnosed as schizophrenic, when the real problem is to get them to quit drinking."

He adds: "They start to drink as a means of escape from the numbness of their lives. Society often does not have a place for young black males. Let's take suicide. I think that blacks are imitating whites, but with a twist. If you examine suicide rates among whites, you find that recently retired white males are at the highest risk of suicide. They find out that society no longer has a place for them, and they kill themselves. This same thing happens to black males, except that it happens at a younger age—at 20 or so."

One group of schizophrenics includes three former black gang members, including one called "the Chief." Bell says: "As long as I've known this guy, he's been a character. He came here seven years ago on a hot summer day—wearing a heavy winter coat and earmuffs. He's doing okay now, but he still remembers the glory days when he was a leader in the Blackstone Rangers, and he'll talk to you all day about the gangs."

The Chief rattles on about his gang days ("Now, I never did none of that fighting with fists and knives; the Chief stood back and watched the Indians fight") and asks a few questions about why he does not seem to be sleeping right. Might it be the six-pack or so of beer he drinks before going to bed? It might, Bell says and explains: "Do you understand that drinking a six-pack is like drinking a half-pint, and if you drink enough, it's going to drive you crazy? Stop drinking." Bell stops him at the door. "Tell me, Chief," he asks, "aren't you ashamed of some of the things the gangs did?" He answers, "Yes, Dr. Bell, you know I really am. We'd be sitting around drinking our wine and listening to the Temptations and giving orders to shoot somebody, and none of it really had to happen."

And so it goes.

Bell lives in a comfortable informally furnished three-bedroom condo in Hyde Park with his wife of three years, Dora Dixie, and their two daughters from her previous marriage, Niki, 16; and Audrey, 13. Parrots chirp from a nearby sun room filled with flowering plants. There is a bookcase lined with medical texts, but standing next to it is a door lacquered with covers of Marvel comic books—the comics he read in medical school.

"I have an entire file cabinet of vintage comics. My favorite way of relaxing is to take a long, hot bath and read a comic or a novel like 'The Destroyer.' When I was in the Navy, I tried to persuade the officers to give comics to all the enlisted men. There are many people who are never going to read 'The Mayor of Casterbridge' who can, nevertheless, acquire an appreciation of language by reading some of the Marvel comics that talk about a 'tryst in the park.' I originally got interested in comics because I wanted to be an artist and I admired the illustrations."

It is a Sunday, and the psychiatrist usually spends it "watching Kung Fu movies, taking a three-hour nap and then going to teach martial arts." A medical-school friend got him interested in karate (Bell has a fifth-degree black belt), and he has taught the discipline to the security guards at the health center to help them cope with disturbed patients without harming them.

"I'm also a big believer in having medical centers try to develop a boys' club, with an emphasis on sports like martial arts, or a Boy Scout troop. I believe that I have done more to influence young black boys away from violence by teaching karate for 15 years than I have as a psychiatrist."

Dora says, "Before I met Carl, I was never into lying around—I always had to be *doing* something—but I've learned that lying around can be okay, too." The family will soon be taking a scuba-diving vacation to Cozumel, Mexico, and Dora says, "Carl makes all the plans; all I have to do is pack."

Bell interjects: "As an eccentric, I guess my clothes head the list. Every year or so I go down to Sears and buy a pile of jeans. And whenever I travel, I buy a T-shirt; I must have about 300. Oh, I have a few nice suits for the times when I speak to business groups or talk to the mayor or present scientific papers—and Dora has taught me how to wear nothing but white shirts—but except for dress-up occasions like these, I go as myself." And such occasions are as rare as he can make them.

Dora Dixie Bell ("no jokes, please," she says) met her husband in 1982 when she was a student at the University of Illinois Medical School pursuing a fellowship on "transcultural psychiatry" at the Community Mental Health Council. She says it was "love at first sight. He was always very gentle and very professional, and he was smarter than I was. He seemed to stand for something and to be motivated by something beyond himself. He had a sense of mission to help his people. He didn't want to save the world—just a little part of it.

"But I'll take the blame. I proposed!"

And was it love at first sight for Bell? "She was my student," he says. "You don't fall in love with your students. But it's weird. It seemed as if I had already known her for a long time."

Dora Bell was divorced when her daughters were very young, and she notes: "I've seen a lot of life. I've been on welfare and I've been middle-class and now I'm a physician. I grew up in Maywood, and I was working as a management trainee for Jewel Foods when there was a mass layoff. I decided that I would never again subject myself to the whims of Corporate America, and I went back to school and got my college degree and medical degree—while raising my daughters. I wanted to be a psychiatrist, too, but Carl forbade it, so now I'm concentrating on family practice, and I'll probably do community work, too."

Bell wonders "how long I can keep up this hectic pace of caring for the severely mentally ill" and talks wistfully about "maybe moving to a rural area and getting a job as a prison psychiatrist—that's the only place where you're going to find a lot of crazy people in the country—and teaching martial arts and letting my wife support me." (He has joined the board of the National Commission on Correctional Health Care to try to prevent violence in prisons.)

Soon he is back to his crusade. "One of our surveys of [black] schoolchildren in Grades 2 through 8 found that 84 percent have seen someone close to them either fighting, shot, stabbed or beaten.

We arranged for these children and their parents to go to a retreat to try to develop ways to reduce family violence.

"Many young black women who are beaten or raped never receive proper medical care and emotional counseling, and years later they end up with severe psychological problems. We have to reach them earlier. And it is unfortunate that so many black women are single parents. I wonder how many corporate switchboards light up about 4 p.m. with calls from black children who just got home from school and are calling their mother to let her know they're safe."

In a paper he wrote for the Community Mental Health Journal, Bell noted that "by practicing community psychiatry it is possible for one man to make a significant difference."

Told that he has, Bell laments, "Yes, but there are only 600 black psychiatrists in the entire country." His wife smiles and says, "There *could* have been 601."

Caring for the Poor

A day with medical resident Charles DeShazer, M.D., at Chicago's huge Cook County Hospital

Chicago's Cook County Hospital, a sprawling colossus on the city's near west side, is the family doctor for thousands of poor patients, most of whom are black or Hispanic. This giant facility, boasting 500 beds, 835 physicians, and a $300 million annual budget, ministers every day to 1000 patients.

Theirs is not an easy lot, emphasizes internist Charles DeShazer, M.D., 32, who is completing his fourth year as one of the hospital's attending physicians.

"This place is simply too big for efficient medical care," DeShazer says. "We are overburdened with too many patients, too little space, and too few doctors and support staff. Most of the patients we see come in very late and only when the discomfort of their illness outweighs the discomfort of having to deal with the hassle of this system."

Still, this public hospital usually delivers excellent medical care without charge. The patients, of course, pay with their time. A typical wait for an appointment at the medical clinic is 4 hours; at the walk-in ambulatory screening center, 6 hours; for x-rays, 3 hours; for the pharmacy, 5 hours. For the patient, going to County is an all-day adventure.

Dr. DeShazer grew up in the neighborhood, or "Hood," as they say, only 5 minutes from County Hospital, and he now finds his medical practice rich in irony, satisfaction—and frustration.

"Growing up," he says, "my universe was bounded by the four-block square area from California St. on the west, Western Ave. on the east, Roosevelt Rd. on the north, and Ogden Ave. on the south." There were three good reasons for this circumscription: the "Disciples," the "Vice Lords," and the "Goon Squads," the teen gangs that brutally protected their turf.

The hero of DeShazer's shrunken universe was his father, Charlie Willie DeShazer, the youngest of 19 children born to a Mississippi sharecropper and his wife. Charlie Willie DeShazer never got beyond grade school, but he and his wife, Alcenia, whom he met in a Chicago church, insisted that their three sons and only daughter acquire college degrees.

The couple shared household duties, with Charlie working days at an auto parts store and Alcenia working nights at a factory. The brightest of their four children, Charles, wanted to be a doctor from the time he was 5.

"My parents always gave me unconditional love and support," DeShazer recalls, "and when I was 5 I received an immunization from our family doctor, a kindly Jewish man named Emanual Feinhandler. He was aptly named, and when I told him that someday I wanted to be on the other side of that needle, he supported me, saying, 'Well, of course, but you gotta do this and you gotta do that along the way.' My father helped, too, telling me, 'Well, of course, you're gonna be a doctor and you're gonna be a good one.' I never encountered any negativism at home."

A bright kid, DeShazer survived the mean streets of Chicago's West Side well enough to earn his M.D. and be on the other side of the needle barely in time to treat some of his former friends.

"I was working the wards a few months ago," he recalls, "when I heard this cry: 'Chuckie, Chuckie.' Well, that was my nickname back in the 'Hood.' It was an old friend named 'A.B.' He had been a star basketball player with great hands. Now, his hands were in police cuffs and his mind was shot with alcohol and drugs. That was the worst thing to see, that this friend of mine who had been pretty with it as a kid, was now gone. His mind was dead. He was proud of me, though. He said, 'You're lucky, Chuckie. You got out.' Of course, then he tried to bum a cigarette."

Most of his friends didn't get out, DeShazer reckons. "In the early teens," he says, "you lose your friends to the gangs. In the late teens, you lose them to alcohol and drugs."

DeShazer managed to escape both the gangs and heavy drugs, though he admits to being "periodically drafted to join the gangs and occasionally fearing for my life. But my brother, Arnold, was a star basketball player in high school and I was good enough at neighborhood sports to be largely left alone." DeShazer ran with a group of 15 like-minded young blacks and he figures that "maybe, three of us got out intact."

Since anyone who made good grades was considered a "sissy," the young DeShazer often "tried to miss questions," but his teachers and older brothers insisted that he bypass the public high school in favor of the private and prestigious St. Ignatius High School. "I didn't want to go at first," DeShazer admits, "because there were no girls at the school, but my father took out a loan and I enrolled."

Some 14 years later, after stints at Chicago's Loyola University and the nearby University of Illinois College of Medicine, DeShazer had his M.D., and he was a long way from his grandfather's Mississippi. And not so far away, too.

His first patient this morning, whom we'll call Mr. Jones, misses Mississippi. Although 90% of Cook County's patients are black, only 10% of the hospital's physicians are black, and Jones, a black man, is happy to be examined by DeShazer, a black physician.

Jones is 30 minutes late for his appointment, which is common, and his chart is "unavailable," which is also common. "The clerical staff is under separate management," DeShazer explains, "and the medical staff always has to fight to try to get our medical records in time for the patient's visit."

Not to worry, though. A few questions quickly establish that the patient is bothered by shortness of breath. At ease, the patient explains, "My youngest daughter, my baby, was givin' me such a fit last night that I got up to whup her, but after two steps of chasin' her across the room, she was laughin' and I was about to drop. I was doin' myself more damage than her, so I decided it was time to lie down."

The physician suspects chronic obstructive pulmonary disease from the patient's history of smoking, and he orders a lung exam and breathing-capacity tests. He also renews prescriptions to treat the patient's high blood pressure and diabetes.

Since DeShazer knows that patient compliance with taking medication depends upon the physician's careful explanation of the need, he patiently explains to Jones exactly how and why he must take his pills. Knowing that these tests and prescriptions will take hours, he allows as to how the patient "has time to slip in some lunch."

For his part, patient Jones muses, "You know, in Chicago, I never have two good days in a row, but when I go back to my folks' place in Mississippi, I just forget about all my aches and pains. Livin's a lot easier there."

DeShazer later adds, "Smoking and drinking complicate about 90% of everything we see here. Yet, when you drive through the ghetto, what do you see—alcohol and cigarette ads on billboards that are pockmarked with bullet holes! Also, about nine of every 10 patients we see have high blood pressure, and about six or seven of every 10 have late-onset diabetes."

While a lot of the footsteps DeShazer hears at Cook County turn out to be horses like diabetes and hypertension, he also sees more than his share of zebras.

"Last night, at the walk-in center," he says, "an elderly Hispanic man came in complaining of a toothache. He didn't speak English, and we needed a translator. His heartbeat was very slow, sounding 'boom . . . [long pause] boom.' We suspected a heart attack, until we finally got his history:

"He suffered from glaucoma, and after experiencing an acute attack of eye pain, he began to take his eye drops every 5 minutes, instead of twice a day. The drops include a β-blocker, and he'd knocked out the heart's natural pacemaker. In a few more hours, he probably would have suffered sudden cardiac death. We got him up to the coronary care unit, where atropine restored the rhythm. Somehow, he had associated the pain in his eyes with a toothache!"

In the meantime, this morning, the next patient is an elderly black lady, Mrs. Smith (another pseudonym), who is experiencing excruciating lower-back pain. She comes quickly to her point:

"You know me, and I'm not one to complain," she tells Dr. DeShazer, "but I can't go home feeling like this. I've been taking

Tylenol No. 3, and it doesn't make a dent in the pain. I'm ready to be admitted."

The woman had recently injured her back while trying to move a stove, and bed rest did not help. She has also lost about 20 pounds and her unspoken fear is that she might have cancer, which is viewed in the black community as the worst curse of all.

Dr. DeShazer asks some questions, then palpates her back muscles, causing great moans of pain. He decides that he needs an orthopedic consultation to determine if the pain is due to a muscle spasm or a disk problem, and he knows that this will be a hassle.

Seeing that the woman is in great pain, he himself finds a wheelchair to take her downstairs to the orthopedic clinic. No luck, though. The orthopedist advises continued bed rest before authorizing a visit to the clinic. He cites the protocol and patient load and so on.

Fuming, Dr. DeShazer decides to admit her to the general medical ward. "She's stayed in bed and that didn't work," he explains. He sticks the admission chart right in her hand, "so nobody can possibly lose it." Then, in a soothing voice, he tells her, "Don't worry. This isn't cancer." Through the pain, she smiles. She will be admitted to a ward so crowded that DeShazer will, a few hours later, have trouble threading his way among the beds to her wheelchair, but she is happy. "You're getting an education, aren't you?" she asks this reporter.

Later, Dr. DeShazer reflects, "The big difference between what I expected medicine to be like and the way it is here is that the medical staff is not in control of medical practice. The bureaucracy controls everything.

"We have to worry about getting charts on time, getting lab tests done, getting consultations, and getting follow-up care. We've been trying to get a Xerox copier up here for 4 years."

It's not DeShazer's way to get mad without eventually getting things better, so he has enrolled in law school at Chicago's DePaul University, which he attends four nights a week. "The real power is legal and legislative," he says, "and I'm preparing myself to make a difference." To relax, he works with his desktop computer and publishes a newsletter on minority health issues.

He also copes with the here and now. "To survive at County," he explains, "you have to be smart and you have to be lucky. I've tried to make friends with all the key people in the specialty clinics, the labs, medical records, and the pharmacy. That's the only way to get things done. If you try to muscle them, watch out. They'll tell you to bug off!"

He is often called upon to talk to patients who are fed up with the County maze. Recently, a young woman with lupus showed up at the walk-in center with what she said was "the worst headache in my life."

DeShazer notes, "The nurse practitioner was smart enough to draw out her history of lupus *and* lucky enough to track down her old medical charts. It turned out that her platelet counts were now so depleted that if she'd bumped into something, she might have bled out.

"Still, she didn't want to go into the hospital because she was in junior college and her final exams were coming up. Also, she hated the way she had been treated before and she didn't trust the system. I told her, 'Look, I don't care what happened before. You have to believe me now. Your life is in danger and you need to be in the hospital. Trust me.'" She agreed to be admitted.

One of DeShazer's friends recently came to County for treatment of complications from a former leg fracture. Due to a clerical mix-up, he was told that he would have to wait 4 months. DeShazer shepherded him through the maze by bringing him to the walk-in center and then obtaining a consultation. The grateful friend related how his girlfriend had recently gone to the emergency room at Northwestern Memorial Hospital, which is a world away on the city's posh Gold Coast.

"His girlfriend had health insurance," DeShazer relates, "and she presented in the ER with an upper respiratory infection and severe headache. While she was being examined, my friend had to wait outside in the visitors' lounge, where he was approached by a woman who asked, 'Who are you?' Well, since my friend was sensitized to the County system, he replied, 'What's it to you!'

"It turns out that the woman was a 'liaison worker,' and she wanted to offer my friend some coffee and doughnuts and answer any questions he might have! That's the good news about the private system. The bad news is that the ER performed several tests on the patient to rule out meningitis and the bill was $1200!"

DeShazer believes that many Chicago medical facilities perform "wallet biopsies" on the patients who walk in, and, "if the result is negative, the patient is told: 'Go to County!'"

And so they do. About 200 walk into the ambulatory screening center every day. On this night, DeShazer is one of two attending MDs on duty, supervising a staff of nurse practitioners, medical residents, and moonlighters. "Be prepared to see a few characters," he says.

One patient presents with an unusual rash, a rash that the nurse practitioner in her beautifully handwritten chart suggests may be a rare form of contact dermatitis. DeShazer examines the man, who is furtive and hostile, and concludes that the rash can be successfully treated. Less easy to solve is the cause of the rash:

"I'm homeless," the man explains, "and I sleep in a basement with five cats. The cats have fleas and they crawl all over me. I'm usually so stoned on alcohol and drugs that I don't much care."

The next nuance is a bit easier to handle. A black female teenager has a pelvic infection, for which drugs have been prescribed. Her boyfriend, however, looks unhappy. DeShazer takes the young man aside and explains that the infection is *not* related to sexual activity and that the condition does not mean that the woman has been "messin' around."

Sexually transmitted diseases, however, including AIDS, do account for many of the clinic's patients. And teen mothers are common, usually raising the children without a father.

DeShazer says, "Four of every five black children are born out of wedlock, beginning a cycle of poverty. Many black women view pregnancy as a way to gain attention and esteem, and if a black woman has not given birth by the time she's 21, it's usually because she's had an abortion."

DeShazer knows the problem only too well, because he fathered two children by the woman he lived with during medical school. It is a touchy subject, and he says ruefully, "I loved the woman, but we grew apart. I had thought that we had agreed that she would practice birth control until I got through medical school. Medical school is a 'jealous bitch,' and you only have time to eat, sleep, and study. I told her that I wanted to focus on school, and I thought that she understood. It didn't turn out that way, though, and I felt angry and trapped."

The mother and two children now live in Florida, and a big chunk of DeShazer's $68,000 annual salary goes for their support. He wishes that he could spend a bigger chunk of his time with them.

He concludes, "Initially, I felt that I had been victimized by a scheming woman, but now I realize that I was irresponsible. I should have also assumed responsibility for birth control and worn a condom. The use of condoms has been stigmatized in the black community by both men and women because 'it doesn't feel the same,' and this attitude has to change. Now, I know."

Sex aside, the big medical problem at County is the *lateness* with which patients present their problems. In rapid order, DeShazer examines a young black man in his late 20s whose uncontrolled high blood pressure has now led to renal failure; a woman with a tumor so large that it engulfs her breast; and a woman with an infected foot callus that has grown so big she can no longer walk. All are referred to specialty clinics.

Shaking his head, he says, "These patients never thought that their problems were worth dealing with until they became unbearable."

The next patient will offer some good news. His legs are weak from diabetes, but he exclaims to DeShazer, "To me, County is the best. This young girl [the nurse practitioner] took all the time in the world to talk to me, and that's more than my private doctor does, and he takes my money. She's pretty, too.

"I've been coming here for years, my children were born here, the doctors are good here, and it's worth waiting for."

Indeed, DeShazer's father was treated successfully at County last year after a heart attack. "I had complete confidence in his care," DeShazer says.

Cook County Hospital recently lost its accreditation because the building did not meet fire and safety standards, thus potentially jeopardizing $100 million in Medicare-Medicaid reimbursements. Still, the huge hospital has managed to fill its residency slots for the coming year, a sign that young doctors still believe in the aging facility. Another JCAH (Joint Commission on Accreditation of Hospitals) inspection is set for this May.

DeShazer himself will soon be moving on, though. By serving at County, which is designated as an official medical care shortage area, he is concluding his 4-year scholarship commitment to the National Health Service Corps. He is now engaged to marry another woman, who is trying to persuade him to moderate his workaholic ways, but he says, "For now, I plan to push on in the direction I'm going until I can make a breakthrough. I want to have a greater impact on a smaller scale."

He hopes to help run a neighborhood health center, and eventually create a network of neighborhood health centers to which County's thousands of patients can be referred for follow-up care. He also plans to continue to spend at least a few days a week at County.

"This place gets in your blood," he explains. "It's not about fire and safety codes. It's about patients and doctors and compassion."

The American Tragedy

Missionary doctor Janelle Goetcheus, M.D., runs a clinic to care for the sick homeless in Washington, D.C.

Medical missionary A. Janelle Goetcheus, M.D., has seen great poverty and human suffering in the heart of Africa, but she has found the greatest medical neglect and despair closer to home:

In this nation's capital, Washington, D.C.

A native of Muncie, Ind., and a 1965 graduate of the Indiana University School of Medicine, Indianapolis, Goetcheus, 48, and her husband Allen Goetcheus, a Methodist minister, always thought that they would work overseas as part of a healing ministry. However, while awaiting a visa to Pakistan in 1975, the couple stopped in Washington, D.C., to visit a church-supported project to provide housing for the poor. They found that the poor also had little or no health care.

"It was a real eye-opening experience for me," recalls Dr. Goetcheus. "Everybody we saw talked about their difficulties in finding basic medical care." Allen and Janelle Goetcheus decided to do their missionary work in America and, in 1976, moved to Washington, D.C.

In the past 15 years, Dr. Goetcheus, a general practitioner, has treated thousands of poor patients and has been caught up in trying to cope with four interwoven American tragedies—poverty, homelessness, AIDS, and addiction.

On this beautiful spring day, she finds all four conditions represented in her first patient of the day, a young black man dressed in a snappy red sweatsuit with matching sneakers. We are at "The Shelter," at the intersection of Second and D streets, Northwest, a scant six blocks from Capitol Hill, where the nation's lawmakers are wrestling with a budget deficit measured in trillions of dollars and where funding for AIDS and the homeless is not in favor.

This shelter, formally known as the federal-city shelter, sleeps 1400 and is the largest shelter for the homeless in the world. Its infirmary has 30 beds, and its medical clinic examines all comers, thanks to volunteer physicians like Dr. Goetcheus.

This shelter is only one of many stops for Goetcheus. As the medical director for the Health Care for the Homeless Project, Inc., Washington, D.C., she oversees the medical care provided in nine shelters; by a mobile van that seeks out homeless persons living under bridges, in the parks, and on street grates; and in the unique Christ House, a haven of healing for homeless people who are too sick to survive on the streets or in the shelters but who are not ill enough to be admitted to a hospital.

On Monday mornings, though, her office hours are at The Shelter. Her first patient, the young black man, has a prescription for eyeglasses, but he doesn't know how to have it filled. He also, it turns out, is asthmatic, addicted to crack cocaine, seriously retarded and psychotic, carrying the AIDS virus—and is homeless.

Goetcheus can only shake her head. "To be seriously ill and seriously impaired is devastating. To be seriously ill and seriously impaired *and* homeless stretches the imagination. We hope that this man has a sense that he is a carrier of AIDS and that he will not spread the disease, but we can only hope. The only other alternative is to institutionalize him, and nobody wants to pay for that."

The next patient complains of seizures, but he is lucky to be able to complain. The seizures are a residual effect of a gunshot wound to the head. The clinic's director, Sister Carol Ann Votruba, notes, "We're like an emergency room, and we see everything—broken legs, fevers, infections, sexually transmitted diseases. Some of the patients don't tell the intake workers the real reasons they're here, but that's OK, too. They'll usually tell the doctors."

Goetcheus adds, "AIDS is becoming so prevalent that every time I see a case of athlete's foot, I suspect AIDS. In time, AIDS will overwhelm us, with half or more of all the people in the shelters carrying the virus and slowly dying." Recently, at a soup kitchen called SOME ("So others may eat"), a screening of homeless persons believed to be at high risk for AIDS found that one of five tested positive for the virus; most are intravenous drug users.

Estimates vary, but a *conservative* guess is that there are 15,000 homeless in Washington, D.C., alone and 3 million across the country.

As a medical student, Goetcheus served a fellowship in Zaire, then the Belgian Congo. "In central Africa," she recalls, "there was great poverty and only one physician for every 100,000 persons or so, but still, the people were hopeful. In America, we're seeing a different kind of poverty. The homeless we see in the shelters are faces of despair. They've been battered down so often that they're broken spiritually. We may be able to heal the broken legs and the frostbite, but we can't heal the psychic scars. We call it the 'Fourth World,' the phenomenon of Third-World poverty within the borders of a wealthy nation. It's a great tragedy."

Almost 90% of the homeless in D.C. are black, and many are becoming increasingly angry. "Recently," Goetcheus says, "we took a Swedish TV crew along with us on the mobile health van, and the homeless people standing in line became so angry at having their plight recorded that the cameramen became scared and left."

Not all homeless are black, though. "The most-photographed homeless man in America," she says, "is a young man who lives 365 days a year on a park bench in front of the Washington Monument. He's white and a college graduate, but he had a schizophrenic break. His illness was controlled by medication, but when he was released from the psychiatric hospital, he went to the streets and quit taking his medication. Now, he lives on that park bench."

A special irony, she notes, is that the energy used to heat the corridors of power in Congress and the federal buildings kicks its steam exhaust up through street grates where the homeless find warmth in the winter. "The government wanted to put spikes over the grates," she says wryly, "to remove this eyesore. As it is, many homeless people get third-degree burns from the heat, if they're not careful."

It is only a 15-minute drive from the White House to Christ House in the gritty Adams-Morgan section of D.C. This four-story building, graced in front by a sculpture of the "Servant Christ," is a monument to Goetcheus' persistence and the vision of the ecumenical Church of the Savior.

Goetcheus has provided medical care for the Adams-Morgan neighborhood poor since 1976, first working out of two rented rooms in a townhouse and eventually transforming a delicatessen into the Columbia Road Health Services, where she became medical director.

Tired of seeing minor medical problems turn into major medical events because they were never properly treated, Goetcheus dreamed of a place where the homeless sick could find care and comfort, a place to eat and rest. She knew that her patients were walking the streets with bronchitis, diabetes, diarrhea, fever, high blood pressure, leg ulcers, and other illnesses and that, in time, they would return in worse shape. One patient who was treated for frostbite on a snowy afternoon was found dead the following morning—frozen in a telephone booth.

Across the street from the Columbia Road medical clinic was an abandoned building, newly occupied by homeless people, who often built fires to stay warm. "While walking to the clinic one morning," Goetcheus recalls, "I stopped in front of the abandoned building and prayed that it could be put to a better use." Years later, a wealthy member of the Church of the Savior donated $2.5 million to transform the rotting building into a place of hope.

On Christmas Eve, 1985, Christ House welcomed its first guest, a homeless man who showed up at the soup kitchen with congestive heart failure. Today, Christ House offers room and board to 34 sick homeless patients, including five with AIDS. The $750,000 annual operating budget is provided by a combination of private-public funds and individual donations.

Allen and Janelle Goetcheus live in Christ House, as do several other physicians, nurses, and social workers. She explains, "So often, the *doing* of things gets in the way of the *being* part of the thing. Allen and I decided to live in the community we are serving. [Allen Goetcheus is president of Christ House.] This is an essential part of our journey of faith."

At first, the move to the inner city was tough on the couple's three sons, two of whom were mugged in the neighborhood. "What kept us going," she says, "is the community of support we have from the church and the joy of helping others."

The odds can be long. Goetcheus recalls one homeless man she found gathered around a fire barrel. "He was only 49," she says, "but he looked much older. He had a high blood pressure of 190/135, but he refused to go to the hospital, saying, 'I'm just an old man dying.' We brought him back to Christ House, and he was in terrible shape. He told us that he had not had water on his skin for at least a year. We had to pry his clothes off, and the stench was unbelievable. The other patients said, 'Don't put him in the same room with me.' He was also alcoholic, and he would often slip back to the bottle. About the fourth time we took him in, however, something seemed to click. He joined our Alcoholics Anonymous classes, quit drinking, and started to take his blood pressure drugs and take better care of himself. He can't read or write, and he's too broken to ever do physical labor, so we're trying to put him in 'SRO' [single-room occupancy]."

Although there are few success stories among the homeless, working with them is a "life-giving experience," says Goetcheus' colleague, David Hilfiker, M.D. In 1982, Hilfiker had abandoned a successful career as a small-town M.D. in rural Minnesota because of burnout and disillusionment. After taking a year off to ski in Finland, his wife's native country, he was persuaded by Goetcheus to help serve the homeless. Today, David and Marja Hilfiker and their three children live in Christ House, but not for long. "Next month," Hilfiker confides, "we're moving into 'Joseph's House,' a townhouse that will provide care and housing for 12 to 15 AIDS patients. For my family, this is the richest way to live right now."

Such enthusiasm is not widespread. The bank, for one, refused to provide the $575,000 mortgage until the Church of the Savior came up with ironclad collateral. And the purpose of "Joseph's House" cannot be told in the community, for fear of reprisals. Still, the Hilfiker family is excited, and recently they had two of their guests-to-be over for dinner. "We want to live with the poor as true peers," explains Hilfiker, "and not relate to them simply as authority figures."

Hilfiker says the root causes of homelessness are "lack of affordable housing, deinstitutionalization of the mentally ill, and addiction to drugs like cocaine."

He adds, "We always used to see homelessness among those who are mentally ill and addicted to alcohol or other drugs. Today, however, the problem is much worse because people who *do* have jobs still cannot afford housing. In Washington, D.C., the cheapest one-bedroom apartment rents for $650 a month, and this is the entire take-home pay for many workers and single mothers. Also, areas like Adams-Morgan are being 'gentrified,' since middle-class people are moving back into the city. The landlords rehab the buildings and triple the rents, and the poor are driven out. And, Social Security disability only pays $218 a month, and the worst rat-infested rooms rent for $50 a week.

"What is worse is the fact that the homeless are only the tip of the iceberg. For every person living on the streets, there are at least 10 who are doubled or tripled up with friends and relatives, or who are living in flophouses. They have a roof over their heads, but they are living on the edge of homelessness. When the district threatened to revoke the leases of people living in overcrowded low-income housing, the renters turned their friends out to the streets."

Hilfiker, who in a 1989 *JAMA* editorial suggested that most Americans consider the homeless to be the "acceptable cost of our affluence," now thinks that the only answer is "a national health system similar to those of Western Europe. The American medical system is so ungenerous that it is strangling the poorest in our society."

He concludes, "Unlike Janelle, I did not set out to be a medical missionary. I have come to the faith *through* my work with the homeless and poor, not the other way around. I have learned that this nation is capable of caring for its homeless and poor, but only if we adopt this attitude:

"We are all family."

Goetcheus, who like Hilfiker is paid about $34,000 a year for her efforts, is too busy to talk much about herself. She looks drawn and tired as she shows this reporter a short videotape clip in which five formerly homeless men talk about what Christ House has meant to them.

One says, "As for me, well, all you have to do is look at me now and then look at a picture of me when I first came here. I have the picture upstairs and look at it from time to time. In everything from my complexion to my expression, you can see the difference. I'm no longer a bag of bones and I'm no longer a wild man. I mean, I used to look so crazy that people would cross the street to avoid running into me. I'm no longer that man. This place is one step from heaven."

As she listens, the weariness lifts from Goetcheus' face and she positively glows. She says, "When we dedicated Christ House, we prayed that it would not be needed for long. But I don't see that happening. The problem is growing worse.

"Still, there are joys in doing what we can. This is home."

Carlton Davis, 46, one of 19 children, always wanted a better life for himself, but when his marriage "went bad," he slowly and surely drifted into a life of decline and drink on the mean streets of the nation's capital.

"I never liked the shelters [for the homeless]," he recalls. "The young 'uns would always be drinkin' and druggin' and throwin' things. You didn't even have to be involved to get hurt. No, I'd rather take my chances on the street." On warm nights, he slept on a platform behind Constitution Hall; on cold nights, he walked the streets.

He adds, "I was always drinkin' and smokin.' Two packs a day and a fifth of liquor a day. I could handle that easy."

His life began to change on December 18, 1987. "The night before," he says, "the young 'uns jumped me and all I remember is wakin' up the next morning pukin' blood. I prayed to God, tellin' Him that I wanted to change my life."

He spent 35 days in the hospital. "The doctors told me I was lucky that I didn't choke on my own blood and die on the streets," he says. The doctors also removed a benign tumor from his larynx. At discharge, he was offered room at a shelter but refused. The hospital social worker mentioned Christ House, and a "light went on. I mean, I wanted to put God first, and this place seemed to have the right sound."

Carlton had never been near the Christ House neighborhood ("They were mostly Hispanic up there and I didn't speak Spanish," he says), but the warm welcome he received turned his life around.

After 2 weeks at Christ House and 8 months at a nearby Samaritan Inn (also run by the Church of the Savior), he found a job washing dishes at a Georgetown restaurant and moved into his own apartment. "But I continued to do volunteer work at Christ House," he says, "workin' in the mail room and the kitchen. At night, I worked for me; but during the day, I worked out of gratitude."

Last November, his right lung collapsed, and the hospital doctors told him it would have to be removed. "I was scared to death," he says, "but I prayed to God that I would survive so I could celebrate 2 years without drinkin'."

He did, and, as an added bonus, it turned out that the lung did *not* have to be removed, only clamped into place. "God was takin' care of me," Carlton says, adding, "While I was in the hospital, the doctors reminded me that I should really quit smoking. Before, the doctors had never put enough fear in me. This time, they did."

Today, Carlton is an adviser to Christ House newcomers. He says, "Whenever I hear people complain about Christ House, I get an attitude. I tell the new people somethin' like this:

"'You know, I see myself in you. You need to learn how to trust a power higher than yourself. . . .'

"And, I used to think, 'What kind of God is this . . . this must be a racist God, because He is not listenin' to me.'

"I used to sit on my park bench and pray to God and expect Him to drop down beside me with pad and pencil and write down my every wish and then He could be on his way—just give me what I want. Well, I've learned that God don't come down here and do no personal favors. . . . No, God does his work through other people, and, for me, He did it through Christ House. I've been blessed."

Carlton is currently living at Christ House, while he recovers from his latest surgery. However, he soon hopes to find a live-in job doing porter-maintenance at a church or apartment complex. In the meantime, he is practicing his singing.

"I used to sing with a gospel group," he says, "but I gave all that up when I hit the streets. The people at Christ House have been after me to sing at the Thursday night service, but I've been holdin' out. Now, I think I'm ready.

"Backup? No, I don't need no backup. I'll be singin' *a cappella*. And I think that it will be well received. I'll be singin' from the heart."

THE HEART OF THE MATTER

Hindsight

Once he was stricken with a heart attack, state-of-the-art medicine was not enough to save former Chicago Mayor Harold Washington. Ah, but* before *the attack . . .

Alton Miller was with Mayor Washington on the morning of November 25, 1987, at a ground-breaking ceremony for the Kenwood-Oakland Community Organization on East 46th Street, not too far from the neighborhood where the mayor grew up and where he was then living, at 5300 South Shore Drive. Afterward, at 10:30 or so, while in the limousine on the way to City Hall, Washington told his press secretary: "I still feel stuffy. I can't shake this virus."

About 30 minutes later Washington collapsed onto his desk in the mayoral office, the victim of this nation's No. 1 killer—sudden cardiac death. Sudden cardiac death, defined as death within 24 hours of an acute heart attack, happens about 1,200 times a day, roughly 438,000 times a year. It works out to almost one American death every 72 seconds of every day. This epidemic is occurring because, ironically, in one of every three cases the first sign of a patient's underlying heart disease is the sudden heart attack itself—and death.

Mayor Washington was one of these cases. He was given state-of-the-art resuscitative care, both by paramedics who rushed to the scene and later by the staff at the Northwestern Memorial Hospital emergency room, but he was essentially dead when he collapsed at his desk. Everything possible that could have been done for the mayor *after* the fact was done, but it proved to be of no practical consequence. Unfortunately, all of the things that the mayor might have done for himself *before* the fact had not been done. What the mayor called "stuffiness" might very well have been the first sign of congestive heart failure, caused by fluid backing up into his lungs.

Harold Washington, who leaves a rich political legacy, also provides a textbook example of how not to take care of your physical health. The mayor, a lifelong heavy smoker who was 100 pounds overweight and suffering from long-standing high blood pressure and high cholesterol levels, unknowingly was walking around with a heart grotesquely swollen to about 2½ times its normal size and coronary arteries that were severely clogged. It was as if a rusty pump were trying to force water through a clamped hose. The mayor's heart, weakened after years of pumping against increased resistance, simply gave out.

His silent heart problem was of such severity that Dr. Robert S. Eliot, the director of the Cardiovascular Institute at Swedish Memorial Center in Englewood, Col., and a leading expert in sudden cardiac death, observes, "If the American Heart Association made house calls to patients in trouble, Harold Washington would have been near the top of the list." But that's hindsight. No one knew the severity of the mayor's problems until it was too late.

The warning signs were subtle and easily missed, recalls Miller. "The mayor did appear to be slowing down, even to the point where he would occasionally take the day off," he says, "but we all missed it at the time. Besides, you simply do not tell your boss, 'You're not looking well.' When you only have a 15-minute appointment with the mayor—which will probably be cut back to 8 or 10 minutes—talking about his health is about No. 70 on the list of 50 most important things to talk about."

On November 25, 1987, Miller was in the mayor's office, checking off some of the 50 most important items on the agenda, when he looked up and saw Washington slumped across his desk. "It looked weird, but at first I thought that there was a logical explanation,"

Miller recalls, "like he might have been reaching for something, but within an instant I knew better. I said, 'Mayor, Mayor?' Then I bolted to the door and told the guard [Frank Lee, the mayor's personal bodyguard], 'Frank, the mayor needs you.' Then I told Delores Woods [the mayor's secretary of 20 years] to start calling people."

The police got the call at 11 a.m., and the Chicago Fire Department one minute later. Miller returned to Washington's office and moved aside the huge mayoral desk so that the three bodyguards could perform manual cardiopulmonary resuscitation (CPR). Next came the CPR efforts of the fire-department paramedics, who within minutes arrived for an all-out attempt to save the mayor's life.

It had been a slow morning at the Northwestern Memorial Hospital emergency room (ER)—until 11:10. The hospital's first patient that day had checked in shortly after midnight, a 49-year-old man with asthma who came in at 12:20 a.m., complaining that he was having trouble breathing. Ten minutes later the first cardiac patient appeared, a 72-year-old woman complaining of chest pain. The ER register indicates that "Washington, Harold," no address or occupation listed, was patient No. 29 on a day the ER would treat 92 people.

At the control desk in the center of the ER is a black phone directly linked to Chicago Fire Department paramedics. When it rang at 11:10, the caller told the nurse who answered, "I need to talk to a doctor." The attending ER physician that morning was Dr. David Kramer, 32, who recalls, "When I was asked to come to the phone, I knew that something was off-base and we were in for an unusual case."

The caller was Ron Smith, chief of the City Hall paramedics, and he came quickly to the point, "The victim is the mayor." Kramer adds: "Well, my adrenaline rose a bit, but we follow a routine that is very ingrained. These paramedics are under the direct medical control of Northwestern, and they work under standing medical orders that follow the American Heart Association's protocol for advanced cardiac life support. Our goal was to try to convert the mayor's heart rhythm from ventricular fibrillation—it was beating more like a quivering bag of worms than like a powerful pump—into a 'perfusable rhythm,' a rhythm that would circulate enough blood to keep the brain and the body alive."

The paramedics continued their work for 12 minutes until, at 11:23, Kramer ordered that the mayor be transported to the ER.

While Washington lay on his office floor, the paramedics pursued the "ABC's" of CPR and advanced life support: secure an airway, assure breathing, assure circulation. One paramedic can provide basic CPR, doing mouth-to-mouth breathing and manually compressing the chest. In the mayor's case, several fully equipped paramedics were on the scene performing advanced life support.

An endotracheal tube was placed into the mayor's mouth, and with the aid of a laryngoscope, it was directed into his trachea, or windpipe. After the tube was taped down, a black Ambu-bag was connected to the tube and squeezed by a paramedic to take over the mayor's breathing in the process known, inelegantly, as "bagging the patient." Meanwhile, with the patient's airway and breathing assured, the efforts to restore circulation continued. Under the best of conditions, manual compression of the chest can provide only 25 to 30 percent of the blood flow circulated by the normal heart. In the mayor's case, there was an added and significant complication: He had a massive barrel chest.

Kramer explains: "We had to convert his heart rhythm from ventricular fibrillation—beating chaotically—into a life-sustaining rhythm. We had initially given epinephrine [adrenaline, to jolt the heart] through the endotracheal tube. Within seconds an intravenous line was placed into each arm under the elbows. After priming the lines with a mixture of dextrose and water, we [introduced] four drugs: additional epinephrine; atrophine and lidocaine, to try to change the chemical environment of the heart muscle so that it would respond to an electrical jolt; and sodium bicarbonate, to counteract the acidosis caused by lack of circulation. As they infused the drugs, the paramedics placed spoonlike paddles from their 'Life-Pak' onto the mayor's bared chest, selected the maximum amplitude and tried to shock the heart back into rhythm."

As the paramedics struggled over the stricken mayor at City Hall, the telemetry hookup at Northwestern enabled Kramer to monitor a video readout of the mayor's heartbeat. The lines remained fuzzy and squiggly, evidence of a continued chaotic rhythm, as opposed to the normal peaks and valleys that indicate the rhythm of life. There was nothing more to be done at the scene, and at 11:23 the ambulance left City Hall and proceeded north on LaSalle Street toward the Northwestern Memorial Hospital ER on East Superior Street. Kramer and his boss, ER director Dr. James

Mathews, 44, sounded the alarm for a full-blown hospital resuscitation, a procedure that Kramer describes as "organized chaos."

The ambulance and the sizable contingent accompanying the mayor arrived at the ER at 11:33, and the paramedics immediately carried their patient on a stretcher into the ER's "hyperacute" room, a spacious, fully equipped facility located right inside the emergency entrance off the corridor leading to the main ER. The mayor would be met by a sea of blue, a medical team that rapidly grew to include 12 physicians, 6 nurses, 2 heart-lung-machine perfusionists and 2 respiratory-care specialists, all in operating-room scrub blues and standing by to provide hands-on care.

As the mayor was wheeled in, the doctor in immediate charge was Mathews, the ER director. He recalls, "Truthfully, I was not that optimistic because in my 15 years of clinical experience I have found that if a heart-attack victim shows no response at the scene, then his chances for recovery are slim."

If the mayor were to have a chance at recovery, his only realistic hope was a state-of-the-art machine being wheeled off an elevator at the same time that he was being taken off the ambulance. The medical device is an innovative version of the cardiopulmonary support (CPS) machine that is used to carry out a procedure called ECMO (for extracorporeal membrane oxygenation). It is, in effect, a portable version of the heart-lung machine used in open-heart surgery that can be set up more quickly and operated more easily than its bulky operating-room counterpart.

Jackie Smith, the clinical nursing manager of the cardiac surgical intensive-care and step-down units, brought the $15,000 CPS machine on a cart from its home in the cardiac-surgery suite on the fourth floor down to the hyperacute room on the ground level at about the same time that heart surgeons John Sanders and Renée Hartz arrived on the scene. On November 25, 1987, this was the *only* portable CPS machine in Chicago. Mayor Washington was about to become only the seventh patient in Chicago to have the benefit of this portable heart-lung pump for an attempted resuscitation from cardiac arrest.

With the arrival of the portable CPS, Sanders took command of the ER effort. The 45-year-old surgeon, who had told his wife that morning that he was "in for an easy day" and was looking forward to an early getaway with his family for Thanksgiving at their cottage in southern Wisconsin, recalls: "Surgeons have no trouble taking charge. It's part of our personality." Sanders is the chief of the medical staff at Northwestern, and at his command was a staff of 21.

Observing the team effort and kept fully informed were the mayor's personal physician, Dr. Antonio Senat, who had been called on his car phone and who beat the ambulance to the hospital and provided vital medical information about the mayor to the ER staff; and Dr. Lonnie Edwards, Chicago's health commissioner.

First, Dr. Richard Davison, a cardiologist and chief of the hospital's intensive-care facilities, intravenously infused some new mixtures of heart drugs, including the potent Bertyllium, to try to alter the chemical environment of the heart and restore a functional rhythm. Kramer, meanwhile, was continuing manual compression of the chest. There was no response, and within minutes Sanders decided to connect the CPS machine.

He observes, "Without this machine, our only option would have been open-chest massage of the heart, and this procedure is at best only 20 percent more efficient than the manual CPR and shocks he had been receiving."

The surgeons—Sanders and Hartz—required only six or seven minutes to connect the CPS machine to the mayor's femoral artery and vein and to get the machine to full circulatory flow. "Actually, the light was very good in that room," Sanders recalls, "the incision and connections went very smoothly, and the patient was on the machine within 15 minutes from the time we were notified by the ER."

Working swiftly, Sanders and Hartz spread iodine over the area of the mayor's right groin, walled off the area with dressings, made an incision, spread aside the fatty tissue with their fingers and fastened it out of the way with metal retractors, located the femoral artery and vein, punctured these two blood vessels with a needle, inserted a guide wire into each and connected the machine's plastic tubings, or *cannulae*, directly to the vessels. Northwestern clinicians have worked with the manufacturers of the CPS machine to try to develop the best cannulae, Sanders explains. "The trick is to have the tubing flexible enough not to rupture the vessel and yet strong enough to flare back and force the needle hole in the vessel into a width about the thickness of a lead pencil."

The principle of the heart-lung machine is simple. Venous blood returning to the heart is diverted into the machine, where carbon dioxide is exchanged for oxygen. Then the freshly oxygenated blood is warmed and returned by the machine into the patient's arterial system. The machine acts as a "heart" by pumping the blood, and as a "lung" by exchanging carbon dioxide for life-sustaining oxygen. The portable ECMO system is about one-half the size of the typical operating-room heart-lung machine, and it can be set up and connected to a patient in about one-third the time. Future models of the machine are expected to be only one-third its current size and to fit at the end of a bed rather than being supported on a cart.

Within seconds after the CPS system was first "purged" by circulating a saline solution to prime the patient's system—to ensure that an air embolus would not occur—it was providing circulation. By 11:45 the mayor of Chicago was on full life support.

Initially, the medical team was guardedly optimistic. "This machine does a better job of pumping blood than does your own heart," Kramer says. Hartz recalls that the previous—and sixth—patient on the CPS system, a woman who arrested during an obstetrical procedure, "made a full recovery. Although she did not, like the mayor, have a true heart attack, she did suffer an arrest of the heart."

For his part, Sanders knew that if there were to be good news, it would come quickly. "If the patient is going to recover," he explains, "he will usually awaken within a few minutes of having his circulation restored, and he will need anesthesia while we continue our work on the heart."

But on this morning the anesthesiologists would not be needed. Harold Washington never awoke, and the next medical services to be required were those of the neurologist, Dr. Onur Melen, who during the two hours the mayor was on the machine, performed a series of standard tests to ascertain if he was brain-dead. While Melen was assessing just how bad things were, nurse Meg Kloster was setting up a bed on the fourth-floor cardiac surgery suite in the hope that the mayor would be transferred there for a possible surgical procedure. Sanders had put everything and everyone in the suite "on hold"—just in case—but it was not to be.

"To be blunt," Kramer summarizes, "there were no signs of recovery. We were able to restore circulation and color, but we were not able to get a cardiac or neurological response." Mathews adds, "The only spontaneous movements the mayor made were a few agonal breaths, or dying gasps."

When the patient did not revive within 30 minutes of being placed on bypass, Sanders was "about 99.9 percent certain that he was dead." Nevertheless, the artificial circulation was continued for another 90 minutes, until Sanders pronounced Washington dead at 1:36 p.m. He explains: "Had the patient not been the mayor, we might have stopped the resuscitation effort after 30 minutes. But we wanted to make absolutely certain that everything possible was done. The CPS machine is licensed by the FDA to provide bypass for up to six hours, but after two hours, there was no doubt that the mayor was irreversibly brain-dead. We were able to achieve full blood flow and convert his heart rhythm from defibrillation into an electrical standstill, but we were unable to achieve a normal heartbeat or any signs of brain activity."

He adds: "In our series of 16 runs with the CPS, we have occasionally achieved cardiac response but not neurological, or neurological response but not cardiac. On four occasions we achieved both, but only one of those, the young woman, made a full recovery. With the mayor, we were unable to achieve either [response]."

After one hour on bypass, Sanders began to tell members of the mayor's entourage, including Edwards and Senat and Washington's family members, that the outlook was dim. Washington's pastor, Rev. B. Herbert Martin, and—at the request of the mayor's companion, Mary Ella Smith—a Catholic priest were called to administer last rites.

"Once the patient is hooked up," Sanders says, "we're essentially operating on automatic pilot, and I had time to talk to the mayor's people who had been allowed in the room. I told them how bleak things looked and that if he were a member of my family, I would not want to artificially prolong life after all hope was gone. We decided that we would run the machine only for two full hours. It was a very emotional scene when I disconnected the CPS hookup. In the confusion, I forgot to dictate notes, and someone had to remind me to check the time the machine was turned off."

The official time of death was given as 1:36 p.m, but Los Angeles Mayor Tom Bradley had offered his condolences earlier, a discrepancy that infuriated many people. Sanders believes that "Bradley called Washington's office that day for another reason, and when he was told that Washington had suffered a heart attack, he mistakenly assumed that the mayor was already dead. I do not believe that one of the mayor's people told Bradley that Washington was dead before I pronounced him dead."

During the two hours the mayor was being worked on in the hyperacute room, the main ER treated an additional 16 patients, including three who came with chest pains and were admitted to the hospital to be checked for possible heart attacks. For the day, 15 patients were admitted to the hospital, including five who had signs of possible heart attacks. "We were able to carry on the normal routine of the ER as well as treat the mayor," Mathews says. "Our security, working with the mayor's bodyguards and Chicago police, did a pretty good job of weeding out the bystanders who had drifted into the ER." Sanders was well aware that he was keeping a pack of reporters at bay outside the ER doors, but he concludes: "First things first. We did everything we could for the patient. Then we told his family the bad news. Then we met the press."

After calling Cook County Medical Examiner Dr. Robert Stein to confirm his hunches about the cause of death, Sanders spent the rest of the night on a "media tour," explaining to various reporters what had happened. Then he drove to his Wisconsin cottage, arriving at 4 a.m. Thanksgiving Day, and found his family still up and waiting for him. He recalls wryly: "My wife, Karen, was very supportive and asked, 'How ya doin'?' My father, John Sr., who is a surgeon in Cleveland and who knows too well how personally we feel about the death of a patient, called the next morning at 7 to say, '0 for 2, huh?' (Sanders had also taken part in the unsuccessful attempt to revive Mayor Richard J. Daley after his heart attack on December 20, 1976). That's the way it goes."

Kramer adds: "I still get very keyed up just talking about our effort to save the mayor. At the actual moment, I tried to be very cool and to suppress my excitement, but it still is a very vivid memory. For a few moments the mayor was *my* patient, and I did everything I could to try to save him. We've been able to bring patients back from the brink of death, and whenever you do, the feeling is almost overpowering. I wish that could have happened with the mayor. Anytime you lose a patient, you have two basic feelings—sadness that there has been a death, and disappointment that you could not prevent it. Whenever I lose a patient, I feel lousy, and I felt very lousy after the mayor died.

"That's why the autopsy was so reassuring. It documented that this patient was unresuscitable."

"Let conversation cease,
let laughter flee.
This is the place
where death delights to help the living."

This passage, in Latin, is on a plaque hanging on the wall outside the office of Cook County Medical Examiner Stein, who has held the post since the county voted to establish it in 1976. He had earlier spent 20 years as a consultant to the coroner and now has a staff of 100 with jurisdiction over all violent or unexplained deaths in Cook County. This means 15,000 bodies a year, and Stein himself performs 500 autopsies a year, as well as supervising the rest.

As a forensic pathologist, Stein is eminently qualified for this grisly but indispensable job. His new state-of-the-art facility was built just a few blocks from the old grim Cook County Morgue in the shadow of the vast Cook County Hospital complex on the city's West Side. Through the halls of the old morgue have passed the mortal remains of John Dillinger, the seven St. Valentine's Day massacre victims, the eight nurses killed by Richard Speck and the 29 young men murdered by John Wayne Gacy. Stein supervised the pathology work on the 1979 Gacy case as well as the identification of the 274 victims of the DC-10 disaster that occurred only six months later. But he is quick to emphasize that his work is much more than simply ascertaining the cause of sudden death.

"What we do here," he explains, "is for the living. The living learn from the dead. I don't want to be known as a doctor of death. I think of myself as a teacher."

The teaching lesson from the death of Harold Washington is very simple, he says. "Harold Washington was a victim of his hypertensive heart disease [one resulting from high blood pressure], his lifestyle and his diet. The message is that we all have to find the time to take better care of ourselves physically."

There are two kinds of autopsies—the simple hospital autopsy that merely lists a cause of death and the definitive medicolegal autopsy performed by medical examiners like Stein. The medicolegal autopsy consists of two parts—findings and interpretations—and it lists both cause and manner of death.

Based on his findings, Stein says that he is "100 percent certain" of his interpretation that the mayor died of a sudden heart attack that was due entirely to natural causes. The mayor's autopsy is a brief document that is "a simple, straightforward exposition of death by heart attack," he says.

The official cause is described as "acute coronary thrombosis due to coronary atherosclerosis with 90 to 95 percent occlusion." What this means, he explains, is that the three major arteries supplying life-sustaining oxygen to the mayor's heart were all blocked by as much as 90 to 95 percent. One of these arteries, the left anterior descending artery, which provides 40 percent of the blood supply to the left ventricle, the heart's main pumping chamber, suffered an acute thrombus, or blood clot, and this triggered a fatal irregular heartbeat. Stein listed as a contributing cause "concentric hypertrophy of the left ventricle." This means that the heart's main pumping chamber was grotesquely swollen from years of having to pump against the greatly increased resistance of clogged blood vessels. The mayor's long-standing high blood pressure caused his hypertensive heart disease, resulting in a swollen heart and narrowed blood vessels. Although it is not listed as a cause or contributing cause of death, the mayor's obesity figured prominently in the autopsy. "Right in my first sentence," Stein says, "I noted that the mayor was about 100 pounds overweight and that this helped to compromise his health."

Stein adds, "The autopsy specimens are so grossly obvious that any sophomore medical student would have quickly diagnosed the mayor's death as I did." Waving his hand toward a microscope in an adjoining room, he says: "Since it was the mayor, we took slides of everything—heart, blood vessels, brain, kidney, spleen. I can send them to any qualified pathologist in the world and have my findings confirmed."

The objective findings of an autopsy can sometimes cloud the interpretation of the cause of a death. In the case of Elvis Presley, for instance, evidence was found *both* of heart disease and of near-toxic levels in the blood of prescription drugs. The Memphis medical examiner, Dr. Jerry T. Francisco, acknowledged the presence of the drugs but concluded that Presley's death was due to heart disease and heart disease alone, with the drugs neither causing nor contributing to the singer's dying at age 42. Other physicians present at the autopsy apparently believed that the death was due to "polypharmacy," or a fatal mixture of the several prescription medications found in the autopsy toxicological tests, but since the autopsy was a sealed document, they were precluded from arguing this view. Only Francisco was empowered by law to state a cause of death, and he chose heart disease. Most experts familiar with the case support his line of reasoning, but controversy nonetheless has surrounded his report.

By contrast, the drug tests on Harold Washington were totally negative. Stein emphasizes, "Our mass-spectrometry drug tests can detect the presence of any one of 30,000 toxicological compounds listed by the National Bureau of Laboratory Standards, and these drug tests were absolutely negative."

Stein rests his case on what he calls the "overwhelming evidence found in an objective autopsy. I had been following the TV reports all day, and the mayor's body was brought in about 4 p.m. I performed a very routine autopsy, requiring maybe 90 minutes, and I knew within about 20 minutes that the clot had caused the arrest.

"The mayor had a huge heart, what we call a 'bovine heart,' weighing 600 grams (a "normal" heart weighs 250 to 300 grams) and indicating the many years his heart had overworked itself pumping against the resistance of severely clogged blood vessels. He also had severe three-artery disease, with the left anterior descending artery, or LAD, which supplies the front wall of the heart and the left ventricle with blood, occluded 100 percent; and with the circumflex artery and right coronary artery, which supply the back wall of the heart with blood, both occluded 90 to 95 percent.

"His atherosclerosis [hardening and narrowing of the blood vessels] was so severe that even the arterioles, or small branches of the circulatory system, were occluded 50 to 60 percent. We found that the blood vessels at the base of the brain were also hardened and narrowed. We also found a small amount of fat in the liver.

"He was only 70 inches tall, and he weighed 284 pounds, which is about 100 pounds overweight. [Nineteen of those pounds, however, may have been due to the intravenous fluids he received during treatment.] This obesity created miles of new capillaries that his heart had to supply with blood. His adipose [fat] tissues were at least three inches thick."

Stein has received hate calls and mail accusing him of covering up the real cause of the mayor's death. It was murder through an overdose of cocaine, according to one version. He has also received numerous freedom-of-information requests for the actual autopsy document, requests that he turns over to county attorneys, contending, "The autopsy belongs to the family, and only the family can release it." He finds the claim that the mayor may have been murdered through an overdose of cocaine especially repulsive. "Medical examiners are always going to be second-guessed," he says, "but this is extremely irresponsible. Personally, I think that someone confused the lidocaine used in the resuscitation effort with cocaine, but there's never going to be a way to end all the rumors. Some people are always going to believe what they want to believe."

He concludes: "The mayor was a victim of some very common causes of death, especially his high blood pressure and heart disease, which was compounded by the way he ate and the way he lived. I never met the man personally, but I can remember seeing him on TV shortly before he died and telling my wife, Elisabeth, 'That man is sick.' He was a big, fat guy."

Patting his own ample waist, the medical examiner adds: "The message is that we all have to practice prevention. But it is human nature to deny things and put things off. That's what the mayor did. Perhaps, if he had [first] suffered a serious scare, maybe severe angina [pain in the chest] or a mild heart attack, he might have been motivated to change his lifestyle. He may have had symptoms and lied to his doctor about them, or he may not have had symptoms. But he exercised the right we all have, and he chose his own destiny."

The mayor's personal physician for his last three years was Senat, who received his medical doctorate from the University of Haiti in Port-au-Prince and specializes in heart diseases. Sitting in his office at Hyde Park Hospital, he speculates: "The precipitating factor of the cardiac arrest may have been the mayor's exertions during the ground-breaking ceremonies that morning. I have seen a videotape [of it], and for a few moments he was making a very physical effort. This may have caused a spasm that helped cause the acute clot in the left anterior descending artery, which was already severely narrowed by the atherosclerosis. The autopsy documented that this was a fresh thrombus, so it [must have] occurred that morning. The mayor apparently suffered from silent myocardia ischemia [temporary disruption in the flow of blood to part of the heart muscle], and this disease can take one of two forms: If you're lucky, you will have warnings like angina or a heart attack in which you have hours to take corrective action; if you're unlucky, you will have a sudden arrest and death. The mayor was not lucky."

Sanders adds: "The mayor's heart resembled the biceps of a weightlifter. It was musclebound to the point where it could no longer function properly. The heart of a superbly conditioned athlete enlarges only marginally in gross size. What happens, though, is that the conditioned heart develops greater efficiency in pumping and relaxing and extracting oxygen. The increase in strength is to be found in its dynamic pulsations, not in its size. The mayor's heart was so large and musclebound and solid as a rock from all that unnecessary work that it had done over the years that it could not regain a normal rhythm following the arrest. Cardiac arrest simply means that the heart stops pumping; the actual cause may be either electrical or mechanical. The clot in the major artery serving the left ventricle shut down his heartbeat and triggered a lethal arrhythmia."

Kramer says: "If the mayor's death does not wake people up to the risks, then nothing will. The narrowing of his arteries took place over a long period of time, and the acute clot delivered the knockout blow. He received superb emergency care, and yet he never had a chance. The only thing left is prevention."

Sanders, who often walks up and down hospital steps to stay in shape for cross-country skiing, adds: "If operating on heart patients day after day does not sensitize you to the risks, then nothing will. I have an exercise stress test every year."

Experts and friends are divided over whether or not the mayor experienced symptoms of his heart disease. In hindsight, Alton Miller recalls that there were warning signs. "The two most impressive things about the mayor," he says, "were his intelligence and the ability to articulate it, and his high energy level. But by last fall he did not seem to have the same energy as before. In the six months before his death, I received at least two phone calls that began, 'You know, your boss doesn't look well. . . .' One was from a physician and the other from a patient who had just recovered from a heart attack. The patient thought that the mayor was showing the same symptoms he had shown before his own heart attack: a grayness of the face, a shortness of breath when talking and an appearance of being overweight.

"Personally, I also thought that by the fall of 1987 the mayor no longer had as much energy as before. Throughout his first term, he had maintained a hell of a schedule, and it had become even more hellacious during his campaign for re-election. But after he was re-elected in April, 1987, he began to slow down, except for the confrontation between the Chicago Housing Authority and the federal office of Housing and Urban Development and the confrontation over the teacher's strike. He always approached political battles like [those involving] CHA and HUD and the teachers' strike as military campaigns, and his energy appeared limitless, but between campaigns he was beginning to slow down, occasionally taking a day off, which was very atypical," Miller says.

"At first, when the word came down that the mayor would 'not be keeping a schedule,' we at City Hall would applaud. We knew that he needed some time off. In the weeks before his death he often was run-down, tired and complaining of a 'cold he couldn't shake.' He took two days off the week before he died and another one the week he died, and his absences were becoming common enough that they no longer surprised his staff. It's not like he was asleep at the ranch or an absentee mayor; he simply seemed to be slowing down. But since he had previously told me that he had been given a complete physical examination, I had put any thoughts of his not being well out of my mind."

Mathews says, "He probably had some symptoms, but as a free-living human, he exercised his right to overlook them." Kramer adds, "Sure, he may have missed the symptoms, but we all would rather think that we are experiencing the flu or indigestion, rather than heart failure."

Dr. Quentin Young, a friend and political associate of the mayor and his one-time acting city health commissioner, observes, however: "I've been a clinician for 35 years, and though I was well aware that he had significant risk factors, I never saw any overt symptoms of heart disease, like shortness of breath. He looked good, considering."

The mayor's chief of staff, Ernest Barefield, says: "It seemed to me that he only had a cold or the flu. Maybe his time was up, just like that runner [Jim Fixx] who ran every day and had a heart attack while exercising. There was no way for the mayor to know what was about to happen—unless he had made an active search to discover the disease."

Delores Woods, Washington's secretary of 20 years, says, "The mayor looked fine on the day he died. Just fine."

Sanders explains: "The symptoms of heart disease can be very subtle, truly silent. It's only in about 30 to 40 percent of all heart attacks that the classic symptoms are present—extreme pain and distress. I've often wondered myself if *I* would know if I were having a heart attack. Recently, I read an article in the clinical literature about heart attacks among cardiologists, the experts in the field. Many missed the initial symptoms. It's absolutely frightening. The mayor would have needed definitive tests to ascertain his heart disease—either an electrocardiogram while undergoing an exercise stress test or the gold standard, which is an angiogram [an X-ray of the heart and blood vessels after they have been injected with a dye to make them show up on the X-ray films]. These tests would have discovered the blockages. In general, though, it's hard for many of our sophisticated imaging techniques to read the blood vessels accurately because of the heart's pumping motion."

Hartz says simply, "This is a patient who should have had an exercise stress test during each of the past 15 years."

In point of fact, the mayor never had any, despite the insistent promptings of Senat and Young and his friend of 55 years, Chicago businessman Dempsey Travis. While it may be unclear whether Washington had symptoms of heart disease, there can be no doubt that he was made well aware of his risk factors.

Senat elaborates: "When I became his physician three years ago, I discovered that for years he had been without a doctor, ever since his previous physician had died. I met him through a mutual friend, and he said, 'I want you to be my doctor, too.'

"I performed a complete physical examination on him in 1985 and discovered:

- "His blood pressure was high at 160/90 [normal is 120/80], and apparently he did not always take his medication as prescribed by his previous doctor.

- "His cholesterol [or fats in the blood] was high at 252 [recommended is under 200, with 160 to 180 considered ideal].

- "He was overweight at 235 pounds [at 5 feet 10, the recommended weight for him would be well under 200 pounds].

- "He had been a heavy smoker, maybe two packs a day, for more than 30 years, and although he said he had stopped, any damage had already been done.

• "He had not taken one day of vacation since being elected mayor in April, 1983."

Appraising these findings, Eliot, the Colorado expert on sudden cardiac death who is also a member of the Prevention Committee of the American College of Cardiology, sums up: "By itself, high blood pressure doubles your risk of heart attacks. If in addition you smoke *or* have high cholesterol, your risk is eight times higher. If you have high blood pressure and you smoke *and* you have high cholesterol, your risk is up to 12 times higher. And if you have all three of these risks factors *plus* being obese, the risk doubles again. So Harold Washington's risk was 24 times the average."

Senat, too, knew these risks and tried hard to explain them to his patient. Just being black was a risk factor because in industrialized societies blacks develop high blood pressure twice as frequently as whites and die from it three times as frequently. Diseases related to high blood pressure kill 100 times more blacks than does sickle-cell anemia.

By complying with his physician's recommendations, Harold Washington might have been a great role model for other patients suffering from hypertension, many of whom frustrate their physicians by refusing to take their medicines as directed. "The reason is simple enough," Senat explains. "Many people are walking around with extremely high blood pressure, but they have no symptoms. If they take the medicine that may save their lives, they suddenly have side effects. So they figure, 'Why bother?'"

For Christmas, 1985, Travis gave his old friend an exercise bike, pointing out that he himself "had as a young man been overweight, and I know the feeling. That's why I now do 140 miles a week on my bike and another 20 miles a week running along the lake." The following June, Senat again gave Washington a complete physical and found that his weight had jumped to 255. He scheduled an exercise treadmill test, but on the appointed day the mayor had one of his guards call to cancel the appointment. The physician tried to reschedule the test but was unsuccessful.

For Christmas, 1986, Travis gave the mayor an exercise treadmill and helped to set it up in his friend's apartment right next to the exercise bicycle. The next year, shortly before the mayoral election, Senat performed another physical and found that the mayor now weighed 265 pounds. He also found a need to increase the mayor's dosage of hypertensive medication. He extracted a promise from Washington to take a vacation shortly after the election and take a treadmill test.

The mayor took the vacation ("He went to Canada, holed up in a hotel and read for four days," the physician recalls), but the exercise test for his heart was again shoved aside. "He actually showed up here last June at Hyde Park Hospital for the test," Senat recalls, "and we were walking to the examining room when one of his aides called to report that the news media believed that the mayor was being hospitalized for a heart attack, and the camera crews were outside the hospital. Well, by the time the mayor had dealt with that crisis, he had used up the time he had allotted for the test. So he was off to his next appointment, and I was again unable to reschedule it."

Travis adds: "I used to be on the board of Northwestern Memorial Hospital, and on four separate occasions I scheduled an exercise test of his heart. The room was set aside, and everything was in readiness, but he canceled—all four times."

Young tells of a similar experience. "I had gone beyond the ethic," he recalls, "and had actually solicited Harold as a patient. He lived close to my medical office on the South Side, and I had convinced him that we would open early one day, at 8 a.m., and quickly put him through the test before we officially opened at 9. It was scheduled for 8 a.m. on Monday, and we were all ready for him when the guard called at 7:55 to cancel. I rescheduled for the following Wednesday at 8 a.m. Same result. The guard called at 7:55 to cancel. I asked, 'Well, when does the mayor want to reschedule?' I was told that at that time he was not prepared to set another date. It must have been an issue of control. Some people never use a doctor, and some people never heed their doctor. Harold simply wouldn't listen."

Senat thinks his patient may also have been suffering from the stress of running the nation's third largest city. "He was a workaholic and a classic Type-A personality," the doctor recalls, "a man intensely focused on what he wanted to accomplish. And I think that the stress of the 'Council Wars' helped to run him down."

Sanders agrees. "You know," he says, "in many ways, the mayor of a large city has as much stress as the President of the United States—without any of the protective devices like Camp David and

Air Force One and an enormous staff and a supportive Cabinet. And certainly President Reagan is a positive role model of how to take care of yourself physically. He exercises, takes his vacations, gets regular medical checkups and has the benefit of a supportive wife. Sure, Washington must have felt the stress of having to wrangle with his own City Council."

Others disagree on this point. "He loved every minute of being mayor," Miller says. Travis says: "He told me that he took to political battles the way a 'duck takes to water,' and that he 'would begin to salivate whenever he was planning a political campaign.' So I think that he handled stress very well."

Senat visited the mayor three weeks before Washington died and found that the hypertensive medication needed to be increased again. "I told him, 'Mr. Mayor, you have been taking two pills a day, and now I need to increase your dose. Since I know that you will not take three pills a day, I am going to change your prescription to one long-acting pill each day.' I also asked him about his diet, and I was told that he was cutting out red meat and was eating only fish. Well, he never filled that prescription, so he probably was without hypertensive medication during the three weeks before his death."

Travis also visited his friend around this time and was surprised to see that his Christmas gifts had been moved from the mayor's apartment into the guards' apartment across the hall. "What's going on?" Travis asked, and the mayor replied, "Well, I put the machines over there because it's easier to work out across the hall." Travis checked and found that in two years the mayor had put less than 200 miles on the bike and less than 100 on the treadmill, and since he himself was doing 140 miles each week, he said, "Harold, that's B.S.!"

At a public meeting attended by both Travis and Washington a week before the attack, Travis prophetically told his friend: "You're going to be mayor as long as you live. Only you can hurt yourself."

The day of the death, Travis "got the call and drove like a fireman from the South Side straight to Northwestern, arriving before the ambulance engine had cooled down." He was promptly collared by reporters from nearby CBS-TV and agreed to an interview that he thought would be in a mobile truck. Instead, he ended up at the CBS studios at McClurg Court, and when anchors Bill Kurtis and Walter Jacobson appeared to be referring to the mayor in the past tense, Travis says he "lost it. I simply couldn't go on. I stood up and said, 'Sorry, fellows, I can't do this one,' and walked out. The minute I had received the call about the heart attack, I had begun to cry. I knew in my heart that he was dead, but I refused to believe it."

Travis had conducted 100 hours of one-on-one taped interviews with Washington for five chapters in his 1987 book, "The Autobiography of Black Politics" (Urban Research Press), and he believes he knows "Harold better than anyone." He muses: "I think that his mental energy simply overwhelmed his physical energy. A few years ago I went to Japan with him for eight days, and he was going, going, 16, 17 hours a day. He wanted me to continue on [with him] to China, but, man, I was beat. I waved them off at the airport, and then I went back to my hotel and slept for a day. I was glad to see him gone because I was tired of trying to keep up. When I got back to Chicago, I was exhausted.

"But the mayor thrived on hard mental work. The night before he died, I was with him at a City Hall reception, and afterwards he almost skipped into the night because he felt so good. Even the guards commented on his energy. Harold was a very private man, and after I had interviewed about 100 people who knew him for my book, I concluded that I knew him best. Everybody would recall being with him and seeing him and talking with him, but nobody really *knew* him. Whenever he would reach for a cigarette, I would put my hand over his and say, 'No.' I was with him the day the Bears won the NFC title game at Soldier Field, and when a lady came around with some food, Harold reached for a 'Fat Mac.' I grabbed his hand and said, 'Damn, man, you can't be hungry!' It was only noon, and we had had a late breakfast. He had a lot of free advice to take better care of himself, but he really believed that nothing would happen to him."

The mayor, a former track star and amateur boxer, had only two passions in his later life—running Chicago and reading—and almost his only physical exercise was turning the pages of a book. He also liked to eat. "How do you get through those 18-hour days?" Young asks rhetorically. "You power yourself with junk food."

Tribune reporter John Kass covered Washington's last mayoral campaign and followed his car and security staff each day. He recalls that the mayor ate constantly, stoking up on fast food en route to campaign stops and eating his fill again only minutes later at whatever banquet he was attending.

In the fall of 1986, Kass recalls, the mayor stopped for lunch one afternoon at the Red Lion on Lincoln Avenue. The restaurant was closed to the public for the day but was set up to accommodate the mayor's appetite and Kass' interview. The mayor said he enjoyed the Red Lion because it reminded him of the food he had eaten on a recent trip to London. Kass reports:

"The mayor ordered a large salad with cream dressing, a steak-and-kidney pie (about eight ounces), and then a second steak-and-kidney pie (again eight ounces). He drank two Cokes to wash the meal down and ordered a large dessert (a trifle). The dessert consisted of pound cake, macaroons, sherry, fruit cocktail and loads of custard and whipped cream. He had another Coke. The mayor finished his early-afternoon lunch with coffee, telling me that he was eating early that day because he was scheduled to hit the campaign dinner circuit later that evening."

Kass describes a typical campaign day: "In the morning at about 10, his entourage would stop at a fast-food place—the favorites were Popeye's Famous Fried Chicken, Dunkin' Donuts or McDonald's—and a bodyguard would be dispatched to bring a large bag of food back to the limousine. A few minutes later we would arrive at a campaign stop, and he would again eat whatever they provided him there. At noon his car would again stop at a hamburger or chicken stand, and again he would eat. Later in the afternoon, at another stop, he would eat again. And again at dinner. Sometimes he would munch the last bite of a fast-food hamburger, pass the wrapper across to a guard and march directly to the buffet food available at a campaign stop."

Sanders adds: "You live alone, and what do you eat? Junk food, of course. But the mayor did not seem overly obese. He was heavily muscled and simply massive. He reminded me of someone who might have been a lineman in professional football."

Yet the Tribune reporter also encountered vivid evidence of the mayor's physical decline. During the height of the campaign, Washington and Kass left a candidates' forum at Daley College one evening and walked up one flight of stairs to reach street level. Kass recalls that after only three or four steps, "the mayor put his left arm around me for support and began coughing, spitting and wheezing.

He stopped walking, rested a minute, and we began walking up again. Washington wheezed the entire time. His staff, who said he did not have a cold, was also concerned by what was happening. Before he made it to the car, Washington looked at me and said, 'You better exercise so you won't end up like this.'"

"This guy *was* a reader," Senat says. "His books were never well-thumbed because he would go through them at one sitting." Miller says the books were usually work-related. "He loved 'The Power Broker' [by Robert Caro], and he liked the books by Gov. [Mario] Cuomo [of New York] and Mayor [Ed] Koch [of New York City]."

Young adds: "He had a great mind. I first met him when he was a state senator and I was the medical director at Cook County Hospital. Now, the county budget is designed to conceal as much as it reveals, and when I went down to Springfield to seek his support for our hospital budget, I was astonished at his grasp of detail. Later we had him over to the house to meet a potential political supporter, and he was making chitchat with my wife, who is the editor of the Bulletin of Atomic Scientists. She told me later that Washington knew more about the issues of nuclear energy than anybody who was not either working in the field or a nuclear physicist. He had charisma, warmth, wit and wisdom and had been well-received wherever he was for most of 65 years, so in hindsight it may be unrealistic to have expected him to change his lifestyle. He was unlucky in that he never suffered symptoms serious enough to motivate him to seek care, but he was lucky in the sense that he escaped suffering a disabling stroke or diminishing mental and physical vigor and died going full tilt on the job."

That job was his life, says Senat. "His first love was the city, and he had 8 million advisers. My visits with him were never complete until we discussed Chicago and what was best for the city. There are priorities and then there are priorities, and Harold's priority was the city. He knew exactly what he wanted for the city, and he was very predictable in that if he thought something was not right for Chicago, he would get very angry. And he loved the job. Haven't you ever heard Harold sing, 'Chicago, Chicago . . .'?"

During the re-election campaign, it was press secretary Miller's job to paint for reporters a picture of a vigorous mayor whose natural stamina allowed him to outwalk reporters less than half his age during the long days and nights. One day recently, fresh from a workout at a downtown sports club, Miller bites into a ham-and-cheese on pita bread and sadly concludes: "Sixty-five is simply too damn young to die. If the mayor's death doesn't point up the need for aerobic exercise and regular medical checkups, then I don't think anything will."

Harold Washington might have had his 20 years as mayor. Sanders says, "He probably needed heart-bypass surgery to replace his diseased arteries, and had he had it, he would have been up and about in six weeks, with a life expectancy of 10 or 15 years."

Others take a philosophical view. Dr. Carl Bell, a black psychiatrist and community activist who knew the mayor, observes: "Harold died right on time. We have a joke in the black community—it's called Social Security. The average black male dies at exactly age 65."

At first, there were general rumors, which soon focused on allegations by Sherman Skolnick that the mayor had been murdered. Skolnick, a self-styled reformer who claims to "research judicial corruption and political murder," achieved a modicum of fame in the late 1960s and early 1970s by using his Citizens Committee to Clean Up the Courts to help oust two Illinois Supreme Court justices for official misconduct.

Through his "Hotline News," a recorded phone-message service he operates from his home on the South Side, through interviews with the black community's Chicago Defender and radio station WVON and later while on the "Dave Baum Show" on WBBM Radio, Skolnick suggested his murder scenario. That scenario includes an autopsy that has been "suppressed" because it revealed "cocaine in the mayor's blood" and concludes that since the "mayor did not use the stuff," he must indeed have been murdered.

Under Baum's intensive questioning, Skolnick was unable to offer any proof of his allegations.

There is nothing more to be known about the death of the mayor. Dr. Stein wrote the autopsy, Dr. Senat, the mayor's personal physician, reviewed it in the presence of Dr. Edwards, the mayor's health commissioner, and of Ramon Price, the mayor's half-brother, who now controls access to it. They all agree: There are no secrets in that sealed document.

Harold Washington was an extraordinary man, but he died an ordinary death. This is the verdict from the best and brightest of

Chicago medical scientists. Yet their message, too, may well go unheeded. Beliefs and habits are hard to break.

Leaving Northwestern Memorial Hospital one afternoon by taxi, I found myself with a driver who was jovial, hefty and talkative. As we sped by a storefront, we could see through its snow-shrouded front window the unmistakable silhouettes of fetching leotard-clad young women swaying rhythmically to the beat of aerobic dancing. The driver smiled and said: "Ah, what a pretty sight, but what a silly thing, this exercise. I get all the exercise I need walking from the barstool to the bathroom."

A Second Chance

This cardiac-rehab program saves lives by changing lifestyles

It is early morning at the coronary-care unit of Swedish Covenant Hospital on Chicago's Northwest Side. The unit is brimming with electronic gadgetry, and patients awake to the machines, medications, technicians and tubes that are keeping them alive after a heart attack. It may not look like it, but these people are lucky—they will have a second chance.

A few blocks away at the gymnasium of North Park College, whose campus adjoins the hospital, there are scores of middle-aged men and women running on a bare hardwood floor, all graduates of coronary-care units throughout the city, and they are literally running for their lives. They are members of the Cardiac Rehabilitation Center at Swedish Covenant, and they are making the most of that second chance.

Cardiac rehabilitation demands much more than exercise, of course; it requires a change in the lifestyle that caused the attack itself. Over the years, many of these patients had busted their guts—and hearts—to earn the good life, and their reward was a hospital bed. They don't want to go back.

Medical science can often pull them through the first crisis. There are medications to regulate the heartbeat and widen the arteries. Angioplasty can clear the clogged arteries that are unable to supply the heart with nourishing oxygen. Bypass surgery can replace the narrowed coronary arteries. A transplant can even substitute for a failing heart.

Motivation, however, is required to maintain a healthy heart and to prevent heart attack No. 2. The person who is healthy today should heed the hard-earned wisdom of the men and women who regularly come to the cardiac-rehab center at Swedish Covenant. The stories of these people who are starting over offer important ways for the person who is without symptoms today to minimize the chances of a first heart attack.

Not risking one is a very good idea, because every year 450,000 Americans die within 24 hours of a heart attack. This amounts to more than 1,200 people each day. In a third of these 450,000 cases, there is absolutely no warning. The first symptom is the last symptom —a sudden heart attack.

The 600,000 Americans, then, who do survive a heart attack every year are very lucky. They have become graduates of a common educational experience—the coronary-care unit. They have in effect been hit over the head by a two-by-four, and many are, for the first time in their lives, ready to pause and consider changing the lifestyles that put them in the hospital. Some will make the necessary changes, some will not.

Among those who are trying to change are the 100 or so men and women who currently are committed to working out at the cardiac-rehab center at Swedish Covenant. They are part of a tradition dating back to 1971 when cardiologist Dr. Noel Nequin teamed up with a heart-attack victim to develop his pioneering belief that the heart-attack patient can regain strength and vigor by exercising and making necessary behavioral changes.

Nequin believes that regular supervised exercise in a support group is the glue that will enable cardiac-rehab patients to stick to their other lifestyle changes. Over the years, he has introduced thousands of recovered coronary patients to the benefits of a rehabilitation program and, though the dropout rate is high, his enthusiasm has never waned. He founded the Coronary Club of Chicago in 1975.

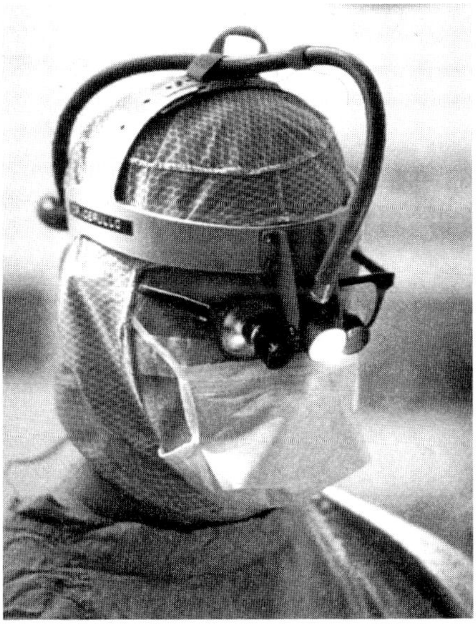

Charles Osgood *Chicago Tribune*

Author Dennis L. Breo (far right in OR photo) scrubbed with (Chicago's) Northwestern Memorial Hospital brain surgeon Leonard Cerullo, M.D. (left), and heart surgeon Renée Hartz, M.D. (below), to observe life-and-death operations. Brain surgeons face tough odds. Cerullo explains: "If the patient wakes up doing the same, I am happy; if the patient comes out of surgery for the better, I am ecstatic; and if the patient wakes up for the worse, I am devastated. Totally, utterly devastated. My self-esteem is shot and I feel as if I should never have been born." Hartz expresses her philosophy this way: "I try to do for every patient exactly what I would do for my own father."

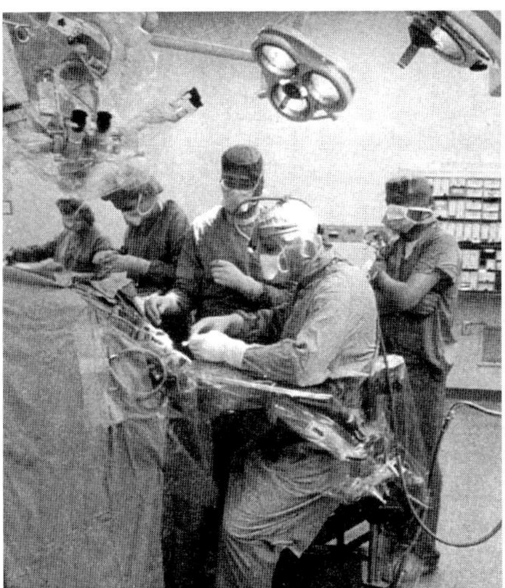

Charles Osgood *Chicago Tribune*

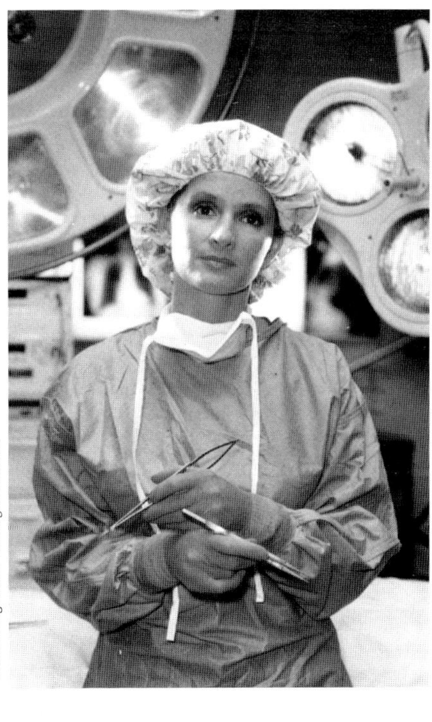

Karen Engstrom *Chicago Tribune*

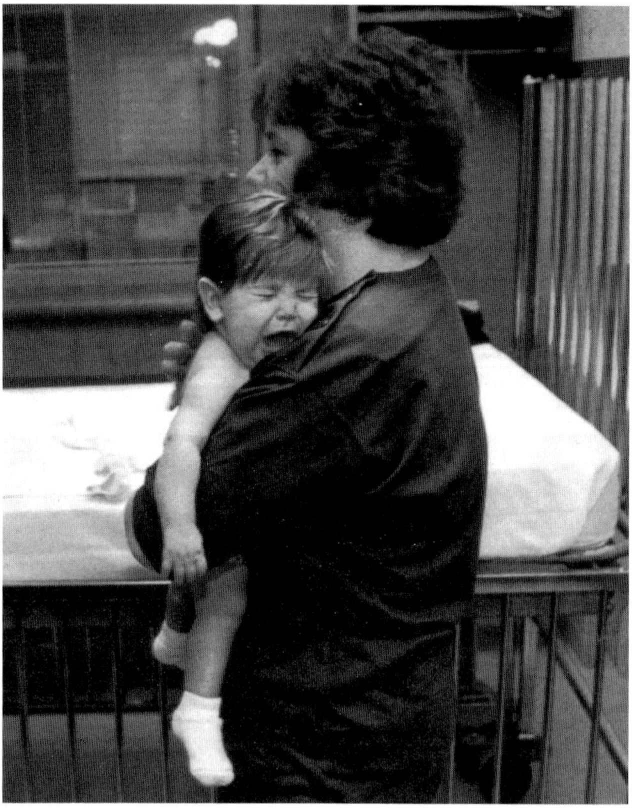

George Thompson *Chicago Tribune*

Janet Aggen comforts her nine-month-old daughter Lauren shortly before a biopsy procedure to determine how she is adapting to her new heart. On Christmas Day, the three-day-old Lauren was near death. Then she got a belated present—a heart transplant at Children's Hospital in Chicago.

John Dziekan *Chicago Tribune*

Chicago psychiatrist Carl Bell, M.D. (above), is out to stop black-on-black violence. "We have got to teach black people," he says, "to stop beating each other to pieces right in their own living rooms." Internist Charles DeShazer, M.D. (below), survived the mean streets of the inner city in time to earn his medical degree and treat his former gang members and friends at Chicago's huge Cook County Hospital—only minutes from the ghetto where he grew up. "This hospital gets in your blood," he explains. "It's about patients and doctors and compassion."

Dennis L. Breo *JAMA*

Dennis L. Breo *JAMA*

If you are both homeless *and* sick in America, that is a true tragedy, say missionary M.D.s David Hilfiker (below) and Janelle Goetcheus (below right), who decided to do something about it by establishing Christ House, which is both a shelter and a medical clinic, located within the shadows of Capitol Hill in Washington, D.C. Hilfiker says, "The American medical system is strangling the poorest members of our society." Goetcheus adds, "There are joys in doing what we can." One grateful fan is resident Carlton Davis (right), who says the "warm welcome I have received turned my life around."

Dennis L. Breo *JAMA*

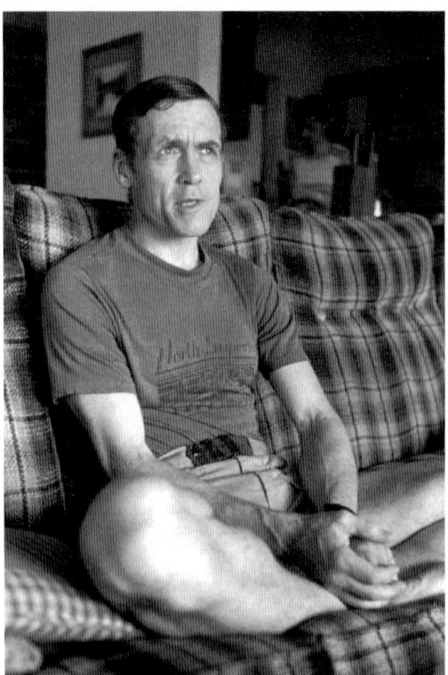

Dennis L. Breo *JAMA*

Dennis L. Breo *JAMA*

Harold Jaffe, M.D. (below), of the federal Centers for Disease Control and Prevention, says he is still " puzzled and frustrated" over failing to figure out precisely how Florida dentist David Acer might have infected Kimberly Bergalis (above) and five other patients with the dentist's strain of the AIDS virus.

Dennis L. Breo *JAMA*

Chris Walker *Chicago Tribune*

Heart disease, to have or have not, the choice is yours—or so say cardiac-rehab experts who save lives by changing lifestyles. Seizing their second chances are John Wagenknecht, who tackles the rowing machine (opposite); and Jane Ridgeway, who does some stretching (above). Ignoring all health advice was the way of late Chicago Mayor Harold Washington (right) — and he paid the ultimate price.

Chris Walker *Chicago Tribune*

Dennis L. Breo *JAMA*

Dennis L. Breo *JAMA*

Kicking butts—AMA leader Lonnie Bristow, M.D. (top right), and anti-tobacco activist Alan Blum, M.D. (above), are among the many physicans who believe that the Joe Camel advertising campaign should be snuffed out.

The best little whorehouse in Manhattan will be converted into a shelter for homeless hookers, if AIDS physician Joyce Wallace, M.D., has her way. Wallace, posing next to the sleek contours of a voluptuous nude in the former brothel, believes that her "impossible dream" will help control the AIDS epidemic. She also drives a custom van into New York's major "whores' strolls" to distribute condoms to the city's streetwalkers and offer counseling and testing for AIDS.

Dennis L. Breo *JAMA*

Dennis L. Breo *JAMA*

U.S. Bicentennial Expedition

Emergency room physician Chris Chandler, M.D., made it to the summit of the world's highest peak, Mount Everest, as part of the U.S. Bicentennial Expedition in 1976 (above). However, his luck ran out when he and his wife, Cherie Bremer-Kamp, tried nine years later to scale another Himalayan peak—Mount Kanchenjunga. Bremer-Kamp is shown in full climbing gear on Kanchenjunga in a photo taken by her husband (opposite, lower left). The photo of Chandler at base camp on Kanchenjunga (opposite, top) was taken by his wife and is the last taken of the climber before his death on the mountain on January 15, 1985; Bremer-Kamp (also shown on the Chandlers' Sausalito houseboat, the *Laylah*, opposite, lower right) survived but lost parts of her fingers and toes. "In the winter," says Bremer-Kamp, "the cold is unbelievable on Kanchenjunga and the jet-stream winds, blowing at up to 200 miles per hour, can blow you right off the mountain."

Chris Chandler

Dennis L. Breo *JAMA*

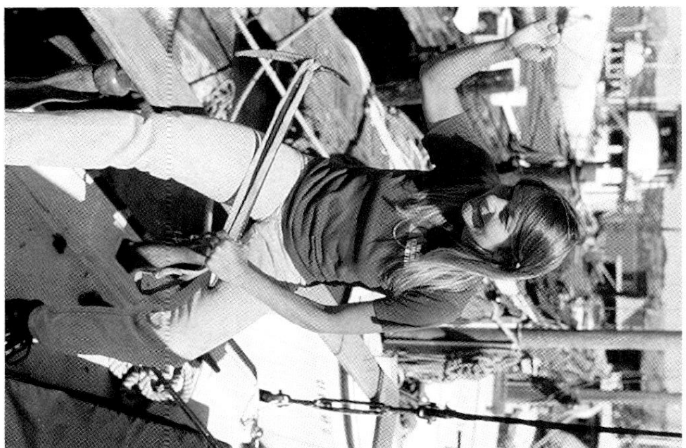

Cherie Bremer-Kamp

Wally Schlech, M.D. (lower left), a former 1960s dropout, became a disease sleuth and solved an epidemic of listeriosis among pregnant women in Halifax, Nova Scotia, by tracing it to tainted cabbage. Millionaire businessman Phil Sokolof (left), known as "Mr. Lean," is determined to make food giants see the lite and to teach Americans the facts of good nutrition. Public health officer Bob Sanders, M.D. (below), pushed a bill requiring kiddie auto restraints through the Tennessee legislature and become known as "Dr. Seat Belt."

Dennis L. Breo *JAMA*

Dennis L. Breo *JAMA*

Top researchers Bert Vogelstein, M.D. (right), Barbara Weber, M.D. (below), and Francis Collins, M.D. (lower right), are leading a revolution in our understanding of the causes and potential cures of cancer. "The revolution of discovery," says Vogelstein, "has proven that cancer is a genetic disease." The next hoped-for revolution, he says, is one of dramatically improved treatments of cancer, possibly even cures.

Dennis L. Breo *JAMA*

Dennis L. Breo *JAMA*

Dennis L. Breo *JAMA*

Bettmann Archive

Among the Allied force of 176,000 men who stormed the sands of Normandy on June 6, 1944—D-Day—to begin the epic push to liberate Europe from Hitler's Nazi Germany were two physician members of the Third Auxiliary Surgical group: Capt. Charles O. Van Gorder, M.D. (shown in full combat gear, opposite, top), and Capt. Treadwell L. Ireland, M.D. (opposite, bottom). Both lived to tell about it and, in interviews 50 years later, Ireland summarizes, "Everybody was scared and everybody who survived was lucky." Van Gorder adds, "It was something we had to do and nobody thought much more about it."

Courtesy of Charles O. Van Gorder, M.D.

Dennis L. Breo *JAMA*

Courtesy of Treadwell Ireland, M.D.

Dennis L. Breo *JAMA*

Courtesy of Cold Spring Harbor Laboratory

Legendary Nobelists Francis Crick (with pointer) and Jim Watson discovered the secret of the double-helix structure of deoxyribonucleic acid (DNA) in 1953, solving the secret of genes and heredity and how like begets like. This "blaze of understanding" is probably the most important find of the twentieth century. It launched the revolution of genetic medicine by proving our genes are made of DNA, thus revealing the secret of heredity, and it made the dream of understanding and preventing genetic diseases, like cancer, potentially achievable. Watson and Crick are shown in front of their DNA model at the Cavendish Laboratory of Cambridge University in Cambridge, England, in 1953 (above). In 1991, the two reenacted the photo at Cold Spring Harbor Laboratory in Long Island, N.Y. (below).

Courtesy of Cold Spring Harbor Laboratory

Next December, on the 20th anniversary of the cardiac-rehab program, the first of its kind in the Midwest and one of the first in the nation, the hospital will be able to move its students down the street from the college gym to a new state-of-the-art fitness facility now under construction. The new "LifeCenter on the Green," made possible by a gift from philanthropists Jack and Dollie Galter, will be affiliated with Swedish Covenant, and its facilities will be open to the community.

For Nequin, it will be a dream come true, enabling him to help more cardiac patients make the most of their second chance.

The coronary arteries girdle the heart muscle like a crown, or "corona." If one of the three major arteries becomes severely narrowed (more than 75 percent blocked) or develops a total block, clot or spasm, the result is usually angina (severe chest pain), heart attack or total cardiac arrest.

Technically, a heart attack occurs when blood flow to the heart muscle slows or stops for a period of time. The portion of the muscle denied life-sustaining oxygen is damaged or destroyed.

Heart disease is our nation's No. 1 killer, and the typical risk factors have been well reported, though not necessarily well understood.

The fixed risks include being male, growing older and a history of blood relatives who developed heart disease before age 65.

Of the major controllable risks, the most important is within one's power to eliminate. "If you only do one thing," says Corinne Murphy, the cardiac-rehab program director, "don't smoke!"

Other major controllable risk factors are diabetes, high blood pressure, high cholesterol, obesity (weighing 30 percent above your recommended weight), heavy drinking (more than 21 alcoholic drinks a week) and lack of exercise. Some experts consider uncontrolled stress to be an independent risk factor, and additionally, it is interwoven with all the others.

What's most important, however, is the combination of risk factors and how each person handles them—or doesn't. For this story, seven patients were selected at random from the Swedish Covenant cardiac-rehab program and asked to tell their stories. All are similar in only three respects: All but one were smokers, all were convinced "it could never happen to me," and all are now determined to make the most of their second chance.

Chuck Carlson, 62, was only 43 in August 1971 when he stood up in his living room to answer his wife's call to dinner and promptly collapsed from a heart attack. "I was totally ignorant of heart disease," he recalls. "There was little or no education in those days. But I knew I was in trouble."

His wife drove him the few short blocks to the Swedish Covenant emergency room, where an electrocardiogram (EKG) diagnosed a mild heart attack. Weeks later, he was given some heart pills, sent home and told to "take it easy."

Carlson, however, was an active man who was used to working 12-hour days as a computer operator, then joining his twin brother, Arvid, then a cameraman for WGN-TV, to photograph football games and horseraces on weekends. He also liked to snow- and water-ski and ride horses. At 6 foot 1 and 175 pounds, he considered himself a recreational athlete who was in excellent shape. He became bored with taking it easy.

Carlson's doctor referred him to Nequin, who was then a 34-year-old Swedish Covenant cardiologist who hoped to help his patients by convincing them to resume physical exercise, but under close medical supervision. The effort started on the hospital's fifth floor in a small room that had been the obstetrical delivery room.

"Actually, my two daughters had been born in this room," Carlson recalls. "Dr. Nequin had persuaded the hospital to give his idea a try, he commandeered the room and borrowed an exercise bike and treadmill. He started me out very cautiously—calisthenics and stretching."

Over the next 20 years, the program has been relocated from the delivery room to the basement of the hospital's nursing dorm to the gym of nearby St. Demetrius Church to the North Park College gym and pool (in 1978) to this year's final destination—the new LifeCenter. The original calisthenics and stretching routines have been expanded to include cycling, aerobic dancing, rowing, long-distance running and swimming. Coronary Club lectures by outside experts have covered such topics as diet, stress-management, post-coronary sex and yoga.

Along the way, Carlson says he has learned and changed with the program. "Today, I am about as knowledgeable about heart disease as a non-physician can be. This program has been a lifesaver, enabling me to totally change my approach to life."

In retrospect, he says, his "workaholic lifestyle" caused the attack. "I didn't smoke (one of the few exceptions in the program), I drank moderately, and I didn't have any glaring risk factors, but I was always working.

"Being engrossed in work was a viable option because the net result was paying the bills, but in the process I neglected my family, usually ate on the run and had to keep pushing—all the time."

Carlson also learned a new word: cholesterol. "The odds are that my cholesterol was high at the time of the heart attack," he says, "but I had no way of knowing it. I had never heard of the word until Dr. Nequin explained later that mine was too high."

Carlson has avoided heart attack No. 2. Over the 20 years, careful eating has controlled his cholesterol, medication has controlled the high blood pressure he developed 10 years ago, and he has controlled himself through "the camaraderie of the cardiac-rehab center. I thought that I was invincible, but I was wrong. Now, I know that I need support to lead a balanced life."

When his twin, cameraman Arvid, suffered a heart attack in 1982 while covering Jane Byrne's campaign for mayor, Carlson gave his brother the message he gives himself:

"Make the choices and find the support you need to change and balance your life and avoid self-destructive habits. I gave up the photography work to have more time for myself and my family. I watched my diet to control my cholesterol and weight. I stopped living in a helter-skelter fashion. I approached job stress as just another day at the office.

Now, Carlson says, "I feel fantastic." Divorced for eight years, he is engaged to marry a woman he met through the cardiac-rehab program. He spends weekends skiing at his cabin in Michigan's Upper Peninsula. He has run "half a marathon." He breaks off the discussion to begin his three-day-a-week routine: 15 minutes of stretching, 30 minutes of cycling, 15 minutes of running. He concludes, "I'm on the program forever."

Other patients offer other lessons. One is: Don't deny your risk.

Jane Ridgeway, 58, says she was "very, very surprised" when she felt a "WHAM!" deep in her chest 11 years ago.

It's surprising that she felt this way, since she was a walking time-bomb: She had smoked 2½ packs of cigarettes every day for 30 years. She drank heavily ("martinis, beer, you name it!") to the point of blackouts. She would stay up half the night and work hard the next day. The job was very stressful—she was one of the first women to work as a field engineer for Illinois Bell, a company she had joined as a telephone operator at 16. "I very much wanted to prove myself in this man's world," she recalls.

She had just gone through a bitter divorce and was a single parent to four children. She had a stressful relationship with her boyfriend. She was 10 pounds overweight. Most significantly, heart disease ran in her family, and both her parents and two of her sisters had previously suffered heart attacks.

Still, she ignored the first wham. "It went away, so I did nothing," she says. Later that day, at 8 p.m., the pain returned, and she went to bed. At 1 a.m., she awoke in a cold sweat and drove herself to Swedish Covenant, where she got the news: heart attack.

That summer, she joined Nequin's exercise program. But she still had one problem. Although she tried everything from acupuncture to hypnosis, she could not shake her addiction to nicotine. "I would run my laps," she says, "then sneak outside for a cigarette.

"Really dumb! I did not listen. I told myself: 'It cannot happen again!'"

It did, though. "In 1985," she says, "I again developed chest pains, and they diagnosed an almost total blockage of my left anterior descending artery—the Big Boy artery." Angioplasty was advised. "They told me there was a 5 percent risk of something going wrong," she says, "but I figured, 'There's a 95 percent chance the sun will shine, so I'm not canceling my picnic, right?"

Wrong. The artery ruptured on the operating table, and her heart momentarily stopped. Emergency bypass surgery pulled her through, but the damage had been done. By 1987, her only option was a heart transplant, which was performed at Evanston Hospital.

"After the transplant, I had to take 13 drugs every day," she says. "I alphabetized them 'A to N' so I could keep them straight. However, the steroids she required to prevent a rejection of the new heart were bloating her body. She was becoming a "steroid cripple" and needed to exercise "to keep from turning into a fat blob.

"I decided to call Dr. Nequin to try to rejoin the program, but I was afraid he wouldn't want me because of the liability risks. Instead, he did back-flips of excitement when he learned I was serious about getting into shape." She rejoined the program for real and, today, she says she's in "the best shape" of her life. The only limitations I have are related not to my heart but to being 58! I cry when I think of all the time I wasted being out of shape.

"Every day, I bike, I walk fast, I swim. At home, I ride an exercise bike religiously. A few months ago, I pedaled my bike for 50 miles—from here to the Botanic Gardens in Glencoe and back. I feel wonderful."

She has become an evangelist. "I ask my transplant support groups, 'Who in the group can bike for 50 miles?'"

She drinks "only to have champagne to celebrate the New Year." She quit smoking—for good. When she catches one of her children "sneaking a smoke," she talks about how stupid it is. She adds, "With all I've been through and all the good luck I've had to still be alive, for me to light up a cigarette would be like putting a match to an $80,000 mink coat!"

She concludes, "This gym keeps me alive—and I plan to be here for many more years."

Another lesson: Pay attention to your family history.

Ed Stone, 58, knew that his father had died at age 51 of a heart attack and that his older brother had recently survived a heart attack, but he never related those events to himself.

In 1976, Stone was a 44-year-old Tribune sportswriter in his 12th year of covering the Chicago Bears. "Those were some pretty lean years for the team," he acknowledges, but he doesn't attribute his problem to the Bears. "The job wasn't particularly stressful," he says, "but I put stress on myself. I was a Type A personality only when I wrote. I was a perfectionist with my writing, and I couldn't write until I lit up a cigar. A lot of us guys in the business then liked cigars."

In 1976, Stone was 5 foot 7 and 163 pounds and, looking back, was "terribly out of shape. I never exercised. I loved red meat, and I ate everything. I knew nothing about my cholesterol and high blood pressure. I hadn't seen a doctor in 12 years."

In March of that year, he left a football luncheon in the Loop, walked to his car and had begun the ride to his suburban home when he felt like his heart "was going to explode out of my chest. I've never felt that kind of pain—before or since."

When he got home, he had to call his wife's physician. He didn't have one.

Weiss Memorial Hospital successfully treated his heart attack and released him with the advice that he look up Noel Nequin.

"I've been in the program ever since," he says. "This gym is critical to me. I'm a runner, and the social support is important for discipline. You start to talk to someone and, before you know it, you've run three or four miles. You know what keeps my discipline—guilt. If you miss a day or two here, people let you know it."

The exercise has slowed but not prevented the progressive narrowing of his arteries. In 1983, he required triple-bypass surgery. Today, however, medication controls his high blood pressure, the running and careful eating has reduced his cholesterol, and he is optimistic that the arteries will remain clear. He can exercise for 11 minutes on a treadmill before reaching his maximum heart rate, which is excellent for a 58-year-old man with or without heart disease.

Some time ago Stone made the switch from sportswriting to copy editing for the Tribune, purely for the sake of regular hours. Since he is no longer writing, his wife will no longer let him smoke cigars at home, and the newspaper's anti-smoking ban prevents him from enjoying a worktime cigar after dinner. "Oh, I could go to the smoker's lounge," he says, "but that's no way to enjoy a cigar. Cigars require more time."

He pauses. "You know, though, I've been lucky. I got an early warning and have been able to watch my health. When you think of people like (former football great) George Allen, who was chairman of the President's Fitness Council and looked like a million bucks and yet died suddenly of a heart attack (at 72), you realize how fortunate I am."

Stone's older brother also required bypass surgery (which was successful). Recently, Stone took his 28-year-old son for a cholesterol test and a talk with Nequin. "He listened pretty good," Stone says, "but he probably forgot it all an hour later. I've learned to like oat bran, but my son loves red meat. I lecture him, but he's got a mind of his own. He thinks he's immune."

Stone shakes his head and heads for the running track.

Yuppies have heart disease, too. John Wagenknecht, 41, is the son of a physician, but he says that his ignorance of what caused heart disease was appalling.

During the early 1980s, Wagenknecht, then in his early 30s, was living the yuppie dream; a beautiful wife and son, big bucks as the financial officer for a leading real estate development firm, a big house in Kenilworth, a sailboat in Burnham Harbor and skiing vacations in Aspen.

It all seemed natural for the oldest of five children in a super-achieving family. In high school, he played varsity football and baseball. He had been an age-group swimming champion since he was 10. He glided through Princeton.

Looking back, though, he can see clearly why it happened. He recalls: "I started smoking heavily in college, and by 1985 I was doing two, three packs every day—the macho brands like Marlboro, Winston. My cholesterol, I later learned, was very high, though at the time I didn't know it. I had never had it checked! I loved junk food, and cheeseburgers were my standard fare. I was 15 to 20 pounds overweight. I was not following a regular exercise program, but I was a weekend warrior, sporadically doing touch football, golf, tennis, skiing. I did not like conflict, and I would keep the stress of job politics inside.

"What's worst is that I was going through a very painful divorce. One day, my wife just walked in and said she wanted out. I had tried desperately to save my family, and I had failed."

In April 1985 he had just completed a ski vacation in Colorado ("some of the hardest skiing I've done in my life") and was living alone in a Chicago high-rise. His heart attack began in the early morning, "as a hard kick in the back, taking my breath away. The pain subsided, and I thought that maybe I had slept on the wrong side or something. Then I broke into a sweat, and a cold wave was running up and down my arms. When I looked in the mirror, my face was ashen and gray. I had recently completed a class at work in cardiopulmonary resuscitation (CPR), and I knew that I was having a heart attack.

"I was scared to death, thinking, 'I don't want to die alone in this apartment.' I threw on some jeans, went down to the lobby and asked the doorman to call an ambulance."

He regained full consciousness five days later, having survived a massive heart attack. He was 36, and slowly he began to battle back.

The first few months were the worst. The attack had knocked out much of the muscle of his left ventricle, the heart's main pumping chamber, and he was developing heart failure. The pumping power of his heart measured only 12 percent, compared to 50 to 60 percent for the normal person and 70 to 90 percent for a trained athlete. Incredibly, at age 36, he was seriously considered for a heart transplant.

Wagenknecht, however, obtained enough expert consultations to convince himself that he didn't need a new heart. In December 1985 four of his coronary arteries were successfully replaced and an arterial aneurysm (or swelling) was successfully resected.

Two months later, he joined the Swedish Covenant rehab program and ever since he has had, in Nequin's words, "an amazingly uncomplicated course." He has easily completed his goal of running 1,000 miles since joining the program, has participated in road races under medical supervision and is pushing to do more.

He has quit smoking and sticks to a low-cholesterol, low-fat diet. A recent treadmill test disclosed that he could exercise for more than 12 minutes before reaching his maximum heart rate, which is normal for his age but phenomenal considering his status six years earlier. Nequin considers him a model patient.

Wagenknecht is recently married to the woman he was dating when he suffered the heart attack, and the couple has two young daughters. He is still living the good life, but with a difference.

"In 1985," he says, "I had no hunch that I was going to have a heart attack. My lesson translates: Know your risks. It's so simple to find out.

"Now, I'm much more aware of the importance of handling stress better. I don't preach, but if someone asks me about my heart attack, I'm very open. Last summer, I took a colleague out on my boat. He had no idea what had happened to me, but once I took off my shirt and uncovered my surgical scars, there were no secrets. Well, this man is a little out of shape, smokes a little too much, weighs a little too much, is under a little too much stress and is a little bit concerned. He asked for advice, and I said, 'Well, let me tell you. . . .'"

Heart attacks can happen anytime, anyplace.

Ellen Schweri, now 49, was sitting in church on November 26, 1989, taking part in a group discussion of world concerns. The topic she introduced was death squads in El Salvador.

Moments later, she collapsed, the victim of a suddenly irregular heartbeat. This is the type of event that usually results in sudden cardiac death but, fortunately, one of her friends knew CPR and was able to maintain a heartbeat until paramedics could shock the heart back into rhythm and prevent brain damage. Nevertheless, she was in a coma for 12 hours and essentially unconscious for five days. Today, working out on a bike in the cardiac-rehab program, she jokes, "I can't remember what I forgot."

Except for a sedentary lifestyle, she had no real risk factors, although she had smoked for 18 years before quitting. Subsequent medical tests could not explain what caused the cardiac arrest. She recalls, "Right before the event, I was going through a middle-aged, premenopausal crisis: depression, sluggishness, sudden rages. Vacuuming the carpet was a lot of activity for me. I begged my doctor to put me on premenopausal hormonal replacement so that I could sleep at night."

She was given the hormones, and the prescription was doubled a week before her cardiac arrest. Today, she speculates that the elevated estrogen levels might have caused a clot in either a coronary artery or the base of the brain and triggered the electrical storm in her heart. Warning labels indicate this is possible, but Schweri is not losing sleep over the possibility. She says she is looking forward, not backward.

For one thing, she is delighted to be alive. She had a cardiac defibrillator implanted in her abdomen to make sure that her heart stays in rhythm. And, this May, she marks her first anniversary of biking and walking in the cardiac-rehab program.

"It's ironic," she says, "but I seem to be getting from exercise what I was looking for with the hormones. I feel much better, I sleep much better, and I handle stress much better. My doctor was willing to put me back on the hormones, but I said, "Not right now.

"This is the first time that I've really exercised in my life, and I feel wonderful. I realize now that I'm responsible for my own health."

It's never too serious or too late to act. Fifty-nine-year-old Al Spielman found that out.

He weighed 360 pounds when he was 42 and suffered from diabetes and high blood pressure. Not surprisingly, he had heart attacks in 1973 and again in 1976. After the second one, he looked up Nequin.

The physician made Spielman the president of the Coronary Club of Chicago and, during one of the group's meetings, pulled him aside for an introduction to the guest speaker—a distinguished cardiologist from the University of Chicago.

The outside cardiologist took one look at Spielman and recommended that he risk a new procedure being performed at the University of Minnesota. The surgery was designed to remove a portion of the intestines to alleviate extreme obesity. The expert said, "You've got nothing to lose, because without it, you'll be dead in six months."

Spielman waited months but submitted to a successful ileal bypass in 1977. Today he weighs 209 pounds, is no longer diabetic, has his cholesterol controlled by the operation and has his high blood pressure controlled by medication.

"I used to be out of control," he says. "I would eat anything and everything. It was like being an alcoholic. Today, I'm in control. Nequin has an unbelievable program. It saved my life."

And, appropriately enough, it saved Nequin's too. But the 53-year-old cardiologist who graduated from the Far Eastern University Medical School in Manila, first became interested in exercise "to help my patients, not myself."

His program had humble beginnings. "In 1973," he recalls, "we had maybe one dozen patients exercising in the basement of our nurses' dorm. It took a lot of laps and a lot of boredom to complete one mile. We turned a broom closet into a shower, and when our only woman patient was ready to shower, the rest of us had to go wait in the hallway."

Fearing a credibility problem because his patients were becoming more fit than the doctor, Nequin decided in 1973 to start his own modest running program—three miles a day, three times a week. "The first time I ran three miles," he recalls, "I almost died."

In April, 1975, while giving a guest lecture about his program to the American Medical Joggers Association at the Boston Marathon, Nequin met Dr. Roger Bannister, the man who in 1954 ran the first four-minute mile.

Nequin, a driven perfectionist, was inspired by Bannister and resolved to run harder. That December, in Honolulu, Nequin ran his first marathon. The next April, he completed the Boston Marathon and has run it ever since. He created a medically supervised long-distance running club for his cardiac-rehab patients.

Nequin was hooked, and he soon graduated to ultra-marathons (26.2 miles or more). On many occasions he has completed marathons of 50 and 100 miles. At 5 foot 6 and 132 pounds, running 50 miles or more a week and regularly competing in ultramarathons, he seemed heartsafe.

Then the strangest thing happened. While running the Western States 100-mile marathon at high altitude in July 1982, he developed chest pains and had to stop at 51 miles. A competitor, he returned the next month and completed the 100-mile course at his own pace—over four days. There were no chest pains.

That September, he noticed disturbing changes in his EKG while exercising. Subsequent tests determined that one of his coronary arteries was 99 percent blocked and another, 30 percent. The third artery was clear.

Angioplasty was then in its infancy, and Nequin went to Emory University in Atlanta, where a tube with a small balloon at the end was threaded into his right coronary artery and the blockage was flattened against the arterial wall, reducing it to a negligible 35 percent. The next year, he ran the entire 100 miles of the Western States marathon.

However, in 1988, while driving to work, Nequin again experienced severe chest pains. His nurses insisted he be rushed by ambulance to St. Francis Hospital in Evanston, where he underwent a second angioplasty to reduce a 90 percent blockage in his left anterior descending artery. The other two arteries remained clear. He immediately resumed running and planned to run the Boston and London marathons this year, unless, of course, he decides to serve as chief medical officer for the marathon along the Great Wall of China.

He explains: "The state of your heart can be different from your fitness. I have always known this, and, unfortunately, it has turned out to be true in my case. This is why everybody should have an exercise stress test. I always knew that I had high cholesterol, but I had deluded myself by believing that my high ratio of the favorable high-density cholesterol would protect me.

"Fortunately, I had enough sense to realize that when it's time to be a patient, you can't self-doctor. My doctors tell me that I am a plaque-builder, despite all the exercise. However, by being aware of this tendency, by taking medication and continuing to exercise to reduce my cholesterol and by constantly monitoring my heart's performance, I have been able to stop potential heart attacks and to escape without any damage to the heart muscle."

The physician-patient adds, "My problem is learning how to handle mental and emotional stress. I am a perfectionist, and I become very intense when I have a deadline to meet. And there are always deadlines. In addition, I was going through a divorce in 1988. My own experiences have made me a believer in stress-management techniques. I am doing much better, and I am optimistic that I will be running well into the next century."

He concludes, "I like to quote (legendary physician) William Osler, who said, 'The secret of a long life is to acquire a chronic disease early in life and then take care of it.' I will continue to work in cardiac rehab, to run long distances, to take my cholesterol-lowering medication and to keep my fingers crossed!"

With that, he steps into his Toyota Celica, license plate "Run 50," and speeds off to his next appointment.

KICKING BUTTS

Take No Prisoners

The war on tobacco and AMA vs. Joe Camel

Babe Ruth, baseball's Sultan of Swat. Charles Lindbergh, the Lone Eagle of aviation. Nat "King" Cole, entertainment's mellow-voiced crooner. John "Duke" Wayne, the "true grit" cowboy of Hollywood. American originals one and all, they became legends famed for their indomitability of spirit.

They also shared a cause of death—lung cancer, from smoking too many cigarettes and inhaling too many contaminants.

But, then, cigarettes were considered "safe" when the Babe, the Lone Eagle, King Cole, and the Duke were first hooked on nicotine, a substance now known to be as addictive as heroin. After all, ads appearing until 1953 in *JAMA* itself were headlined, "More doctors smoke Camels than any other cigarette!" The ad's artwork pictured a concerned pajama-clad physician who has grabbed a bedside telephone from its old-fashioned cradle on his nightstand, where his watch, black bag, and prescription pad stand at the ready. The caption reads, "I'll be right over!" The text elaborates, "24 hours a day your doctor is 'on duty' . . . guarding health . . . protecting and prolonging life. . . ." Presumably, the physician grabbed his black bag and prescription pad, lit up a Camel, and dashed off into the night to make a house call. This was the world of the 1940s.

It was during the 1940s, especially during World War II, that women began to smoke in large numbers, a habit bolstered by their assembly-line work to help the war effort. Equal to men on the assembly line, women were also free to smoke. Nowhere was this trend more pronounced than on the West Coast, where Kaiser shipyards aggressively recruited women workers. Kaiser's wartime needs led to the growth of the first medical group practices, or health maintenance organizations, and, today, the first Kaiser medical clinic remains in operation at Richmond, Calif., across the bay from San Francisco.

The clinic is only a few miles from the medical office of Lonnie Bristow, M.D., the Chairman of the American Medical Association (AMA) Board of Trustees and a practicing internist in San Pablo, Calif. Earlier this year, as part of AMA's campaign to ban the highly popular Joe Camel ads that AMA—and others—believe are targeting young people to begin smoking in record numbers, Bristow issued an unusual challenge:

He invited executives of the major U.S. tobacco companies to walk with him through hospital wards to see one of the results of smoking—lung cancer patients and other pulmonary cripples.

There were no takers—except for this reporter from *JAMA*, who volunteered to go in their stead.

My escort was Herman Bruch, M.D., a specialist in diseases of the chest and the senior member of the four-physician East Bay Pulmonary Group at Brookside Hospital in San Pablo, right across the street from Dr. Bristow's office. Dr. Bruch is also a consultant at that Kaiser clinic in Richmond, and the first patient we see is Margaret Smith (not her real name), a 63-year-old woman who "smoked up to three packs of cigarettes a day from the age of 12 until the day I walked into this [Kaiser] clinic with acute pneumonia 3 weeks ago. That's 52 years."

To tell her story, she must first stop breathing the aerosolized medication that was prescribed to help unclog her lungs. The device continues to make a rhythmical wheezing sound as we talk. She is only recently weaned off the ventilator, which had been breathing for her ever since she was admitted. The ventilator, Dr. Bruch observes, "is a key prop of my practice." Speaking in a soft, raspy voice, Mrs. Smith says:

"'Why'd I start?' I guess I was just a smart teen and I wanted to keep up with my friends. And, I listened to all those tobacco ads on the radio. You know, like 'I'd walk a mile for a Camel.' Funny, but now I can barely walk across this room. I didn't want to come in [to the hospital], but things had gotten so bad that I couldn't walk without becoming breathless. I enjoyed smoking, especially after a meal, and I had a cigarette in my hand from the time I got out of bed until the time I went back to bed. Oh, I smoked everything—Camel, Chesterfield, Winston, lately the generics because they're cheaper.

"'Will I quit when I get out of here?' I pray every day that I will. My husband doesn't smoke and he's promised to help me. My four kids, they all smoke, but, thank God, my granddaughter, who is 17, refuses to look at a cigarette. Me, even now, when I know I have to quit, I still have that feeling that I want to light up." Spent from the brief interview, she returns to her breathing apparatus.

Dr. Bruch thinks Mrs. Smith can beat the killer weed—"if she stops smoking and if she hasn't already developed a lung cancer that has yet to present. Lung cancer takes 8 to 10 years to grow to visibility."

Back at his office at Brookside Hospital, the first outpatient is 72-year-old Luella Brown (not her real name), another 52-year smoker and a survivor of lung cancer. She is with her daughter, Becky (also a pseudonym), who is there to help her walk. Dr. Bruch congratulates Mrs. Brown—it has been 5 years since lung surgery to remove her cancer. It has also been 5 years since her last cigarette.

"I started when I was 13 or 14 or so," she recalls. "Remember that little voice on the radio—'Call for Philip Morris!'? That and my girlfriends got me started. During World War II, I smoked away while working at Kaiser Shipyard 3. Over the years, my daughter and every doctor I ever met—they all begged me to quit, but I couldn't. About 5 years ago, I was down in Texas visiting my family and my 4-year-old grandson saw me light up and said, 'Grandma, you're dying. Those cigarettes are killing you.' I puffed away, anyway. I thought, 'I'm 67 and if I don't have lung cancer now, I never will.'

"When I found out I had lung cancer, I was scared to death. I was having a cup of coffee and a cigarette in the waiting room and when I got the word, I just snuffed out my cigarette and told my daughter, 'I quit.' She said, 'Oh, I've heard that before!' But I meant it. Now, I can't even remember what it's like to hold a cigarette. I think cigarettes stink and [with a chuckle] I don't allow them in my house! Imagine that. Thank God, my daughter quit one year before I did. The pain I've been through with lung cancer is enough to make you want to put a gun to your head. Every time I get a cold I want to rush to the doctor."

She is asked about her health since surgery and with the denial typical of smoking patients replies, "Oh, fine. Nothing major." Dr. Bruch reminds her of her four hospitalizations for pneumonia, joking, "We have a discount plan—the fifth time is free." She laughs and says, "Oh, those. Well, I'm happy just to be here." Daughter Becky is asked about cigarette ads targeted to kids and replies, "I don't see how the tobacco people can live with themselves. They should be made to see what they're doing to people." Then, she assists her mother to her feet and helps her walk down the corridor—very, very slowly.

Dr. Bruch says of Mrs. Brown: "She is very, very impaired and at risk of lung failure."

Our third patient, Eloise Jordan (another pseudonym) is a 70-year-old woman who has been admitted after a heart attack scare to a hospital in nearby Pinole, Calif., where Dr. Bruch also consults. She had complained of dizziness prior to her hospitalization and Dr. Bruch has requested cardiology and neurological consults. He now suspects a treatable heart arrhythmia, but is puzzled by her chart notation reading, "chronic airway obstruction." He explains, "Breathing problems usually mean smoking, but this patient says she hasn't smoked." Indeed, Mrs. Jordan volunteers for the *JAMA* reporter who is doing a story on smoking, "Oh, I did a little when I was a kid, but it was just a 'keeping up with the Joneses' type of passing fancy."

Later, rifling through her thick patient chart back at the admitting station, Dr. Bruch says, "I'm stymied. Given her condition, she should have been a smoker. Aha! Look at this. When I saw her on a consultation back in 1985, she was coughing and wheezing and could barely walk. At that time, she told me she'd smoked half a pack of cigarettes a day for 50 years, but was going to quit. Now, she's forgotten she smoked for 50 years. Unbelievable!"

One of Dr. Bruch's partners, Carolyn Ray, M.D., emphasizes, "As pulmonary specialists, we're dealing with the real hard-core smokers. They'll joke it off, if they can, and blame everything for their medical problems except cigarettes. You can take hard-core smokers and show them patients hospitalized with smoking-related problems until you're blue in the face and all you'll accomplish is to make them deny their addiction and smoke even more. The antismoking message is very threatening to them.

"I have one woman patient who suffers from severe emphysema and, yet, she used to sneak cigarettes in the hospital bathroom! Nicotine may be the single most addictive chemical we know. Hard-core smokers won't listen to you until their smoking prevents them from doing what they want to do. In the case of my emphysema patient, I finally got her off cigarettes by convincing her that the only way she could continue to do the thing she liked—going to Vegas and visiting her grandkids—was to quit smoking. She quit a year ago."

A knock at the door interrupts the interview. Dr. Ray has been summoned to a "code blue." A patient in intensive care is in crisis—one of her smoking patients.

Dr. Bruch picks up the narrative. "Without tobacco, we'd probably be out of business," he says. "About 80% of what we do is smoking-related, and about 20% of all the patients in this [Brookside] hospital have a smoking-related illness.

"Heart and cardiovascular disease is the No. 1 smoking-related killer. Cigarettes injure the blood vessels and help cause arteriosclerosis, which can lead to heart attacks and strokes, but these problems are seen by other medical specialists. In our field, lung cancer is the No. 1 smoking-related killer among men and it recently replaced breast cancer as the No. 1 killer among women, as well. COPD, or chronic obstructive pulmonary disease—asthma, acute bronchitis, and emphysema—is the most common smoking-related disabling disease among both men and women and the No. 3 smoking-related killer. It is also the 10th leading cause of death overall. We are born with tremendous lung reserves, and before a smoker develops mild emphysema, 50% of his or her lung capacity has to be first destroyed. Loss of an additional 10% leads to moderate symptoms and 10% beyond that to severe symptoms. A high number of smoking patients suffer from both COPD and lung cancer.

"Our practice is consultative and it is grim in the sense that we don't see healthy patients, but it is rewarding in the sense that we can help people cope and see them get better—if they stop smoking!

"So, obviously, I'm against smoking. The tobacco firms are on record as saying that if they knew their product was 'unsafe,' they wouldn't sell it, and I think that this causes them to deceive themselves so they can feel they are honest red-blooded Americans. In my opinion, what they're doing is immoral, but if they were to admit that cigarettes are dangerous, it would jeopardize their prominence in the community as 'honest businessmen.'

"Why do they persist? Money. The same thing with the magazines and newspapers. They should be as rough on cigarettes as they are on Bill Clinton, but they're not. They want to keep those millions of dollars in cigarette ads."

Dr. Bruch, 56, has never smoked, "except during World War II when I was 7 or so and the cool thing to do was to pick up cigarette butts and try to puff on them!" His colleague, Dr. Ray, 43, says she only smoked "on and off during college—Tareytons, I believe. It was the cool thing to do." Dr. Bristow, 63, had a tougher time kicking the urge to smoke.

"I quit in 1970," he recalls, "after smoking a pack a day for more than 20 years. I guess it was peer pressure that made me start—thinking that smoking made me grown-up, mature, attractive, successful, and suave—or at least I thought so.

"The kicker was when my 5-year-old son, Robert, saw me light up one day and asked, 'Daddy, why are you smoking? Don't you love me?' Well, there was no way I could let down my son (now a physician), and within 6 weeks I had phased out my smoking."

Dr. Bristow, a black physician, refers to medicine's fight against the forces of tobacco as a "black-flag" battle. He explains, "During the civil war, when some Union troops with black soldiers went into combat against Confederate troops, both sides would wave a black flag. This meant the opposite of a white flag—a fight to the death, with no surrenders, no prisoners. Mercy was neither expected nor given. That's what it's like fighting against tobacco interests."

As a prominent AMA spokesman, Dr. Bristow knows from firsthand experience what medicine is up against. "Money talks," he says, "and the tobacco forces have used vote-trading to make great inroads into government.

"Tobacco is one of only three American products that enjoys most-favored trade status. Autos, for one, don't have this status, which means that tobacco firms can use the clout of the U.S. State

Department for their overseas exports. They're far from stupid and, looking down the road, they've had the foresight to go abroad and build their export market. And, since in many ways they've already kissed off the U.S. market, these exports are becoming more and more important." And, for some reason, tobacco is regulated by the Food and Drug Administration as a food, not as a drug, despite the fact that tobacco contains 400 chemicals, of which 40 are known carcinogens. And, groups like the truckers of North Carolina, who make their living by hauling tobacco, simply don't care about health issues when it's time to testify on legislation."

He deplores the Joe Camel campaign because "to kids, cute cartoon characters mean that the product is harmless. That's why Kool cigarettes used a penguin 30 to 40 years ago. But cigarettes are not harmless and I find it exceedingly cynical and shallow for the tobacco firms to say, 'If we believed our advertising caused children to smoke, we'd drop the ads immediately.' They have to know that their advertising is influencing youth under 18 to begin smoking. That's why we're in a black-flag battle."

In Chicago, as one exits the southbound Kennedy Expressway at Ohio Street and heads east toward the lake, a rise in the road offers an excellent view of two side-by-side silhouettes:

Painted on the side of a dingy hotel is a towering likeness of Joe Camel, the "smooth character" from R.J. Reynolds who is depicted as a debonair dromedary, decked out in white tuxedo, black tie, and black shades, a cigarette insouciantly dangling from the side of his mouth as he tickles the black-and-white keys of a piano, the top of which sports an enormous pack of Camel Lights, a few butts stylishly protruding toward him. A few yards south of Old Joe, across an alley and a small parking lot, looms the sleek 30-story exterior of the headquarters of the AMA. One has to drive a mile or so farther east, under enormous overhanging ads for Philip Morris' Marlboro Man, before the fine print under Joe Camel becomes visible—the Surgeon General's warning that "Smoking causes heart disease, lung cancer, and emphysema."

Taking issue with the explicit nature of this warning is R.J. Reynolds biochemist, Sam Simmons, Ph.D. Simmons told this reporter that his reading of 30 to 40 years of the scientific literature on smoking and health, notably animal studies and human epidemiology, leads him to the "scientifically derived position that smoking is a risk factor, but not a proven cause of human diseases like heart attacks, lung cancer, and emphysema." He says, "The evidence has not converged on proof of causality."

Warnings aside, tobacco firms spend $6.5 million *a day* on characters like the Marlboro Man and Joe Camel. They say it's to reinforce brand loyalty and/or to shift smokers among brands, but antismoking forces are mobilizing in the belief that the ads target young people under 18 to *begin* smoking. The ads are everywhere. The front door of the coffee shop across the street from AMA is festooned with images of the "smooth character," showing Old Joe and his sunglasses basking in a hammock on a Hawaiian beach and striking a studly pose in work boots, jeans, and aviator's jacket while profiling against a country skyline. But, then, why all the fuss over a cartoon camel?

Since the tobacco firms want to hold on to their dwindling market share and the antismoking activists want to persuade youth not to replenish the tobacco pipeline, Joe Camel has become a symbol of the battle.

It began with the December 11, 1991, publication in *JAMA* of three antismoking articles, reporting that 6-year-old children find Joe Camel as easy to recognize as Mickey Mouse; that since the 1988 introduction of Joe Camel into the U.S. market, Camel's share of the illegal children's cigarette market (under 18 years of age) has increased from 0.5% to 32.8%, representing a sales increase from $6 million to $476 million; and evidence from California that cigarette advertising encourages youth to smoke and should be banned. In an accompanying editorial, California Representative Henry Waxman, chairman of the U.S. House Subcommittee on Health and the Environment, wrote, "Enticing children, Third World populations, and disadvantaged members of our own society to smoke is the only way for tobacco companies to make up for the number of smokers who quit or die. We should be especially alarmed at the tobacco industry's efforts to recruit children to nicotine addiction."

In early 1992, San Francisco family law attorney Janet Mangini filed a lawsuit, argued by her office and legal colleague Alan Caplan, calling for a statewide ban on the Camel advertising campaign. The suit argued that the advertising violated state business practices by giving out Old Joe T-shirts, beach towels, baseball caps, running shorts, and other items designed to lure youth into smoking—without warnings on the paraphernalia about the hazards of smoking.

That May, San Francisco Superior Court Judge Lucy McCabe refused to grant Mangini an injunction banning Joe Camel, ruling that the 1965 federal laws regulating the advertising and labeling of cigarettes preempted state courts. In a headline typical of the media's cutesy, flippant coverage of the Camel controversy, the *San Francisco Chronicle* headlined, "Cigarette's Joe Camel clears a legal hump."

In June 1992, on the opening day of the AMA Annual Convention, AMA President John Clowe, M.D., and U.S. Surgeon General Antonia Novello, M.D., led a parade down Michigan Avenue and over to AMA headquarters, urging spectators (and TV cameras) to "Say No to Old Joe!" Dr. Bristow finds it objectionable that shortly after the antismoking articles appeared in *JAMA*, the enormous ad for Joe Camel appeared next to AMA headquarters; that the ad was whited out shortly before the AMA parade to "Say No to Old Joe" marched under it and repainted shortly afterward; and that an AMA attempt to buy counter-advertising space next to the camel was prohibited because of R.J. Reynolds' contract banning competing ads within the same geographical area.

Responding for R.J. Reynolds is Peggy Carter, manager of media relations at the tobacco firm's headquarters in Winston-Salem, NC, who told this reporter that the timing of the events involving AMA and the Joe Camel sign was pure coincidence. "The building next to AMA is a highly desirable advertising location," she said, "and we were on a waiting list for it long before the *JAMA* articles appeared. The whiting out of the sign was part of the regular maintenance to refurbish it, and the codicil forbidding competing ads in the nearby area is standard industry practice."

So it goes, and several events this past summer have intensified the battle and forced attorneys to work overtime. First, the federal Environmental Protection Agency (EPA) issued a report calling "environmental tobacco smoke" (the inhaling of the smoke of others' cigarettes), which is often referred to as "sidestream" or "passive" smoking, to be a Class A carcinogen and cause of lung cancer. Documenting that this inadvertent inhalation of others' smoke puts the nonsmoker at a 30% higher risk of lung cancer and causes an additional 3000 lung cancer deaths a year, the EPA struck a hammer blow at the tobacco industry.

Dr. Bristow believes that the EPA report is the "torpedo below the waterline that may sink the tobacco industry in the U.S., since it will lead to a smoke-free workplace." Switching his metaphors, he continues, "If this were a 15-round boxing match, we're in the ninth or 10th round and tobacco has been hurt very badly."

Fearing nonsmoking mandates throughout American workplaces, the tobacco firms promptly filed a lawsuit to invalidate the EPA finding.

A few weeks after the EPA action, the staff of the Federal Trade Commission (FTC) recommended that the FTC seek an outright ban of the Joe Camel campaign on the ground that it entices minors to smoke. If the FTC's five commissioners accept the staff recommendation, a trial, expected to take years, will be held before an administrative law judge. The attorneys general of 27 states have urged the FTC to proceed. Helping tobacco fight the FTC call to arms are various newspaper editorialists who claim federal action would violate the First Amendment guarantee of free speech. Typical was the editorial in the *Chicago Tribune* that concluded, "Old Joe is none of the government's business."

On the other hand, Dr. Bristow believes that U.S. tobacco ads should be limited to "tombstone" presentations of bare facts, which is a far cry from the bronco-busting, cycle-riding, piano-playing, sky-diving, youth-appealing images Old Joe projects. R.J. Reynolds' Peggy Carter says, "All our advertising is designed either to reinforce loyalty to our brands and/or to persuade smokers to switch to our brands. Since Camel has only 4% of the adult market of 46 million smokers, the Joe Camel campaign has ample opportunity to penetrate the adult market. And, we feel that we have the right to run ads showing lifestyle pastimes and pursuits that our adult customers find enjoyable. We neither need nor want the youth market and, as a matter of fact, are on record as urging youth not to smoke. Our target is Philip Morris' Marlboro, which is sitting on the lion's share of the adult market—67%."

On September 1, the federal Centers for Disease Control and Prevention (CDC) issued a report on tobacco and health, concluding that 418,690 premature (before 65 years of age) deaths in the United States in 1990 were attributable to cigarette smoking. Comparing the average number of cigarettes the victims had smoked with the number of years they'd lost, the CDC reported that every minute spent smoking had robbed the smoker of one minute of life. Since 7 minutes is about what it takes to finish a cigarette, the report prompted headlines, "Seven minutes closer to death." The Tobacco Institute declined to comment on the CDC report.

For antismoking activists, there was good news and bad news in the CDC's findings. On the one hand, the number of smokers has declined from 42.4% of all adult Americans in 1965, when the Surgeon General's office issued its first warning, to 25.5% in 1990. On the other, the number of teen smokers has not declined since 1980, and it's in their teens that people become addicted to smoking. Some 90% of all smokers start before they're 18; the average age for a new smoker is 13; and each day 5000 children light up for the first time.

And, smoking remains a potent economic force. The Tobacco Institute estimates 1992 tobacco sales at $47.5 *billion* (the sale of 510 billion cigarettes accounts for 95% of this figure) and 46 million Americans still smoke (there are 44 million exsmokers). The 1992 sales include $4.8 billion in exports.

In the meantime, attorneys Mangini and Caplan have cleared their own legal hump by amending their lawsuit against Joe Camel and persuading a California state court of appeals to allow their case to go forward. In a joint interview, they told this reporter that they are "ecstatic" about the appellate court decision that will allow them to advance their argument that Old Joe illegally targets—and influences—underage smokers and should be dumped. As we talk, the windows of their conference room afford a commanding view of Market Street, where a fleet of taxis are driving by with Joe Camel signs adorning their roofs.

Mangini begins, "When I read press reports about the *JAMA* articles, I was stunned. I mean, Mickey Mouse is a pretty important character and to think that 6-year-olds find Joe Camel just as popular, well, I was outraged. I'm a solo practitioner who shares office space with Alan [Caplan] and others, and I filed the suit as an individual plaintiff, asking for relief under the California code governing unlawful business practices. We won the first round, stopping the Reynolds' attorneys from moving the case into federal court. But when we lost round 2, the superior court decision that federal laws preempted state action, we were devastated. Now, I think the round 3 ruling that we can proceed is wonderful."

California Appellate Court Justice Donald King accepted Mangini's amended complaint and, while throwing out her failure-to-warn argument on tobacco and health, upheld her contention that the Camel campaign has violated its more general duty not to deceive the public. King's ruling states, "Mangini's 'targeting of minors' theory of unfair advertising is not based on 'smoking and health,' but on the more general duty not to engage in advertising that is against public policy, oppressive and unscrupulous, and harmful to consumers. . . . This theory is not subject to preemption by the Federal Cigarette Labeling and Advertising Act."

R.J. Reynolds requested relief from King's ruling in an appeal to the California Supreme Court, which voted on September 30 to hear the case and decide if it should go to trial. The Mangini lawsuit is supported by the California Medical Association, five other medical groups, and former Surgeon General C. Everett Koop, M.D., and current U.S. Assistant Secretary for Health Philip Lee, M.D. Caplan says, "We think the case will go to trial and that we have an excellent chance of winning. We are asking three things:

"An injunction to ban the Joe Camel campaign in California; a corrective ad campaign, paid for by R.J. Reynolds and supervised by the court, to undo the damage caused by Joe Camel; and the refund of all monies earned by R.J. Reynolds from the camel campaign to be used for court-supervised charitable and research activities."

Mangini is brimming with corrective ideas. "I'd have Joe Camel die of lung cancer," she says, "and replace him with a nonsmoking camel, Joe Jr., who would educate children about the dangers of smoking, perhaps on Saturday morning TV cartoon shows!" She says, "I'm irrelevant to this lawsuit, but I'm sure the R.J. Reynolds attorneys will do everything they can to discredit me."

Caplan, who describes himself as "relatively new to the tobacco wars," is also involved in a San Diego lawsuit charging eight tobacco firms, their advertising agency Hill & Knowlton, and the Research Council on Tobacco with not disclosing all the smoking-related health risks known to them over the past 40 years. The case is scheduled for trial in 1994. "From what I've seen," he says, "the tobacco lawyers follow a 'scorched earth' policy. They are given two orders—'don't settle' and 'don't lose.' Well, we're following the same policy." Mangini concludes, "Nobody's brought them down yet, but there's always a first time."

All of the preceding is irrelevant and "frighteningly awful," according to the ultimate antismoking warrior, Alan Blum, M.D., who believes medicine and the government are "flogging a dead camel."

It's not that Blum doesn't hate the tobacco industry—he does with a passion—it's just that he thinks current antismoking efforts are misguided.

Blum, now a family practice physician in Houston, is an important figure in the antismoking movement for several reasons and his evangelism borders on obsession. Driving up to my Houston hotel in a car overflowing with various tobacco ads, exhibits, and research papers, Blum waves me inside and speeds us off to his favorite Chinese restaurant—talking nonstop all the way and throughout the dinner to follow. Tall, thin, and intense, he pursues his tobacco prey with conviction and the provocative barbs of a born phrasemaker.

His father, a Long Island physician, suffered a heart attack after a lifetime of smoking three packs of cigarettes a day. He recovered, quit smoking, lived another 15 years, and took young Alan to many baseball games, where he pointed out the ubiquitous ads for cigarettes. "Let's see," the son recalls today, "it was Lucky Strikes at Ebbets Field, where the Brooklyn Dodgers played, Chesterfield at the Polo Grounds, where the New York Giants played, and Camel at Yankee Stadium, where the New York Yankees played. My father told me, 'Someday, historians will look back at our era and think how stupid we were to pursue medical research at the same time we were killing ourselves with tobacco.'"

Later, his father handed him the Surgeon General's report of 1965, the one with the first cigarette warnings, and Blum promptly wrote an editorial for his high school paper, entitled, "A Childish Habit." Following medical school at Emory in Atlanta, Ga., he began a residency at Jackson Memorial Hospital in Miami, Fla., and founded "Doc," for Doctors Ought to Care (about smoking). In subsequent years, he was a Fishbein Fellow at *JAMA* and served as editor of medical journals for the Australian Medical Association and the Medical Society of the State of New York, where he devoted two entire issues to an antismoking crusade and was later fired for having, in his description, a "very, very messy office." An entertaining public speaker, Blum has, by his own count, delivered 1600 antismoking speeches to various groups, "which is 1300 more than the next nearest guy."

As a believer in free speech, he believes that the answer is "not to take on a cartoon character," but "to launch a national counter-advertising campaign that will laugh the pushers out of town."

He adds, "We have three main goals at Doc. First, to obtain funding for our tobacco archives, which right now are scattered throughout my car, an annex of my home, an office I rent in the family practice department [of the Baylor College of Medicine], and in the home of our executive director, Eric Solberg. Ideally, this would become a 'museum of what it was like when people used to smoke,' sort of a 'Marlboro Park.' We need $550,000 to $700,000 to obtain enough space, install a computer system, and hire two people to inventory and display all the materials we've accumulated.

"Second, we want to laugh the pushers out of town through the use of satire and ridicule. If smoking killed baby seals, it might be opposed more vigorously. The reason I founded Doc was to have a base to promote antismoking advertising. The devil does not like to be mocked."

Blum has outdone himself on this score. He helped create the "Barfboro Barfing Team" van, which shadows the Marlboro Adventure Team van across the country, carrying an antismoking message to all who will listen. He has created ads for "Emphysema Slims" and "Dead Man Chew" and is prepared to put them on bus benches, if newspapers refuse to carry them.

"When R.J. Reynolds chose Houston a few years ago to test-market its new brand, Dakota, targeted toward underemployed, undereducated 'virile females,' ages 18 to 24, who attend tractor pulls with their boyfriends, Blum responded by designing a counter-ad. The Dakota ad, displaying the new Reynolds' brand next to its target competitor, Marlboro, was headlined, "Houston is known for conquering space, great barbecues, and individuals who make up their own minds. You decide." Blum's creation juxtaposed Dakota against a pack of "Barfboro" and ran the headline, "Houston, home of the largest medical center in the world, asks you to make up your own mind. DaKota . . . Da Cough . . . Da Cancer . . . Da Coffin." The Houston newspapers refused to run it.

Blum calls it "hush money," the millions paid by tobacco firms to advertise in magazines and newspapers, who return the favor by refusing to run strong antismoking articles. In his video, "Medicine vs. Madison Avenue," he says, "It doesn't matter what the magazine is, whether *Time* or the *National Enquirer* or what the cover content [the "high cost of health care" in the former, "headless man found in topless bar" in the latter], the odds are high that you'll find a cigarette ad on the back cover. . . ."

Doc's third major goal, Blum says, "is to attack the tobacco allies, also through satire and ridicule. I mean challenging companies like Kodak, which makes the cigarette filters, and Kimberly-Clark, which makes the cigarette paper."

For that matter, Blum questions AMA's wisdom in taking money from Fleishman's Margarine for a program of cholesterol education. "There is no Fleishman Margarine company," he says. "It's simply a division of R.J. Reynolds and I'm concerned that AMA can't seem to do anything unless it can get someone else to pay for it. I wrote a letter to AMA this year, urging it to make worldwide headlines by refusing to do business with a long list of tobacco allies, whose names I provided, but I never heard back." He adds, "From 1964 to 1978, AMA did nothing on smoking except 'study' the issue, and this 14-year gap puts Nixon's 18½-minute Watergate tape gap to shame."

Despite his criticisms, Blum still thinks the AMA has a role to play. "AMA would be perfect," he says, "to launch a strong national campaign of counter-advertising. Right now, we don't have one and the tobacco firms are beating our brains out with a three-pronged strategy:

"They spend billions every year to directly reach the public with favorable advertisements; they've portrayed the antismoking forces as a powerful lobby out to curtail their constitutional rights, enabling them to attract great support from civil libertarians, when, in fact, there is no strong national antismoking movement; and they've played for sympathy by creating smokers' rights groups."

The most effective countermeasure, he says, "is to enforce the existing law against advertising cigarettes on TV. By that, I mean preventing the tobacco firms from sponsoring sports events that prominently advertise their logos. The telecast of the 1989 Marlboro Grand Prix race included the showing of 5933 Marlboro logotypes [Blum hired a medical student for 6 hours to count them!], and this should be illegal under the 1969 law banning cigarette advertising on TV. The second best thing would be to deny the deductibility of such advertising, and in 1992, such a bill was beaten back in the Senate by only 56 to 38."

The other answer, Blum believes, is an amply funded, powerfully supported national effort to ridicule the tobacco pushers, a potent effort led by an effective national spokesman who is someone like, well, like Alan Blum. In the meantime, he's off to Ireland to make antismoking speech No. 1601.

This battle has been smoking for a long time. When Christopher Columbus discovered the American Antilles in 1492, he found the native Indians using tobacco in much the same manner it is used today. The French diplomat Jean Nicot, in whose name nicotine comes down to us, sent the seed of *Nicotiana tabacum* to Catherine de Medici, the queen consort and regent of France, and, in short order, British, French, Portuguese, and Spanish sailors took tobacco from Europe to all parts of the world. The very existence of some of the original American colonies depended on the tobacco leaf, and it has been intertwined in American commerce ever since. Weeding it out will not be easy.

In his history of the National Cancer Institute, Michael B. Shimkin, M.D., noted that the first public health warning on tobacco by the Surgeon General was published in *JAMA* on December 12, 1959. Shimkin wrote, "The impact of its conclusion that smoking is a principal factor in the increased incidence of lung cancer was practically nil, especially as an editorial in that same issue took the teeth out of the report by labeling it as 'conjecture.'" He also recalled an antismoking lecture he gave about that time to members of the "Lost Chord," a society of individuals whose vocal chords were sacrificed to smoking-related cancer of the larynx. "The air was thick with tobacco smoke," he wrote.

Richard Bordow, M.D., the fourth member of Dr. Bruch's East Bay Pulmonary Group, knows how hard it is to go up against the tobacco lobby. A historian of smoking and health, he has written sections of the Surgeon General's annual report on tobacco and has edited textbooks on smoking's relationship to pulmonary diseases. He has also testified in an antismoking trial.

"Every time I see a tobacco ad," he told this reporter, "I feel it's another fraud against mankind. The evidence linking tobacco to human disease is so overpowering that we should never have to do another study. But I have a very healthy respect for the ability of the tobacco people to find a loophole to justify what is disgraceful behavior on their part.

"Years ago, I was called by the prosecution as an expert witness in a trial alleging that tobacco firms caused the lung cancer death of a heavy smoker. I had to endure 30 hours of pretrial depositions from a battery of 29 high-powered tobacco firm attorneys. They went over everything in my background to try to impeach my credentials and to try to assassinate my testimony that smoking causes lung cancer. It was exhausting, but it was something I had to do. I held my ground, but we finally lost the case because the prosecutor failed to get an autopsy report from the treating physician, showing the cause of death as lung cancer.

"I question the morality of this type of behavior by tobacco executives who are bright enough to know better, but I accept it as an unfortunate part of capitalism.

"But times are changing. The tobacco firms and their attorneys are learning that you can't impeach the truth."

TWO EPIDEMICS—AIDS AND AFRAIDS

Living with AIDS

Courageous AIDS patients tell what it's like to live on Death Row

Safe sex."

Whoever thought that these words would have to be coupled—"Safe sex."

Well, with AIDS, they have. Indeed, it often seems that the retrovirus that causes acquired immune deficiency syndrome (AIDS) is much smarter than the humans among whom it spreads.

AIDS is caused by the human immunodeficiency virus (HIV), which is found in human blood and semen and which is spread by homosexual anal sex, the sharing of needles contaminated with blood carrying the AIDS virus, and transfusions of AIDS-tainted blood. And, of course, anyone who has sex with someone who has acquired HIV through any of the above high-risk factors. And, saddest of all, children born to a mother with AIDS.

The stakes are very high because science has little with which to fight the virus and the diagnosis of AIDS is also the prognosis—death. By knocking out the protective immune system, the virus makes the body naked prey to a bewildering variety of opportunistic infections that are normally held in check. The two leading AIDS killers are *Pneumocystis carinii pneumonia (PCP)*, which is caused by a fungus, and *Kaposi's sarcoma*, a rare skin cancer that usually strikes only elderly men of Mediterranean heritage.

The sobering reality is that medicine has *never* cured a viral disease, although vaccines have previously been successful in *preventing* such viral diseases as measles, mumps, and polio. It takes eight to 10 years, on average, to develop a new drug in America and there are few prospects in the pipeline that promise to stop the AIDS epidemic. A nation raised on the miracles of penicillin and the other "wonder drugs" is learning to live with failures, and of the 100,000 Americans diagnosed so far with AIDS, half are dead and the other half are dying.

Nathan Birnbaum, MD, a psychiatrist who counsels AIDS patients at Chicago's Northwestern Memorial Hospital says, "AIDS stirs up primitive feelings because it involves all our taboos: It's contagious; it's incurable and fatal; it mainly strikes the young; and it is tied up with drugs, sex, morality. Also, it strikes the brain. It leaves nothing out. You could not invent a disease more likely to stir up anxiety among people."

Still, with 96% of all AIDS cases concentrated among gay men and drug addicts, plus recipients of tainted blood transfusions, it is hard for the general population to identify with the disease. Birnbaum says, "The collective mind-set is one of both fear and fascination, but, primarily, it is one of not thinking about it. Most people feel compassionate about those with AIDS, but they also feel that it is a disease that only involves 'someone else.' This will not change until AIDS strikes closer to home."

Whether it will or not remains an open question. Nationally, women comprise only 7% of all AIDS cases, with the majority of these—51%—having acquired the virus from intravenous drug use. Another 28% of these women acquired AIDS from heterosexual contact—the vast majority from sex partners who were drug addicts and most of the rest from bisexual men. The remaining females with AIDS were either sexual partners of hemophiliacs with AIDS and/or born to mothers who carry the virus. Only 2% of all males with AIDS acquired the virus from women, and most of those were drug addicts, including prostitutes.

So, although the primary risk factors—homosexual anal sex, intravenous drugs, and contaminated blood transfusions—are relatively rare among the general population, anyone who has sex with a partner who has put himself at risk through any of these means also runs a risk. This is the threat of spreading AIDS into the general population and it accounts for a second epidemic—"AFRAIDS."

This year alone, 1,000 babies will be born with AIDS in New York City. Dr. Robert Murphy, a member of the AIDS Treatment Service at Northwestern Memorial Hospital, says, "What amazes me is that AIDS should be a huge women's health issue, and so far it isn't. The risk of a woman acquiring AIDS from an infected male sexual partner is 10 times, maybe 100 times, the risk the other way around . . . for a woman, having unprotected sex is a little like playing Russian roulette."

What, then, can be done? In addition to an intensified search for new drugs and vaccines, doctors and patients on the frontlines of the twin epidemics call for sexual caution, condoms, the sharing of clean needles by addicts—and, above all, compassion.

Jim de Lacerda, a nurse on Chicago's Cook County Hospital AIDS Service, emphasizes, "We cannot just blame the victims. I get so upset when I see people on our hospital staff treat AIDS patients badly. We see hospital graffiti that makes fun of them, and we see hospital staff treating them rudely. I confront the staff members and they usually get defensive. I think that most are just denying their own fear and guilt about sexual indiscretions. You know, heterosexuals are not perfect, either. People must understand that the gays and the junkies did not *create* this virus. . . ."

In the meantime, the clock is ticking and the suffering is very real. In remarks before a congressional hearing, Dr. Marcus Conant, director of the California State Dept. of Health AIDS Leadership Project, made these remarks:

"I have diagnosed about 1,000 AIDS patients. And there is a period between diagnosis and death, a lengthy period of anguish and hopelessness. Young men who were healthy and vibrant, who were running 5 to 8 miles a day and working out at the gym two to three times a week, are now seeing themselves literally waste away.

"If they're lucky, they'll come down with Pneumocystis pneumonia, which is like smothering to death, but they die quickly. If they're unlucky, they'll come down with Kaposi's sarcoma, which lets them live longer and which does not hit the brain, which means that they must remain conscious through their pain as they watch their bodies become tattooed with hideous purple blotches. I treated one Kaposi's patient who had a horribly huge lesion in his throat. He had to sit bolt upright in his hospital bed so he would not choke to death.

"Before I left California to come to this hearing, I was visited by a young male patient who had just discovered a purple lesion on his thigh. I sent it off to biopsy. Well, he knows what it is, and I know what it is, and you know what it is, and when I return tomorrow, I'll have to tell him: He has AIDS.

"He, like all the others, is trained by our American culture to be brave and to fight. But he will have nothing to fight with because I will have nothing with which to offer him hope. The only tools I have are AZT, which means that he may live a little longer and suffer a little less, and aerosol pentamidine, which is not approved by FDA but is widely used in California.

"He wants to fight this invader, and he will turn to me for help—and I have no treatment. We may be able to reduce our drug development from eight years to five, but this will not help my patient.

"In five years, I must tell him, he will be dead."

"Victims" is a word that AIDS patients do not like, because as persons with AIDS (their preferred term) they are trying to learn to live with the disease, not die from it. And, they are unsparing in their appraisals of how they acquired the disease. In candid interviews with this reporter, five PWAs, four gay males and a former user of IV drugs, agreed to talk—anonymously—about their previous lifestyles. They were interviewed at the AIDS clinics at Chicago's Northwestern Memorial Hospital and Cook County Hospital. And a woman who was married to a bisexual who died of AIDS also agreed to talk—anonymously.

Here are their stories:

Jim is 50 and works as an academic librarian. He is bearded and bespectacled and neatly dressed in a three-piece suit. His weight is 131 pounds, down from his normal 137 but up from the 123 to which he had fallen after a bout of severe diarrhea. He is scolarly and loquacious and is the proud caretaker of a voluminous library relating to gay history and the gay-rights movement. He explains: "Gay activism actually started as a response to the Prussian penal code that inflicted severe penalties for homosexual behavior. Later, in England, gays were often called 'Mollies' because they tended to hang out in the bohemian neighborhoods where the prostitutes, or Mollies, did their business. . . . "

He turns from this historical digression to the issue at hand.

"I've always been what is called a 'vanilla' gay, which is to say pretty conservative. Chicago gays often refer to the rest of America as a bicoastal society, and we in Chicago thought that we were pretty insulated on our conservative Midwestern island from what was happening in California and New York. I can remember giving an interview in 1982 to a CBS reporter from Los Angeles to try to explain the anomaly of why Chicago gays were not coming down with AIDS in anywhere near the numbers being seen on the coasts. I talked about things like Midwest conservatism and so on and actually appeared almost smug about it all. To the degree AIDS was occurring in Chicago, it appeared to be among the 'leather set,' the boys who played mean and tough, and that was never me. I recall saying to a friend, 'AIDS appears to be driving through Chicago on a motorcycle.' I felt fairly safe.

"In 1984 a friend of mine persuaded me to enroll in the prospective study of gay men being conducted in collaboration between the Howard Brown Clinic and Northwestern. The idea was to track gay lifestyles and sexual practices and to see how they related to the development of AIDS. I didn't see a real need for it, but I was persuaded that it was a way to get free health check-ups. In spring, 1984, my blood was drawn and frozen, but even after an antibody test for the virus became available, I chose not to be tested.

"My first real fear came in November, 1985, when I learned that a man with whom I had had sex the previous November was hospitalized with AIDS. I spent a sleepless night trying to reconstruct what might have happened that night. He was a younger man and appeared to have been attracted to me because I was a 'Daddy' figure, an object or type rather than a person. This is fairly common among some gays, but I figured, 'Oh, what the heck, why not?' I remember that when we left the bar and reached his apartment, I was struck with all these photos lining the wall and showing him dressed in leather and masks and so on. I thought, 'Oh, brother, what have I gotten into?' but the rest of the evening was rather uneventful. Now, a year later, I was up all night, my heart racing, worrying about what we might have done. I recall that it was mostly give and take, give and take. For the next three or four days and nights I was a basket case, frantically trying to come to terms with the fact that I might be at serious risk. As always, I went home for Christmas, and I remember being almost maudlin around my parents, hugging them every time I saw them and thinking that this might be our last Christmas. My parents are fundamentalist Christians and have no idea of the way I am sexually.

"I was the person in our family to get off the farm and come to the city, and I've always known I was gay. I remember being 13 and going to the theater in Kansas City and having an older man sit next to me, spreading out his raincoat, and over the next hour or so proceeding to masturbate me. I thought: 'Hey, I'm not the Lone Ranger. There are others like me out there.' After he left, I remember going into the lobby and trying to find him. I wanted to do it again, but it was very crowded and there was no way. I didn't think much about sex again until I got to college and I was seduced by an older man to whom I was introduced by a gay professor. We became lovers, and I was faithful to him, but I was to learn that he was a notorious playboy. About a year later I noticed these spots on my hands and feet—secondary syphilis. The doctor at the student health service said, 'How did this happen?' and I began to concoct this wild story about meeting a woman at a bar and going off with her and so on, but I couldn't carry through with the charade. I told him the truth. He said, 'We can cure syphilis, but you'd better get psychiatric help or your life is not worth a dime.' Well, after he told me that I was a worthless piece of junk, I sought out the school's psychiatrist. She was very kindly and understanding and completed an evaluation that said I was perfectly normal psychologically and emotionally. Anyway, I showed it to the doctor, and he wouldn't have anything more to do with me.

"I continued on my way. During the 1970s and the sexual revolution there was a tremendous burgeoning of gay consciousness and gay sexuality, and gay bars sprang up all over the city. I've always been somewhat of a loner, but I guess I took advantage of the situation. For years, I was often on the prowl or on the phone, and I imagine that I've averaged about one different partner a week for years and years. They say that receptive rectal intercourse is the riskiest behavior, and I've done that. Yet, during those years, all I really came down with was a case of hepatitis and some intestinal infections.

"So here it is Christmas, 1985, and I'm scared to death. I couldn't tell my parents, so I told some close friends back home who know I'm gay, and they told me that I was feeling sorry for myself, to buck up. It was good advice, and I put the fear out of my mind.

"By March 1986, however, I was very fatigued and could hardly make it to work. I was coughing uncontrollably and loudly, and, finally, my friends called me aside to tell me how terrible I looked. They suggested I take some time off. Well, I went to the hospital and was diagnosed as having PCP, or AIDS. My doctor wouldn't believe it. He said, 'Everything in your chart looks fine . . .' but my worst fears had been realized. I took it pretty well, though, because the real fear had come the previous November when I realized that I might be at risk. I spent three weeks in the hospital to knock out the pneumonia."

Right before Jim was discharged, his doctor came into the room. "I can still see him sitting on the window ledge. 'Give it to me straight,' I said. He told me that the average survival time after PCP was 18 months. I might live longer or I might die sooner. I asked, 'Is there any hope?' He replied, 'Well, if you'd asked me that a year ago, I would have had to say no. But I think that yours is the first generation of AIDS patients for whom we might have effective experimental drugs.' He also gave me some good advice. He said, 'Jim, don't worry yourself about how you might have picked this up. It's not important.'

"Afterwards, I had my blood from spring, 1984, defrosted and tested for antibody. It was positive." He frowns. "You know, I might have infected my young partner, rather than the other way around.

"The level of insanity out there can be frightening. After my diagnosis, I lost interest in sex. Whether it's apathy or self-preservation, I haven't had or thought about sex at all. Occasionally, though, I'll get a call from an old friend. One wanted to come over for sex and I told him upfront. 'No, I have AIDS.' He didn't care, he said. I thought, 'Is Tom insane?' I just couldn't do it; I would feel as if I were a murderer.

"Last summer I made an inventory of my personal possessions. I've always saved archival things, like the newspaper headlines that read, 'Man Lands on Moon' or 'President Kennedy Assassinated' or 'Big Snow Hits Chicago.' I told myself: 'Jim, give it up. You no longer have any use for these things.' I began to plan to turn all my papers and gay-history memorabilia over to various libraries. I was very down. One night I saw a MacNeil-Lehrer report on AZT, but I didn't think that I was eligible.

"That fall I began to experience oral thrush [a fungal infection that causes white patches in the mouth] and constant diarrhea. The diarrhea was not only dehydrating—my weight dropped to 123—but the mental terror was overwhelming. I'd have to go to the bank or the grocery, and I'd wonder, 'Can I make it?' Often, I didn't, and I'd have to grit my teeth, go home and take a shower and change my clothes. My cleaning lady was aghast. I can remember once having to fly on Air Canada and nervously chug-a-lugging Pepto Bismol before I boarded. 'Please, God,' I prayed, 'let me make it without embarrassing myself.' I had called ahead to check with the airline about medical equipment aloft, but they began to ask about my condition, and I thought, 'Oh, no, I'd better back off.' That time, I made it during the flight, but not during the drive from the airport.

"When I started on AZT this January, I was a wreck, but within days my thrush had cleared up, the diarrhea had stopped and my weight began to go up. So far, my blood counts are okay. What worries me is the possible spread to the brain. I've always been somewhat of a klutz, but now, every time I bump into a door or have trouble getting out of a chair I wonder if this is the first sign that my mind is going. I'm scheduled for psychological tests, putting square pegs into square holes and so on, and I'm hoping for the best.

"Two of my closest friends have died in the last few weeks. Both had been diagnosed with PCP, and both were hoping to get on AZT. But their luck ran out. Now I'm wondering if the ax will fall a third time. I still haven't made out a will. But I have no complaints. I feel that I have been lucky and that my doctors have given me tremendous care.

"And, you know, although 50 is not so old, I am a bit of an old geezer. I've lived a full life. I really feel sorry for the young ones, the men in their 20s who are just setting forth in life and who have been told that they have AIDS."

Frank, 46, is a former body builder, and this day he still looks powerful, with a bullet-shaped head and chest bulging through a shirt that is open almost to the navel. He used to enter contests at 145 pounds and now weighs in at 182, "fat for the first time in my life."

His appearance is a mirage. His blood counts are bad, and he may soon need a transfusion. He speaks in a soft voice, almost a whisper. He appears breathless. He was diagnosed as an AIDS patient in May 1985, after coming down with PCP and cryptococcus meningitis, an inflammation of the lining of the brain. The meningitis was so severe that for one solid year he did nothing but stay at home and endure eight hours every day of intravenous drip to fight the meningitis.

"Man, that was the worst. Eight hours every day with an IV stuck in your arm and vomiting and shaking with the chills when it's 90 degrees outside. I've got to tell you the truth: I almost cashed in my chips. One day, though, they finally got the meningitis."

He is an unrepentant "fast-track" gay and is totally at ease with a sexual lifestyle that may shock the general public. "Man, I never had any choice," he says. "This is just the way I am. Nobody ever said it's easy being gay."

By day he was an investment banker at a major Chicago bank, a banker so successful that in 1978 he could retire to an apple orchard in the Illinois countryside. "I did the whole bit," he recalls. "By day I wore the three-piece suit and did business; at night I put on the other costume and went into the leather bars.

"I was a child of the 1960s, and I was into some very heavy things, sexually and with drugs. Part of it was a head trip, and all the sex was associated with drugs. I'm from the Timothy Leary school of drugs—the more the better—and I tried acid, coke, poppers, you name it, but nothing intravenously. Sexually, I was a pig.

"I was very selective in my sexual tastes. I went out only with extremely good-looking, well-built men. Wednesdays and Sundays were my days off, and I would party on Tuesday and Saturday nights. I needed the rest of the week to recoup, because the body literally cannot take what was going on more than two or three times a week."

Frank was into fisting, or anal fist-f——ing. He says, "The whole point was, How much can you take?" What's the appeal? "How do I know? What's the appeal of anything? All I know is that it was a very macho world.

"It was wild out there. There was a handkerchief code, and cards were handed out in the bars to make sure that you understood the game. A red handkerchief meant fisting, and if you wore it on the right side, it meant you preferred being receptive. Black was

S&M [sadomasochism], gray, bondage; and green, a hustler. With me it was an experimental thing, and one thing led to another in a sort of natural progression. I did this kind of thing two or three times a week for maybe 20, 25 years. Of course, I was at high risk of something like AIDS. And if it weren't for AIDS, I'd still be chugging along.

"You know, Chicago's always been something of a finishing school for gays. The young kids come in from Des Moines and Indianapolis, learn a few tricks and move on to Manhattan or California. Among Chicago gays, you usually find only the very young or the very old, but you don't have the cross-section you have in San Francisco or New York. After I retired from the bank and bought my orchard, I used to winter in California. Chicago has everything that California does, but it's just that there's so much more on the Coast. By 1984 I began to worry about AIDS, and I had the antibody test taken in Chicago. Then I left for California. A few weeks later I found out I was positive. I felt terrible, but with time it passed. I continued to have sex, but safe sex, no exchange of fluids. I believe that I was exposed to the virus in Chicago.

"I've been gay ever since I can remember. I got syphilis from an older guy when I was in the sixth grade. It took eight shots of penicillin. For days, I couldn't walk. Oh, over the years, I had everything—gonorrhea and herpes and hepatitis and syphilis and rectal bleeding and intestinal tears. But everything healed. It went with the territory.

"I'd say that most people would never recognize three-fourths of gay men as being gay. And about one of every three gay males is into the kind of thing I've been into. That's the way it was. I've been all over the place—Amsterdam and Paris and London and Berlin and Munich and New York and Los Angeles and San Francisco, and it's all pretty much the same. By comparison, Chicago is pretty tame, probably 10 years behind the other cities in the extent of the action. But you can find it here, if you're looking.

"Right now, I'm feeling pretty lousy. I'm very tired, and I'm having trouble breathing. I think I'm anemic. My parents? Of course, they know I'm gay; I can't convince them I'm Haitian. What it boils down to is when they find out you're gay they're p——, and when they find out you're sick, they're there for you. That's the way it works. Out in the country where I live, they still burn crosses into the ground, but nobody knows I'm gay. The home-care nurses are absolutely wonderful, and I enjoy being alone, watching TV and pruning my apple trees and working on my pumpkins and raspberries. Today I'm through with sex. If somebody hits on me, I simply say, 'No, thanks. I have AIDS.' If they still want 'safe sex,' I say, 'No way, not with me.' I'd feel like I'm taking somebody's life into my hands.

"To readers, I'd say, 'Don't judge me.' We only go around once in life, and it's up to everybody to make their own decisions. You either want to do something and you do it, or you don't. Everything that's found in the gay community can be found in the straight community, too, with a few modifications. And I'd hate to tell you how many bisexuals, married men, I've had sex with. There used to be bisexual baths in San Francisco.

"Me, I'm hanging on, but if the pain gets too bad, I'll tell you the truth: I'll end it. I don't have time for the pain."

He smiles. "See, you learned something."

Derek, 40, was nearing his peak as a successful architect/designer when he was hospitalized last fall with PCP and encephalitis and diagnosed as having AIDS. He recalls "feeling like a leper and wanting to run and hide.

"I'd traveled all over the world, Amsterdam and London and Tokyo, and back in 1982 when I was in San Francisco on R-and-R from Tokyo, I remember picking up a kid on the street—really he was just a street urchin—and going to a room for sex. Afterwards, he said, 'You know, I have these swollen glands in my neck and in my crotch, and they say that this is the 'gay cancer.' I was really disturbed that he would tell me *after* the fact, but I also decided that it was time to calm down my lifestyle. I'd been a premed student, and I knew enough biology to figure out that these kinds of symptoms could be the result of sexual transmission. I decided that it was time to get out of California and get back to the Midwest. I spent two years in St. Louis, and in 1984 I came back to Chicago, my hometown. It felt great to be back in the town where I had grown up as a kid, seeing Marina City and the Wrigley Building and Tribune Tower and Michigan Avenue.

"When they told me the diagnosis, I was just numb. I don't think that I really began to deal with it until just before I left the hospital. And then I wanted to run and hide. I was angry that I was being cut down right at the peak of my career, but I was also ashamed at the stigma. But I've worked myself around to accepting my disease. What I'm angry about is that Chicago is not doing the job it should to help people like me to live with this disease, as opposed to dying from it."

The interview is resumed later in his apartment, a fourth-floor walk-up that he will soon have to vacate. Too many steps to climb. The designer's eye is evident, and the apartment is tastefully arranged, with exposed brick and striking angles and contemporary furniture. Everything is orderly and in its place. Tucked out of view is a chalkboard where he keeps messages to remind himself of appointments. "I've had some short-term memory loss from the encephalitis," he explains, "and I have to keep reminding myself of appointments, or I forget."

Taped down in meticulous Letraset—"Actually, it's architect's tape, which is firmer than Letraset," he explains—are reminders for "Acupuncture" at 2 p.m. on Tuesday and "Group" at 8 p.m. on Wednesday and "NW" [for the Northwestern AZT clinic] on Thursday a.m. Scrawled in chalk is the entry, "Tribune" for 10 a.m. Friday.

He has quit his job to devote full time to his fight for life, and he spends his days on the phone talking to friends and going to various support groups. He is giving this interview, he says, for two reasons: "to persuade Chicago to provide more services for AIDS patients and for the emotional satisfaction of standing up and doing something, of trying to make a difference."

A beeper goes off. It is time to take an AZT capsule, a ritual that must be followed every four hours for 24 hours, every day. His beeper will also remind him at 3 a.m.

He confides that he was bisexual and once was married. "What's important to me is affection and love and caring and support. That's why I don't want to be in isolation. If I don't feel well enough to go out, that phone is always burning. Support is very, very important to me.

"That was the best part of being married. I was married for six years while I went to school at Toronto and Berkeley, and it was great for love and stability. My gay experiences during those six years were clandestine. We broke up after we moved to San Francisco."

Regrets? "No," he says. "That implies that I would have had some message from the future telling me what was coming down. And I never got any such message.

"My sexual life is very calm these days. I've given it up. I've been to the bars, but I feel uncomfortable. Maybe 10 percent of the people in a gay bar have AIDS, but everybody thinks, 'Oh, well, the people with AIDS are at that end of the bar, not this end.' But, they're wrong. The AIDS patients are usually at both ends of the bar."

He was divorced well before the AIDS virus came to America, but he allows that, "Sure, bisexual men are a major threat to spread AIDS into the heterosexual world. And there are a lot more of them out there than you would ever think."

Derek begins to pursue the point, but his attention is wandering. A man with an IQ high enough to qualify him for Mensa, the high-IQ society, Derek cannot now remember if he has a dinner engagement or not this evening. Or if his talk on AIDS to Chicago's Gay Mensa society is next Monday or Tuesday.

"You worry about this forgetfulness," he says. "If you lose your mind, you lose everything."

At any rate, he now needs to take a nap. It is noon.

She is a middle-aged counselor, and she is dressed in a prim, no-nonsense fashion. As she tells the story of how she finally came to terms with her husband's bisexuality and his death from AIDS and her subsequent volunteer work with PWAs, she speaks in a soft, flat monotone that occasionally yields to bursts of passion.

"In the spring of 1984 I could tell that my husband was not well, though he tried to keep it hidden. He was fatigued, he was losing weight, he had a case of shingles, he was taking Tylenol every day for low-grade fevers and he had scheduled a bone-marrow biopsy. I said, 'John, I have to know what's going on.' He wouldn't tell me. A few weeks later, he was hospitalized. When they told me the diagnosis was Pneumocystis pneumonia, well, it took me about 15 seconds to figure out, 'He's gay, he's been sexually active and he's going to die.' The fact that I might be at risk didn't hit me right then. We were both very active in the church, and my husband had asked not only that the pastor come to the hospital but that he bring his wife, too. John told me, 'Mary, there's something you have to know. I have AIDS, and you don't have to stay with me.' Well, we'd been married for 35 years and had six grown children, and I wasn't going to leave him then. Besides, I still loved him.

"But I told him, 'John, you have to tell the kids. I'll go nuts if I try to keep this secret.' We called the children into Chicago from around the country and told them the bad news. Two were angry, but they all said, 'You're still our Dad.'

"In 1984 there was no test for the virus and there was no AZT to treat the Pneumocystis. John was dead within seven weeks. The memorial service was held back in our hometown in Ohio, where John had been a highly respected member of the church and the community. I gave the eulogy, and I insisted on telling the mourners, 'He died from AIDS.'" Her voice rises. "Now, everything was out in the open, and this stopped the gossipers in their tracks. I made a conscious decision to tell John's secret because I wanted people to have to wrestle with the issues posed by AIDS. I wanted them to know that a man they had loved and respected had died of this terrible disease. There was nothing left to wonder about, and it opened the way for others to come up to me and discuss their own marriages to gay men or their own gay children. It required a lot of courage because our church teaches that homosexuality is sinful.

"Those seven weeks between John's diagnosis and his death were like a soap opera. That's half the story. The other half was very positive. We bridged the emotional gap between us. Oh, I had known for about 18 years that John was gay. Or, I should say, I knew as much as I could allow myself to know. He always held me at a distance emotionally, and I had often wondered if we would be able to talk honestly before we died. After he came down with AIDS, he told me that he had always known he was gay, but in our day and in our community and in our church, this was not an option. We had met and married while attending a church school. He told me that as he got older he felt more and more of a need to explore this side of himself and to act out his impulses."

Her voice rises again. "I would never sleep around—those are not my values. But I think that straight society's intense condemnation of the gay community has encouraged people like my husband to intensely act out their impulses. What I have learned from all of this is that my belief in Christian compassion is greater than my belief in the church's rules about human behavior. It has been a transforming experience. I cannot approve of what my husband did, but I accept his behavior as that of another human being. I still love him, even though he did not live up to my values.

"In a way, finding out about his gayness was a good thing for me. At last, I knew that I was not crazy. For years I had known that he was not particularly turned on by me sexually, and this had driven me into therapy to confront my own sexual identity. Finally, I knew it was not me. I've never had the antibody test for exposure to AIDS. Right after John's death, I went in for a physical check-up, and everything was normal. If I ever develop the symptoms of AIDS, of course I'll get angry all over again, but I'm not living with this fear. I've poured my energy into trying to understand the gay lifestyle that drew my husband. What I've discovered is a whole new world that is largely hidden from society. And I must say that they have accepted me—a middle-aged, straight church woman—with open arms.

"I can't bring John back, but I still love him, and I feel that I now understand him a lot better."

Among the many AIDS patients at Cook County Hospital is Leonard, a young black man. Leonard, who in drag goes by the name Lisa, is peeling a tangerine. He estimates that he used to average 200 sexual partners a year, "oh, maybe more; I never had any trouble finding men, and I used to fly with friends all over the place." He worked 15 years for a Loop accounting firm before AIDS sapped his energy and forced him to take disability. "I never thought anything like this would happen to me because a lot of the men I went out with were married men with families, and I know they're not into drugs and all this, you know."

He's given up sex. "Oh, if they ask. I just smile and say 'Not today.'" Now he babysits with his younger brothers and sisters. He says: "I've rediscovered God and I put my trust in him. In my mind, I just have another form of cancer."

Other than sexual promiscuity, the big threat of spreading AIDS into the general population is intravenous drug abuse. Coming to terms with a sexual partner who has put himself at risk by sharing needles can be difficult, especially within a marriage.

Sally is married to Sam, who has AIDS, and she has agreed to an interview. On the day of the interview, however, Sam is also there.

His daughter lies sprawled across a sofa, sound asleep and blissfully unaware of the discussion. In the other room, the couple's son is crying for attention. They have given up an afternoon at the zoo, maybe even the aquarium, for this interview.

"All right, man, what's this about, now?" Sam asks. He is mollified and agrees to tell his story. He is in his 20s and in jeans and plaid flannel shirt resembles a lumberjack. Indeed, in high school and college, he both played football and wrestled. He appears the picture of health.

"Back in the summer of 1981," he says. "I got involved with a girl from the neighborhood. She was into intravenous drugs and was a hooker on the side to make the money. I knew she was doing tricks and all that, but I was intrigued by the drugs. I have to admit I was curious. I had my own apartment, and we spent that entire summer getting high on coke and heroin. We weren't real tight or anything, but the sex went hand in hand with the drugs. What can I say? I was just acting crazy. I'd say we shot up maybe 25 to 30 times that summer, and we used only one needle between us. I mean, I cleaned it after every session, but we never thought to use fresh needles.

"What did she look like? Well, like I say, we weren't real tight."

Sally interjects: "She always looked gaunt. Real gaunt and real sickly."

Sam agrees. "Yeah, she was thin as a rail and real pale. Toward the end of that summer, I began to notice that I had painful, swollen glands in my neck, under my arms and in the groin. Now, I was a pretty good student in biology, and I knew that something was going on, but I figured it was related to the drugs. I mean I've never been sick a day in my life. No colds. Nothing. I was into sports and bodybuilding. Even today I'll go out twice a week and run five miles. Oh, I was a little concerned, what with her being a druggie and turning tricks who knows where, but I was only worried about maybe getting VD or hepatitis, never anything like this. I have to take responsibility for what I did, though. I was curious to know what the drugs were all about. I'd had some heavy problems at home, and it felt nice to catch a buzz and escape a little.

"Anyway, my Dad finally stepped in and demanded to know what was going on. I guess I looked pretty bummed out, and after he made me roll up my sleeves and he saw the track marks, he made me return home. He went to the girl's house and told her to stay away from me or he'd turn her in to the police. She was only 15 or 16, she had one kid and she was living at home.

"So, I proceeded to put my life back together. I got into college, and I got back together with Sally. We've been in love since about sixth grade—she's from the neighborhood, too—but during that summer of '81 she was down in Kentucky with her mother. We got married in 1984 and had two children right off the bat. Everything was going fine until one day last February, when I got a notice in the mail from the blood bank. I'd donated blood back in the fall of 1981 and on Palm Sunday in both 1984 and 1985. At first, I thought it was just junk mail or else a 'thank you' for giving blood. I almost threw it away, but I noticed that it gave a phone number and asked that I call. I made the call, and they said they couldn't talk to me on the phone, that it was so serious that I had to come in and talk face-to-face. I thought, 'Oh, wow, I must have some strange blood disease like [former Bears' running back] Brian Piccolo's.

"Then, they told me." He laughs. "I mean it almost blew me away. This is a killer."

Sally says: "By 1986 they'd passed a law to make it legal to notify blood donors if their blood tested positive for AIDS. At first, after he came and told me, I thought he was kidding. But then I saw all the brochures and pamphlets, and I thought, 'Oh, no.'"

Sam: "Thank God that Sally knew about my having used drugs and all and knew that this other girl I had been involved with was as loose as a goose. Of course, I was a basket case worrying about Sally and the kids. But, thank God, prayers were answered. All three tested negative. Now, Sally and I have safe sex—condom, lubricant, spermicide, the whole shot. We keep everything separate—coffee cups, razors, toothbrushes. Sally gets tested every two months."

She adds: "I got my results yesterday. Negative."

Sam: "I go down to Northwestern every six months or so to get my blood tested. I feel fine, but every once in a while the glands swell or there's fatigue. Maybe it's a psychosomatic type of thing. The last time, my blood counts weren't that good—the helper cells were down to 700, and Sal's are something like 1,500. But what are you going to do?"

Sally interjects: "He's always said that if he gets sick, he'll just go away and die."

Sam: "That's right. There's nothing they can do for you, and I don't need to die in a hospital. I can die on my own.

"You know, I get so tired reading about all this AIDS stuff, especially about it being a gay disease and all. That really bothers me. And you can't get away from it.

"I'm a religious man, and I believe in the Second Coming of Christ. I think that this whole decadence thing with the drugs and the sex was getting out of hand, and this is God's way of straightening people out, of saying, 'All this flagrant stuff with bisexuality and homosexuality and drugs is against my law.'

"This whole thing has been like a kick in the pants to me. It's helped me straighten out my life with the little drugs, too. Before I found out I was positive for AIDS, I was smoking a joint of marijuana every day and doing a lot of alcohol. Now, I'm off the marijuana and I'm in Alcoholics Anonymous.

"I've put my life in God's hands, and I try to live a normal life. The tough thing is the *knowing*, but what are you gonna do? Sometimes it all seems like a bad dream. I go to work every day and I work outside in a job that requires heavy physical activity. I'm out there in the cold, and I've never gotten sick. Nobody knows about this AIDS except my wife, my doctor and now you. I fall back on prayer, and, of course, my No. 1 prayer is that my family stay healthy.

"What's the message to readers? Repent! This decadence has got to stop. If you live a moral life—no needles, no sleeping around—you have nothing to fear."

Sally concludes: "I still feel the same way about him, and I still love him just as much. The only difference is that now we don't have to argue about how many children we're going to have. We're only going to have the two we have. Sam wanted a whole house full."

Mean Streets

AIDS warrior Joyce Wallace, M.D., is on a crusade to convert a former Manhattan brothel into a shelter for homeless hookers

The best little whorehouse on Houston St. in lower Manhattan is now shuttered, about to be converted into a shelter for homeless streetwalkers.

The magician attempting this trick is a matronly physician named Joyce Wallace, a 50-year-old internist who practices a few blocks away in Greenwich Village.

She raises a metal curtain, festooned with graffiti, and gingerly unlocks the inside door to the former brothel-hotel. We climb a narrow flight of stairs and come upon a room whose walls are colorfully frescoed with male and female nudes in various motifs of lovemaking. The art was a great prop for the former business. Now it will be scrubbed away for the new shelter.

Backing up against the sleek contours of a voluptuous nude painted on the wall, Dr. Wallace talks excitedly above the noise of a burglar alarm that refuses to shut off:

"This is going to be the reception area," she says. "In the back, we'll have kitchen and shower facilities.

The upstairs floors will be converted into residences for 18 women."

Party balloons are snuggled up against the paintings of the nubile nudes. "Oh, these are from my birthday party," the physician explains. "We celebrated it here and in lieu of gifts I asked everybody to donate money to the cause."

The cause is to help the homeless female prostitutes of New York, most of whom are drug addicts and one third of whom carry the AIDS virus. Dr. Wallace is president of the Foundation for Research on Sexually Transmitted Diseases (FROST'D), and the foundation's main project is "Off the Street," an ambitious effort to create lifesaving shelters in the major areas of New York City where prostitutes ply their trade.

Her critics call this an impossible dream, adding that she is crazy. She smiles.

"Let me tell you a story," she begins. "I grew up in Queens, a borough that now seems a distant province from Greenwich Village. My parents were both schoolteachers, and after my younger brother died of leukemia my mother became a speech therapist for brain-damaged children suffering from cerebral palsy."

One night, her students performed *My Fair Lady*, and the girl who played Eliza brought down the house when she sang, 'I Could Have Danced All Night.' She was in a wheelchair.

"It never would have occurred to my mother that this girl could not have played that part while in a wheelchair. She had the ability to see past the defect to the real person. I'm the same way."

From the unique vantage point of her medical office-home in Manhattan's Greenwich Village, Dr. Wallace has witnessed the unfolding of the AIDS epidemic from the very beginning.

"When I opened my office here in 1977," she says, "the sexual scene was wide open. My practice was one third gay men, and we used to order penicillin by the boxcar. My nurse and I could diagnose a case of gonorrhea in 30 seconds flat, since we were seeing so many.

"Everybody figured, 'So what?' Penicillin could cure gonorrhea and syphilis, as well as the 'gay bowel syndrome.' My patients figured that *Shigella* was the worst thing that could happen to them, and it, too, was treatable."

With the aid of the Armed Forces Institute of Pathology in Washington, D.C., and the nearby St. Vincent's Hospital of Greenwich Village, Dr. Wallace helped diagnose one of this nation's first cases of Kaposi's sarcoma in an immunosuppressed promiscuous gay male. The year was 1981, and she recalls:

"Once it was apparent that sexual promiscuity can kill, we knew that we either had to find a magic pill or that sexual promiscuity had to go."

Back in 1981, as the toll that would eventually be identified as the AIDS epidemic began to widen and its mysteries deepen, Dr. Wallace had a bright idea.

"This appears to be a sexually transmitted disease," she told the New York City Board of Health, adding, "I've heard that women are known to have sex, and prostitutes are known to have many sexual partners, so why don't we study the city's streetwalkers to assess what's happening with them?"

With these words, this middle-aged, middle-class, white physician launched her own personal crusade to try to help the estimated 10,000 prostitutes who walk the mean streets of New York, trying to survive on the fringes.

For the past 3 years, Dr. Wallace has been cruising the "whores' strolls" in a customized van donated by a condom maker. By sheer personality—and the payment of $20—the physician has persuaded the city's prostitutes to be counseled about AIDS and to consent to a backseat blood test for the fatal human immunodeficiency virus (HIV).

Before she was given the van, she tracked the hookers down by foot, taking her boyfriend along as protection. She has had to stare down both hardened streetwalkers and hardened city bureaucrats alike to keep her research alive, but the results are instructive.

New York's streetwalkers, she has subsequently documented, represent a special universe:

The average age is 30. One half are black, one quarter are Hispanic, and one quarter are white. Two of every five are homeless. Four of every five are using or have used intravenous drugs. Nine of every 10 have children, though only one of every 10 of these mothers lives with her children. One of every three carries the AIDS virsus. And the majority of these AIDS-infected streetwalkers neither use condoms nor seek medical care.

Now, her goal is to take these homeless prostitutes off the streets and put them on a new path. She knows it won't be easy, and, indeed, a community backlash may yet dash the dream.

Dr. Wallace lives the old-fashioned way—in a six-room apartment above her medical office.

"I had the sense to buy this brownstone," she explains, "after my rent was tripled at my former office down the block. In 1984, the *New York Times* carried a story about the $238,000 grant I had received to study AIDS among drug-addicted prostitutes. The next day, my rent went sky-high."

On this night, her downstairs medical office has been rented for the night by an AIDS support group whose members are pursuing homeopathic remedies. As they wait to be treated, and as this reporter waits for Dr. Wallace to arrive for an interview, there is much talk among the patients of spiritual mediums and other help from the beyond.

Later, as we speak over their heads, Dr. Wallace observes, "Most of these men were unknowingly infected from 1979 to 1983, when the virus silently spread through drug addiction and homosexual sex. The future spread of AIDS will be among heterosexuals, and the city's streetwalkers may be spreading it even as we speak."

As we talk, her son Ari, age 10, impatiently bounces up and down on the living-room trampoline, asking for money for a pizza. Her daughter Julie, 23, is off pursuing a Ph.D. Twice divorced, Dr. Wallace now has a special relationship with a male friend, a sculptor, but she is so busy with her crusade that she sees him only "very, very late, or not at all."

She continues, "The idea that streetwalkers are not entitled to a second chance infuriates me. Streetwalkers are as varied as people you find anywhere.

"My first female AIDS patient was referred to me back in 1981. She was a bright, lovely young white lady from Kansas. For 9 months of the year, she was an engineering student; for the other 3 months she was a prostitute. She died of AIDS at the age of 23—1 month before she would have graduated.

"She referred seven of her friends to me, all of whom were lovely young women and all of whom were streetwalkers. Two were found to have clinical evidence of lowered immunity. I reported this in a 1982 letter published in *Lancet*. These girls are not atypical. A few blocks from here, on Eighth Ave., there's an area called the 'Minnesota Stroll,' in honor of the streetwalkers who have come here from the Midwest."

There are no firm figures on how efficiently prostitutes pass HIV to their male customers, but Dr. Wallace believes that they do. "Thank God for the Japanese cars, though," she exclaims. "They're so small that there's no room for fornication, and the prostitutes can only provide oral sex to men who mostly have intact penile skin. This means that the risk of transmitting the virus is low.

"However, as the nation's recession deepens and medical care becomes less available, more people will develop genital ulcers, and we may easily see in New York the type of explosive situation that is found in Africa, Asia, and India.

"There is very little difference between the homeless streetwalkers of New York and the poor people of the Third World. And studies show that in certain African cities, one of every five males with genital ulcers who has sex with an infected prostitute will acquire the AIDS virus from a single encounter! This is very sobering to contemplate."

Returning to the New York scene, she says, "Generally speaking, the streetwalkers we see are unloved, unwanted children. All their experiences with mainstream America have been punishing. They turn to prostitution to survive and to feel loved. They turn to drugs to escape reality.

"If we can create an oasis where they can learn to trust again and acknowledge their despair, then they can be helped. All we're talking about is a hot meal, a clean shower, a warm bed. My hope is that clean sheets will prove addictive, and that we can redirect these women to drug-treatment, job-training, and parent-training programs."

Her foundation is seeking to create shelters in each of the city's 10 major whores' strolls. The test pilot shelter on Houston St. was scheduled to open late last year with funding from the city's Division of Substance Abuse Services (DAS), but a backlash from the community and its elected politicians now threatens to defund the project.

Dr. Wallace works a 70-hour week, and lately she has been awakening in the middle of the night in a cold sweat. "We've signed a 10-year lease to convert the Houston St. brothel into a shelter," she says, "and the rent is $5600 a month. Since DAS has not yet kicked in with any funding, I'm borrowing from my son's college account to pay the rent. This is very nervous-making."

She describes the problem as "NIMBY," or "Not in my backyard." She adds, "The communities don't want prostitutes and the politicians don't want prostitutes. The prostitutes don't vote and they don't make donations to political campaigns. I mean, in his recent State of the Union address, President Bush did not even mention AIDS. It was as if AIDS disappeared on August 2, 1990, when Iraq invaded Kuwait.

"Well, AIDS didn't disappear. Half my practice is now AIDS patients. I have 400 AIDS patients and 160 are women. Yes, women, and these women are neither drug addicts nor prostitutes. How did they get AIDS? From men, of course. They are women who acquired AIDS through sexual intercourse with men.

"One of my best girlfriends was divorced and took up with this gorgeous guy who was a reformed drug addict. This was back when nobody knew what was going on. Now, she's dying of AIDS.

"My office has given 5000 tests for AIDS, and we're seeing more and more positives among heterosexuals, especially women. And it's happening right in our backyard."

It's 11 PM, and Dr. Wallace takes this reporter and an assistant in tow and nimbly maneuvers her oversized "LifeStyles Care-Van," a gift from the people who make Ansell condoms, into the chaotic New York traffic.

She is heading out to counsel prostitutes on the notorious 11th Ave. stroll in west Manhattan, but first she gives this reporter a quick tour of the city she loves:

"Down that alley there, almost out of sight, why that's the first Jewish cemetery in New York. It was dedicated way before the Revolutionary War . . . and over there, where you see the five streets coming together, that's the site of the famous 'Five Points' riot during the Civil War . . . Greenwich Village itself was founded during the Civil War when residents fled the uptown area to escape an epidemic of yellow fever. The village began as a shantytown and gradually evolved into an artists' colony where the rule was live and let live . . . and, over there, see that tiny door, well, that's the smallest house in Greenwich Village. The poet Edna St. Vincent Millay used to live there, and she was named after St. Vincent's Hospital, which saved her father's life."

Soft snow is turning to hard sleet as we dodge speeding taxis on 11th Ave., when Dr. Wallace suddenly hard-curbs the van against the corner. Reflected in the rear-view mirror is a familiar sight:

A young girl in a violet miniskirt that leaves nothing open to question is sashaying through the nasty weather, her long legs and deep cleavage precariously balanced on extra-high heels.

Dr. Wallace always travels with an assistant, but she does the tough work herself. Now, dressed for the weather in heavy wool slacks and overcoat and sturdy clog shoes, the 50-year-old physician jumps from the van and tracks down the young girl. Her introduction is no-nonsense: "Hi, I'm Dr. Wallace and I'm looking for girls who want to be tested for AIDS."

This one does not, but she accepts the multicolored condoms the physician is dispensing. Soon, a crowd gathers as prostitutes and their pimps emerge from the darkness to claim the condoms. A corner pep rally ensues as Dr. Wallace tosses batch after batch of condoms to the group, shouting, "Use them in good health!"

Later, back in the van, she explains, "Next time, they'll be expecting me and more will come forward. We used to pay the girls $20 if they would be counseled about AIDS and agree to a blood test. This is about what they would earn for oral sex and it only takes as long, too. But the city decided that paying the girls was illegal, so now we can only give them McDonald's coupons. This makes our work harder."

Other heath educators may worry about cholesterol, saturated fats, and a fast-food diet, but this one observes, "I only hope that these girls live long enough to develop heart disease."

A few blocks later, emerging from the deep crevasse under an overpass, two young prostitutes come forward—one black, one white. "We know what you're doing about AIDS and we think it's good," says the one. "Do you have any condoms?" says the other. As the conversation continues, small cars circle the block and our large van. These are customers on the cruise. Eyes narrowing, one prostitute cuts off the conversation: "Bye, bye. Now, we have to make some money."

The next girl, however, comes directly to the van and the point: "Are you giving AIDS tests? Good, I want one."

"Sheila" is cocoa-skinned and baby-faced, outfitted in a black beret, blonde wig, and toreador slacks. Removing her bright green greatcoat, she asks Dr. Wallace's assistant, "Will you please hold my hand while the blood is drawn?"

First, she is counseled about the AIDS test and its implications. "If I have AIDS, I'll kill myself," she says matter-of-factly. "Well, what if I told you you could live 20 years or more, even with AIDS?" Dr. Wallace counters. "Well, then, maybe I wouldn't kill myself," is the reply.

The encounter is entered into Dr. Wallace's register, and Sheila becomes prostitute No. 2165 to be tested for AIDS. Asked her date of birth, she smiles sheepishly. The midnight hour has come and gone and we are into a new day. "Actually, today is my birthday," she says. She is now 22. Within minutes, the girl disappears into the night, clutching her new condoms and McDonald's coupons.

Dr. Wallace has also given her a card, asking her to call for the test results. "Most don't," the physician says, "and it's hard to track them down. When we were able to pay them to come to my office for the test results, many did. Not now." She adds, "Sometimes, I dream of retiring to Miami Beach and eating stewed prunes."

This night, however, the physician still has a parade of prostitutes to see. "Remember," she reminds, "you're only seeing the cute girls, the ones who are still young and have their looks and can command $20-$30-$40 for sex. Some of the ones we see in the outer boroughs are so broken down it breaks your heart. They need help, and unless we get our shelters, we're forced to remain 'medical gypsies,' visiting them only from time to time in the van."

Dr. Wallace's house calls continue into the early morning of this new day. By the strangest of coincidences, it is Valentine's Day.

Murder or Mystery?

Federal epidemiologist Harold Jaffe, M.D., is asked whether or not Florida dentist David Acer intentionally infected six of his patients with the AIDS virus. He answers, "Yes, no, and maybe!"

For the past 3 years, Harold Jaffe, MD, has been the man in the middle of the extraordinary controversy over how a Florida dentist might have infected six of his patients with the acquired immunodeficiency syndrome (AIDS) virus. As the deputy director for AIDS science of the federal Centers for Disease Control and Prevention (CDC), Jaffe has had to broker the often-conflicting concerns of health professionals and their patients.

At the heart of the controversy are these questions:

Did the dentist, David Acer, D.D.S., now dead of AIDS, intentionally inject six patients with his own AIDS-infected blood or did he accidentally infect them with his own blood by unknown means? Or, in terms of the larger issue, did he murder them in a scenario unique to him or did he accidentally spread his AIDS virus in an unknown manner that theoretically can happen *again* to dental and surgical patients of other health professionals infected with the human immunodeficiency virus (HIV)?

In an interview with this reporter, Jaffe, an epidemiologist of grave demeanor and circumspect speech, summarized:

"I don't know what happened and we may never know what happened. I personally think that it's clear that the dentist is the source of these six infections and that it is unlikely that the infections were transmitted from patient to patient within his practice. DNA sequencing matched his AIDS viral strain to that of the six patients. If the dentist is the source, there are three possibilities:

• "He somehow contaminated his dental instruments with his blood, failed to properly sterilize them, and exposed patients to his blood by reusing the contaminated instruments.

• "He somehow injured himself and exposed patients to his blood.

• "He did it intentionally, or, in other words, he murdered them."

But which, the reporter presses?

"I haven't a clue," Jaffe concludes. "There is no direct evidence for any of these three theories.

"Acer was known to have oral Kaposi's sarcoma and he might have used his dental instruments to treat himself and then reused them on patients without proper sterilization. However, no one in Acer's office ever saw him treat himself in this manner.

"Or, he might have injured himself while his fingers were inside the patient's mouth, possibly while palpating the tip of the anesthetic needle, and his blood spilled directly into the patient's mouth. Although there is no documented neuropathy in Acer's medical records, his AIDS might have made his sense of touch less than normal. If so, he might have put his finger and the anesthetic needle into the patient's mouth at the same time, stuck himself, and spilled infectious blood into the patient's mouth.

"Or, he might have committed murder through a variety of ways. He might have kept a syringe in his pocket, filled with a mixture of anesthetic and his own blood, and used this to infect the patient. I don't pretend to understand all the possibilities by which he might have intentionally infected patients. However, all six patients were fully awake during their procedures and neither they nor anyone on Acer's staff ever noticed anything unusual."

He emphasizes, "We have no direct evidence to support any of these three possibilities. If it were murder, either nobody saw what he did or nobody has been willing to come forward and tell what he might have done."

The CDC has spent more than $1 million and thrown two dozen investigators into action to try to figure out what happened in Acer's dental practice, and, though theories abound, the six deaths remain an official mystery.

"I'm puzzled and frustrated," Jaffe says. "Obviously, we'd really like to know what happened, but at this point I'd be surprised if we ever get the answer."

The controversy began on July 27, 1990, when the CDC published an article, "Possible Transmission of Human Immunodeficiency Virus (HIV) to a Patient During an Invasive Dental Procedure," in its *Morbidity and Mortality Weekly Report*. Within weeks, things heated up. The CDC convened a panel of 72 AIDS consultants, including representatives from the American Medical Association (AMA) and the American Dental Association (ADA), to consider the policy impact of what some observers called "an accident waiting to happen." And the previously anonymous dental patient, Kimberly Bergalis, 22, came forward, filed suit against Acer and her dental insurer, and went public with a crusade to require mandatory testing of health workers for HIV. She also granted an interview to this reporter, which was published in *JAMA* on October 17, 1990.

Bergalis died in 1991, and five more of Acer's patients in Florida have since been identified as having contracted AIDS, including a 62-year-old grandmother, a woman who has subsequently relocated to Michigan, two men, and a 19-year-old woman. Investigators have established that, like Bergalis, none of the five has any risk factors for AIDS other than dental treatment by Acer. Sophisticated genetic sequencing tests have documented that all six patients share the same AIDS viral strain as Acer.

Congress considered mandatory testing of health workers for HIV, but compromised on voluntary CDC guidelines that call for universal precautions during invasive medical and dental procedures and that urge HIV-infected health workers to submit to evaluation by expert panels and to modify their practices, if necessary. In the meantime, the controversy continues.

Bergalis' attorney, Robert Montgomery of Palm Beach, Fla., is continuing her crusade for mandatory testing of health workers.

David Lewis, Ph.D., an environmental microbiologist based at the University of Georgia, Athens, has gone public with his claims that dental handpieces attached to a leaky piece of dental equipment known as a "prophy (lactic) angle" can transfer 50 times or more blood than a needlestick with just 5 minutes of operation during routine treatments to clean and polish teeth. The prophy angle, which is connected to the head used to clean and polish teeth, is a metal joint that gives a dentist the proper angle to maneuver within the mouth. Lewis theorizes that Acer treated himself or some of his sexual partners with this dental device, failed to properly sterilize it, and oral detritus, including blood and saliva with HIV, was passed from patient to patient by the leaky prophy angle.

Heat sterilization kills HIV and other infectious agents, but Lewis fears that 5% to 10% of dentists are like Acer and do not adequately sterilize their devices. With this assumption, he theorizes that AIDS and hepatitis B cases not documented to traditional risk factors may, in fact, be due to infection in the dentist's office. "It is terribly difficult to track these unidentified AIDS and hepatitis B cases back to the dentist's office," he told this reporter, "and that is why dentists must be made to comply with heat sterilization procedures."

(A spokesman for the ADA, Chris Martin, responds, "We are very confident that the overwhelming majority of dentists employ universal precautions and effective infection-control procedures. However, it is always a wise idea for the patient to insist that his dentist employ such protections.")

Douglas Feldman, Ph.D., a medical anthropologist in the department of psychiatry at the University of Miami (Fla.) School of Medicine, has done extensive research on the social aspects of AIDS, including talking to a number of dentists in an attempt to measure whether AIDS patients have access to needed dental services or not. He concludes that Acer "murdered six of his patients," probably because "for some reason he had been upset by them." Acknowledging that the murder theory is "politically correct" to dentists and surgeons, he told this reporter that it is the "only theory in which you cannot punch holes." Feldman says that a grand jury with subpoena powers should investigate Acer's friends and former sexual partners and that contact tracing should be done on the dentist's 1400 patients who have not been tested for HIV. "If this contact tracing were done," he said, "I'd bet we would find another five or six cases of AIDS caused by Acer."

The news media have reached different conclusions about the mystery. The American Broadcasting Company (ABC) interviewed one of Acer's male friends and concluded from his comments that the dentist had murdered the six patients out of anger over society's indifference to AIDS patients who are gay men like himself. On the other hand, the British Broadcasting Corporation rejected the murder scenario, followed Dr. Lewis' lead, and reported that the deaths were due to patient-to-patient infections carried through the unsterilized dental devices known as prophy angles.

Jaffe, the man on the spot, is unpersuaded by all of the above. He says, "I agree with Dr. Lewis that dental instruments should be heat-sterilized, but his theory on patient-to-patient infection goes far beyond any data. I think that this theory, which is a subtheory of our contaminated-instrument scenario, is the least likely way by which Acer's patients might have been infected. And the man interviewed by ABC-TV told a different story in his sworn deposition. He said under oath only that Acer was angry about his AIDS infection, and he specifically said that Acer did *not* tell him that he was going to intentionally infect patients."

It remains an irony of the CDC investigation that Bergalis, a college student, a virgin, and an innocent victim, was put through the wringer with questions about her possible drug and sexual habits, while Acer, the source of her fatal infection, was able to stonewall investigators. The Florida dentist died on September 3, 1990, shortly after Bergalis' AIDS infection was reported, and he went to the grave known only by media descriptions that he was "kind, gentle, boring, and reclusive." The answer to his mystery may have died with him.

Jaffe explains, "We had to be critical with Bergalis, or none of our peers in epidemiology would have taken us seriously. As it was, a lot of people didn't believe our report, anyway. Originally, we did the DNA sequencing in the expectation that the tests would *disprove* a link between Acer's viral strain and that of Bergalis. Instead, the tests confirmed that the dentist was the source.

"We were only able to interview Acer once. When our investigators showed up the next morning, he had retained an attorney and refused to answer any more questions. In that one interview, he seemed cooperative, said that he did not recall doing anything that might have infected his patients, and volunteered a sample of his blood, which is something he did not have to do. We do not have police powers and we were not able to subpoena Acer's testimony or to subpoena the testimony of others to develop Acer's 'biography,' as law-enforcement investigators might have been able to do.

"And, the state's attorneys office in Martin County, Fla. (where Acer practiced in Stuart, Fla.), has consistently said that there was not enough evidence to go forward with a murder investigation and that, in any event, there is no point to it since the supposed perpetrator—Acer—is dead."

Jaffe also touches on a sore point—the way dental and medical organizations reacted to the CDC's initial announcement of the Bergalis case and its convening of a meeting of AIDS consultants to develop public policy.

"This was an extremely difficult case for CDC," he says, "and raised some extremely difficult policy questions. The question of a dentist infecting a patient with AIDS and the possibility that other health professionals performing invasive procedures, like surgeons, might do likewise is one that pits the interests of patients against the interests of health professionals.

"The dental and medical groups, including the ADA and the AMA, wished the whole thing would go away, but we had no choice but to convene a meeting. Although the risk might be remote, it is not zero and AIDS is a fatal disease. It is very difficult to communicate the idea of remote risk when people are hysterical about AIDS. We could not just say, 'Well, this is a one-in-a-million happening, so let's not worry.' The case had to be taken seriously. And, at the time, Congress was considering legislation to mandate HIV tests for health workers.

"So, the CDC was in the middle of a very tough situation and it still is. Our cause was not helped by the reaction of the health professionals. The dental and medical professions were very ambivalent about the Acer case. At the beginning, they wanted to pretend it hadn't happened. The ADA and the AMA had to be dragged very reluctantly into the process of designing some kind of guidelines to make sure that this didn't happen again.

"The attitude of these health professionals did not endear them to their patients, who were left with the impression that the dentists and doctors were only looking out for themselves.

"That was my impression, too. It was wrong of them to imply, 'It never happened,' and to imply, 'This is not a problem,' because 'we know better.' This comes across as patronizing and self-serving and simply does not work. It might have worked 20 to 30 years ago, but it does not work today.

"It seems to me that the right approach might have been for the ADA and AMA to have said: 'We're not sure what has happened here, but we take it very seriously and we are going to work closely with the CDC to get to the bottom of this and then to report back to our members.'"

Will it happen again?

"It could," Jaffe says, "but I certainly hope it does not. In the past year, there have been four clusters of hepatitis B being transmitted from surgeons to patients during invasive procedures; three in the United Kingdom and one in the U.S. The fact is that the current CDC guidelines for evaluation of HIV-infected health workers are voluntary and we have no way of enforcing them. And dentists and surgeons do stick themselves with needles and under current technology this risk cannot be reduced to zero. So, another case *could* happen. And, if we do get another documented case of HIV transmission from health worker to patient, there will be a tremendous public demand for mandatory testing of health workers. So, I hope that this does not happen again."

He concludes, "Whatever happened with Acer has to be very unlikely because as far as we know it never happened before and as far as we know it has never happened since. With Acer, all the possibilities we are picking over seem to be wrong, and, yet, one has to be right.

"I wish I knew which one. Maybe, if Sherlock Holmes were a CDC employee, I could tell you what happened."

THE CABBAGE DIAGNOSIS

Beautiful Dreamer

Asked to solve a deadly epidemic, '60s dropout Wally Schlech, M.D., seized the day

Beginning in January 1985, almost 150 cases of food poisoning were reported in the Los Angeles area and more than 40 people died. Federal investigators traced the outbreak to contaminated soft cheese manufactured in the California plants of Jalisco Mexican Products, Inc., which promptly shut down. The Food and Drug Administration began to sample all imported cheeses and dispatched inspectors to more than half of the nation's remaining soft cheese plants to search for the pathogen responsible, resulting in the recall of tens of thousands of packages of Brie, Camembert, and Liederkranz in addition to the Jalisco products. By August the crisis was over.

The Jalisco cheese epidemic ended in short order largely because, four years earlier, an unlikely medical detective from the U.S. Centers for Disease Control had spent most of his summer tracing the fatal course of a similar outbreak in Halifax, Nova Scotia. In discovering a route by which a deadly bacterium could infest food, the investigator solved a 64-year-old mystery and became something of a hero in the albeit obscure lore of epidemiology, the study of the distribution of disease. The bacterium he tracked is called *Listeria monocytogenes*; the sleuth is Wally Schlech.

Wally Schlech: The name itself bespeaks ordinariness. And Schlech the man is nobody's archetype of a hero. Short, bearded, and bespectacled, he looks the part of the avuncular physician and father of five that he is today. But the sparkle in his blue eyes hints at a past that was something less than domestic. A self-described hell-raiser, Schlech was a member of the class at Williams College whose activities in the late Sixties forced the institution to ban fraternities—until he flunked out, that is. An experience junkie, he then joined the Navy as a hospital corpsman and dodged mortar fire in Vietnam before returning to the United States to finish his college education in relative tranquillity. Deciding that a career as a physician might keep him on the straight and narrow, he studied medicine in New York—occasionally satisfying his craving for pure thrills by rappeling down the sides of Manhattan high rises.

In 1980, when he was thirty-four, he signed on for a two-year tour of duty with the CDC's Epidemic Intelligence Service, the department responsible for uncovering the causal agents of disease epidemics. The stakes at the EIS suited Schlech's high-risk ambitions: Mysterious new killers—Legionnaires' disease, toxic shock syndrome, and the very first cases of AIDS—were offering challenge, opportunity, and possible fame to brash young staffers. "I was hot to trot to prove myself," he says.

Instead, Schlech was assigned to an outbreak of an obscure disease called listeriosis that was making a rare appearance in the Maritime Provinces of Canada. The disease attacked animals far more often than people: It had wiped out South African river rats in 1917 and New Zealand sheep in 1935, and devastated populations of North American chinchillas, European cattle, hogs, silver foxes, and Hungarian geese in the Fifties.

Its human offensives had been far less dramatic: The most recent included 9 cases in Pennsylvania between 1976 and 1977; 23 cases in Boston in 1979; and 22 cases in New Zealand in 1980. Although *L. monocytogenes* had been isolated in 1927, no one had succeeded in figuring out how the bacterium got from its customary habitat of soil, water, and vegetation to people it infected. Generations of EIS investigators had tried to identify the mode of transmission and failed. A listeriosis epidemic was considered a graveyard assignment.

But regardless of the assignment's lack of glamour, Schlech understood that the disease spelled disaster for the people it struck. The flulike symptoms of listeriosis weren't easy to distinguish from those of many other disorders, but the bacterium could attack the brain, causing encephalitis and meningitis, and, in women, the womb, causing abortions, stillbirths, and sometimes fatal defects in newborns. In the Canadian epidemic, listeria was appearing in pregnant women, and it was killing their babies. The epicenter of the outbreak was Halifax, where ten cases had been documented in one month alone; ordinarily, the city's only maternity hospital would see one case every year or two.

When he got there, Halifax authorities told Schlech that 34 pregnant women and 7 other adults had come down with the disease. Most of the patients presented textbook symptoms: The pregnant women suffered sudden, very high fevers, and many had abortions, stillbirths, or seriously ill newborns. Seven children died. Six of the other infected adults had meningitis; three of them died. Schlech had designed a questionnaire to try to find the common thread among the patients, but none turned up. Instead, the clue that excited him came from the one atypical case: an eighty-one-year-old man who was recuperating from *L. monocytogenes*-induced pneumonia.

Knowing that pneumonia was almost unheard-of in the literature on listeriosis, Schlech carefully questioned the man and his wife. Some of Schlech's luckless predecessors had hypothesized that listeriosis was a food-borne disease, and the EIS agent decided to pay special attention to the diets of the victims. The couple told him they lived on a tight budget and ate their meals at home. When the man's wife showed Schlech around their apartment, he made a beeline for the refrigerator and sent all of its contents to a lab for culturing.

Meanwhile, Schlech learned that the man with pneumonia had previously suffered a stroke and, because his gag reflex was suppressed, had difficulty swallowing. In what proved to be a brilliant conjecture, Schlech figured that the man had choked on some contaminated food, sending the bacterium straight to his lungs. When a package of leftover coleslaw from the couple's fridge turned up positive for *L. monocytogenes*, Schlech begged his CDC supervisors for more time. "I think I can crack this case," he told them.

Schlech distributed a new questionnaire with an item on coleslaw. Two thirds of the survivors remembered eating it. He then compiled two lists. The first was of all the Maritime Provinces' farmers who had reported recent cases of listeriosis among their animals. The second identified all cabbage suppliers for the plant in Middleton, Nova Scotia, that had shredded the coleslaw Schlech found in the Halifax couple's kitchen. One name showed up on both lists: a cabbage farmer on Prince Edward Island. When Schlech paid a surprise visit to that desolate area, he found the listeriosis connection.

The farmer had conscientiously reported the deaths of two of his sheep to the local authorities, who had determined the cause to be listeriosis. He had also used his animals' manure to fertilize his cabbage patch. The farmer told Schlech that, after harvesting his cabbage, he had kept it in a cold-storage shed over the winter of 1980-81. The following spring he sent 5,000 pounds of his harvest to the Middleton coleslaw manufacturer.

Schlech knew that *L. monocytogenes* is one of the few organisms whose growth is actually enhanced by cold—whether generated by Mother Nature or a refrigerator. The overwintering of the farmer's cabbage could only have made the bacterial brew more potent. Schlech took samples of cabbage, soil, and especially manure and rushed back to Halifax.

Back in the city he bought several unopened packages of the Middleton coleslaw and sent them off to the lab. The cabbage in each 49-cent package tested positive for *L. monocytogenes*. Finally, Schlech phoned the listeriosis survivors who had not remembered eating the coleslaw and described the coleslaw packages. "It was wonderful," he says. "The packages jolted their memories and they all said, 'Oh, yeah, I did have some of that . . .'"

As part of his celebration Schlech bought a crate of Canadian lobsters and flew back to Atlanta. His name was in the record books. By understanding the mode of transmission of *L. monocytogenes*, medical investigators were able to answer a host of related questions about how the bacterium spreads and who is most susceptible to it. Years later, when listeriosis was diagnosed in the first several victims of what became known as the Jalisco epidemic, medical detectives knew the vehicle of infection was something edible, and solving the epidemic was just a matter of finding out which foods the patients had ingested in common.

Listeriosis not only made Schlech a legend in his field; it also led him and his family to a new home and a new way of life. In the fall of 1982, Schlech joined the staff of Victoria General Hospital in Halifax, the last place he'd imagined he'd want to be just a year and a half before. Mellowed perhaps by success, he began raising hay, not hell, and now collects stamps, coaches Little League baseball, and serves as an elder in his church.

As chief of infectious diseases at Victoria General, Schlech is getting a second shot at those elusive and career-making pathogens that were so new a decade ago. He spends about half of his time caring for AIDS patients, bringing his usual bravado to the front lines. "We're going to beat this disease, too," he says with typical enthusiasm. "I believe that by the year 2000 we'll be well on our way to having a vaccine and a combination of drugs that will keep the virus in check. AIDS will become just another chronic disease that we can control indefinitely, like diabetes and high blood pressure."

Sometimes, Schlech longs for the good old days when there were clear-cut answers like tainted coleslaw in the fridge. Even now his ambitions aren't entirely typical of a physician and family man. "I might try to make a go of my hay farm, maybe raise cattle, too," he says, elaborating on a daydream of early retirement. "Or maybe I'll become a medical missionary to Third World nations." Whatever he chooses, it's hard to doubt that Wally Schlech will succeed.

NEVER MARRY A DOCTOR?

Serious Condition

The gains and pains of a medical marriage

Her favorite restaurant was Chicago's Shangri-la, but the early days of her marriage to a physician hardly measured up to the name.

"I must have seen half the movies in Chicago," she recalls. "There were no beepers in those days, but they always knew how to find my husband. I always told him that I married him despite the M.D., and the first years of our marriage were really rough. He was doing general practice, treating heart attacks and delivering babies, and he worked at least four nights a week. The only times I saw him were on Wednesdays, Saturday nights and Sundays—and then only if he didn't get an emergency call.

"It got even worse when at age 35 he decided he didn't want to keep up this pace. He decided to switch from general practice to dermatology; that meant taking a three-year residency at Cook County Hospital. He would spend the afternoon he was off back at his clinic caring for his old patients; he had to spend his nights sleeping at the hospital. For three years he spent only one night a week at home.

"But that's the way it was for a medical wife of my era. We were married in 1946, and men were expected to work hard. Their wives were expected to stay home and uncomplainingly raise a family. All my friends who were married to doctors lived the same way."

This medical couple, who prefer anonymity, have now been married for 40 years. The rewards of their sometimes-painful life together are obvious: Their Lake Shore Drive condominium takes up the entire top floor of a prestigious building, commanding an awesome view of Lake Michigan and Oak Street Beach. He is a noted art collector, specializing in "works on paper," and the walls are lined with original lithographs and drawings by Picasso and Van Gogh. Antiques and fine china complete the decor. When one walks in the front door, he is standing face to face with a priceless oil nude by Matisse, the only oil in the doctor's discriminating collection. Coffee is served by a housekeeper.

As she reminisces he sits in another room, working the phones. At age 66, he says he is "retired," but he still finds time to run two Chicago hotels and two Chicago banks (real estate and banking are also among his passions), as well as spending two nights and Saturday afternoons practicing dermatology at the large group practice he established on the city's Southwest Side. Not to mention his leadership role in civic, commercial and cultural activities.

She is a bit wistful. Waving her hands, she says: "Oh, if John [as we shall call him] were not so intense—obsessed really—we probably would not have all this. I'm into comfort, but I also like simple things. Sure, the art collection is nice, but we don't need all of it. And we don't need *all* these antiques. Sometimes I think that our life gets cluttered up trying to impress a lot of people who really don't care that much about us and about whom we don't care that much. It can be a waste of time.

"I like to get away to our condo in Miami Beach because it's so much simpler. This year we'll be going for the Christmas holidays and taking two of our grandchildren. I'm going to stay in Florida right through the middle of February. I've found that when I return to Chicago with John, he never wants to go back to Florida; if I stay in Florida, he'll come back to join me. I used to love to walk on the [Miami] beach, but it's no longer safe, and John refuses to take walks with me. He thinks that if you take strolls on the beach, you must be a 'surfer.' He will only walk *to* places where he can *do* things. So now I no longer walk on the beach; I swim in a pool instead."

Theirs was marriage made in an era when the doctor was married to medicine. The patient came first—and often last. Their three children, two daughters and a son, were born during the first five years of marriage, and the family quickly got used to the doctor's absences. He switched to dermatology so he could have a "more orderly" life, but he quickly got into real estate and banking to fill up his time.

He was always a good provider, and the family lived in a lovely five-bedroom suburban home, where Mary (as we shall call her) "became a full-time gardener," in addition to chairing committees for numerous civic groups, teaching school and working in her husband's office. "I was always good at finding things to do."

Both John and Mary stressed education to their children, and John—to Mary's occasional dismay—also demanded self-reliance. The children are all achievers: The son is an attorney and bank president, as well as a pianist, sailor and musician; one daughter is an attorney, the other a teacher and real-estate appraiser. All three are married; John and Mary have six grandchildren.

Since Mary used to be a social worker and teacher, she respects achievement and its rewards, but she adds, "I guess I like low-key. If we do something, fine; if we don't, that's fine, too. John tends to be consumed by his passions, and this can cause problems."

The object of her ruminations enters the room and promptly takes over the interview.

"When I was younger," he begins. "I'm still young, but I used to be younger. Well, sure, in the early days I worked very, very hard. But today nothing bothers me. I used to think that Mary was much calmer than me, but now I think it's the other way around."

She interjects: "Aha, that's what you say, but I don't believe it."

He tells a story. "I love to listen to loud music. Our neighbors used to think I was nuts, turning the stereo up full blast; but with classical music I wanted to hear everything the treble and the bass and the cymbals. That's the way it sounds in the orchestra. My son told me, "You know, Dad, I think I owe my love of music to your putting Horowitz on full blast. It made me appreciate the passion of the music."

Mary says: "You could hear it a block away. The neighbors thought he must be off his rocker. I guess I just like my music a little softer. He could use a little gentleness, a little softness."

John explains: "I'm a very forceful, opinionated person, but so is she. That's why we've stayed together for 40 years. My passion is life, and everybody says of me, 'He loves what he does.' Well, you could be known for things a lot worse."

Mary: "I've always done what I wanted to do. I had to or John would have overwhelmed me. We even vote differently. I've liked a lot of losers."

John interjects: "I'm a capitalist to the core and a limousine liberal, but I've backed a few losers, too."

He softened a little. "You know, Mrs. Smith [as we shall call them] is a very wealthy woman for one reason. When we decided to get married in February, she insisted that it be February 15, not February 14. She wanted two presents every year, for Valentine's Day *and* our anniversary. That decision has made her a wealthy woman."

Mary smiles. "Oh, yes, I have a lot of wonderful gifts. John is very successful at what he does, and it is very important to him to be consumed by what he does. His work is his passion. My passions are family and friends."

John: "On our 30th wedding anniversary, we had a party for 130 people, and about 50 were people who Mary knew *before* we met. She has a genius for friendship, and some of her best friends today she knew when she was 10. Oh, I picked her because she was self-reliant, and pretty and smart and with a sense of humor, too. I knew that she could put up with me, and, besides, I never thought of myself as the hardest-working guy in the world anyway."

He says he'll never give up medicine. "I'll tell you why. It's the only area in life that is not adversarial. In medicine the patient and the physician are working *together* for the same result. A few days ago I saw a 14-year-old boy with an anal wart the size of a cauliflower. It was red and angry and painful, and he was afraid to tell his parents. At first, I thought that it was an (sexual) abuse situation, but it turned out not. With drugs, I've been able to shrink it. I can't explain how gratifying this is. It's like the teenager with psoriasis who's afraid to go out of the house. I cleared up his face, and he thought it was a miracle. I thought we both might cry.

"You know, I've practiced for 40 years in a Bohemian section of the city, and these people live differently than the folks on Lake

Shore Drive. They're not as fortunate, and I pay close attention to their skin. You see babies with blotchy skin, signs of poor hygiene and nutrition. When my son's daughter was born, I told him how fortunate she was to be born in a good hospital with good genes and to have a loving family to take good care of her.

"I don't get aggravated by anything anymore because when you've seen people who are sick and dying, you realized that all the rest of it is unimportant."

What drives him?

"You mean the monkey on my back?" he responds. "My father was a doctor, and he taught me to be self-reliant. Maybe I'm trying to please him. Whatever I do I want to do right. I got out of general practice because that 20 or 30 seconds you wait for a baby to start breathing after delivery was starting to seem longer and longer. I didn't want to do it when I was 50."

Mary interjects: "You said you wanted to retire at 45, but that was before the real estate and the banking."

John: "I got into the hotels and motels to help out Mary's father and brother, who were in the business, and we quickly realized that to buy a hotel you had to pay a lot of interest to the banks. So we bought our own bank. And I had a good business mind because we had always operated a medical group practice. I never felt any particular stress."

Mary: "Well, you had a heart attack."

John's voice rises: "I did not have a heart attack. There were some enzyme changes, perhaps indicating some ischemic changes, but all I know is that the EKG today doesn't show any damage to the heart muscle and I'm rated 'normal' by my life insurer."

Mary: "Well, the medical records said it was a heart attack, and you started to cut out the red meat and the eggs and the salt."

What would he call it? John concludes: "I had a cardiac event, but there was no neuromusclar damage. I feel terrific."

John continues: "I don't play golf, so I've always found other things to occupy my time. Sure, I wish I could have done more. I would have liked to spend more time with my family."

Mary's voice rises: "Don't forget those three years you spent at Cook County with only one night a week at home And our house was robbed once when I was all alone."

John responds: "Well, you weren't in the house and nobody was hurt. That's the important thing." Reflecting on the early days, he smiles: "You know, after we had been married for five years, I said to Mary, 'Jeez, don't you ever wear anything but a nightgown?' I never saw her except very late at night and very early in the morning.

"Later on, I wished that Mrs. Smith would have included me more often at the family dinner. I ate a lot of meals at home alone."

Mary: "Well, it was your choice. You never made it home on time, and the kids had to eat at a regular time. I said, 'Give me a time, and we'll eat together,' but you could never make it."

The happiest times, they both agree, were vacations with the children.

Mary adds: "Sometimes I wanted to go without the kids, because if they came along it wasn't a vacation for me, but he would say, 'No, I don't see enough of them, and I want to bring them along.' Our family was always last on his house-call list. When our children got sick, he would *tell* me what to do. When his partner's wife had to go to the hospital to have a baby, the neighbors had to take her. Her husband was delivering a baby! It was a way of life."

John leaves the room, and Mary sums up: "Sure I'd do it all over again. We've been mostly happy. What I like most about John is his loyalty and his passion. What I would change in his obsessiveness."

She is growing impatient: "I have to cook an ethnic dish for Thanksgiving dinner tomorrow, and I'm running late. We've had some problems with our children and our in-laws because of competitiveness—sibling rivalry and rivalry between the in-laws. I wish it were otherwise, but I'll make the best of it. I enjoy my time with my daughters, and when I'm with my son, I enjoy that, too. I wish that we could all be together, but I can't tell 40-year-olds what to do."

John returns to conclude, "It was always thus."

ACTS OF COURAGE

Hooked on Danger

Cardiac nurse Cherie Bremer-Kamp, R.N., lost her fingers and toes while futilely trying to save the life of her late husband, Chris Chandler, M.D., when the daring duo made a fatal attempt to conquer a Himalayan peak

The gentle rocking of the boat, docked in San Francisco Bay, gives off a steady background groan. Softly, in a clipped Australian accent, critical-care nurse Cherie Bremer-Kamp, R.N., describes the tragic morning of January 15, 1985, when she and her husband, Chris Chandler, M.D., awoke at 26,000 feet on Mount Kanchenjunga, the world's third-highest peak, and realized to their horror that he was suffering from a fatal swelling of the brain.

Bremer-Kamp and Dr. Chandler were adventurers, united in their bond to live life on the edge, hooked on danger. In the winter of 1985, they were, by climbing without oxygen, "meeting the mountain on its own terms." That January 15 was their 49th day on the Himalayan peak, and when they awoke they were only 2,000 feet shy of thc summit. "I was very excited," she recalls. "We were optimistic that we would make it that day to the top."

She is sitting below the deck of their 36-foot sailboat, the *Laylah* (which in numerology, the study of the occult significance of numbers, means "love"), her elbows resting on the table where earlier this year she laboriously wrote a book describing her adventures with Dr. Chandler, and she stares out at the sea. Waving her hand toward the magnificent San Francisco Bay, she says, "Oh, this is beautiful, but it is a different kind of beauty. It doesn't give you a charge. Chris and I both were deadened by the routine of normal everyday living, and we enjoyed putting ourselves to the test of climbing and sailing adventures. Danger was an essential element."

Pointing to the reporter, she adds, "Right where you're sitting, well, three years ago our boat was capsized in the North Pacific by hurricane-force winds, and that entire area was swamped with water. We had intended to head for Valdez, Alaska, to do some ice-climbing in our own backyard, but the boat was severely damaged, and we were lucky to be able to limp into San Francisco harbor. The boat's been here in Sausalito ever since, and I live here now with my daughter, Annapurna. Chris and I built the boat in Puget Sound, Wash., and before the accident we sailed it down to San Diego and on to Hawaii. It was so boring that we came to call it the 'geriatric cruise.' Chris and I were not the type to sail to Tahiti. No, we wanted to sail to Antarctica."

Brushing the hair from her eyes, she continues: "Non-climbers are uncomprehending of what I have to say, but to Chris and me the mastering of danger offers insight into life. The word for 'thrill' comes from the Greek words meaning 'to penetrate,' and for us climbing mountains was a way to cut through the farce of everyday living. It was a cleansing process."

There are photos of Mount Kanchenjunga lining the side of the boat and to an untrained eye the summit looks benign. "Ah, but you see with the eyes of a non-climber. That rise there is 500 feet of solid ice, and it is pure hell to try to climb it," she explains.

When you are high in the Himalayas, the highest and loneliest place on Earth, the air is very thin and very clear and the distances are very hard to judge. On that fateful morning in the winter of 1985, the summit of Kanchenjunga looked very close, indeed, but it was to remain very far away.

In 1985, the 38-year-old nurse and the 36-year-old physician possessed imposing credentials to challenge the mountain.

Dr. Chandler, an emergency-room physician from Seattle, had made it to the summit of the world's highest peak, Mount Everest, as part of the 1976 American Bicentennial Expedition.

The Australian-born Bremer-Kamp had been climbing in the Himalayas since she was 24, and her daughter, Annapurna, 15, is named after the Himalayan peak across the valley in Nepal from Mount Dhaulagiri, which Bremer-Kamp climbed when she was five months pregnant with her daughter-to-be (from a first marriage to American-born climber and anthropologist Terry Bech; their son, Daniel, lives with his father in Holland. Dr. Chandler has three sons from a first marriage).

The physician and nurse had met and fallen in love in 1978 on an expedition to Pakistan's K2, the world's second-highest peak. It was during that climb, which was a large expedition, that the two turned their backs on large, highly organized mountain-climbing efforts, opting, instead, for two-person expeditions, with minimum support from Sherpa cooks and porters. In the summer of 1981, climbing in this minimalist style, Dr. Chandler and Bremer-Kamp had without oxygen made it to 26,000 feet on Kanchenjunga, but an avalanche buried their equipment and prevented a move on the summit. The government of Nepal granted permission for a new attempt in 1982, but Bremer-Kamp broke her foot while training. The next available climbing time slot was the winter of 1985.

Bremer-Kamp says, "In the winter, the cold is unbelievable on Kanchenjunga and the jet-stream winds, blowing at up to 200 miles per hour, can blow you right off the mountain. But there is less risk of avalanches than there is in the summer and there is almost no snow. The risk evens out, just as it does for climbing without oxygen. It is harder to breathe, sure, but, on the other hand you can move faster because you don't have to carry all that heavy oxygen equipment."

On the morning of January 15, 1985, the two were at almost the identical spot they had reached four years earlier. The beckoning summit of Kanchenjunga was thrown up millions of years ago when the Earth violently crumpled and formed a mountain chain stretching 1,500 miles wide and 150 miles deep across the subcontinent of India. The spectacular Kanchenjunga massif, located on the Nepalese-Tibetan border, has five major summits, four of which are above 26,000 feet, an altitude at which a curtain appears to descend, above which mortals intrude at the greatest of risk. In Tibetan mythology, the name "Kanchenjunga" translates as "five treasure houses in the snow." It is believed that the five summits hold the treasures of the gods: gold, silver, copper, corn, and sacred books. Bremer-Kamp, Dr. Chandler, and their Sherpa porter, Mongol Sing Tamang, were only 2,000 feet below the main 28,168-foot summit.

On this brilliantly sunny day in Sausalito, Bremer-Kamp closes her eyes and tries to bring it all back, the way it was that frightful morning on Kanchenjunga. She says, "You know, when I wrote my manuscript I was almost in a state of hypnosis. I would lie awake nights recalling the climb, and although the next morning might be warm and sunny I would be sitting here shivering in a sweater while I wrote. Retelling the story she wrote, she says:

"We were climbing the north face of the summit, and we were largely protected from the wind, blowing from the south and southwest. The temperature—without wind—was about 60 below.

"We had spent the night sleeping in an ice cave. The next morning Chris had the assignment of melting ice on the butane stove so we could have some water to drink. We all were profoundly dehydrated and the cold was deep within us.

"At this altitude, we knew that we all were functioning with an impaired IQ. All climbers know this, and we cope by instinctively following the rules we have drawn up down on the ground. The cardinal rule is to descend at the first sign of high-altitude sickness.

"I was outside the cave when I noticed with horror that the stove's light had gone off and Chris was breathing gas fumes. At 26,000 feet, the oxygen is only one-third normal and, now, the carbon monoxide fumes were competing with Chris for the available oxygen. I began to scream at him when it hit me that he was in a bad way.

"He was unable to dress himself and unable to fasten his crampons. I moved inside the cave to try to help him, and then he said, 'I can't see anything. I'm blind.'

"My heart froze and my fingers turned into claws. My body must have gotten a sudden surge of adrenaline—the most potent vasoconstrictor of all—and the blood vessels to my hands and feet tightened up as if a clamp had come down on a garden hose. It was so cold that my fingers were frostbitten within seconds. And I had been blaming the gas fumes for Chris' deteriorating condition, and now I instinctively realized that he had probably developed cerebral edema.

"Panic-stricken, I tore off my gloves to look at my hands. My fingers had become white, like marble. I knocked them together and it sounded as if I were banging two pieces of wood against one another. I showed them to Chris. He giggled, 'They are pretty bad, aren't they?' He was like a little kid.

"I left my gloves off, because my claws needed to be exposed to dress Chris. I thought that I would have to sacrifice my hands to save our bodies. I imagined that my hands would have to be cut off at the wrists. Chris, too, sensed the danger. He said, 'Yeah, we'd better go down; we'll try again tomorrow.'

"Chris was acting as if he were punch-drunk, but we placed him in the middle of the rope, between Mongol and me. But Chris began to topple over and the Mongol couldn't support him. I had lost my ice ax and we fell 300 feet before the rope snagged on a frozen snowdrift, stopping us only 30 feet before a cliff. If the rope hadn't snagged, we would have fallen off the mountain to our deaths.

"Righting ourselves, we continued down the mountain, but I had to watch Chris every step of the way.

"I wanted to make it farther down the mountain, but since it was getting dark, we decided to stop. Mongol dug out a platform on a gentle snow slope and I lay down next to Chris to try to warm him up.

"Chris kept sliding off the platform, and I couldn't control him. Fearing that he was in danger, he stood up and tried to run, but he got caught in his own sleeping bag. His last words were: 'Will somebody help me?'

"Then, he fell to the snow. I tried to do mouth-to-mouth resuscitation, but I couldn't open the zipper to his sleeping bag. It was frozen solid, coated in ice."

As death and love met on that Himalayan peak, Bremer-Kamp contemplated going with him. She recalls, "I wanted to go with Chris, but there were two things holding me back—my children, Annapurna and Daniel. I turned toward them."

She didn't know what to do with Chris. She was repulsed by the traditional climber's burial, placing the body in a crevasse, and pushing the body over a cliff was equally disgusting.

Instead, she propped him up against the ice platform so he could sit where he was, in dignity, with his pack and ice ax beside him, gazing out over one of his favorite sights—the vast plateau of Tibet. "I would like to think," she says, "that he remains there today—frozen forever above this holy place."

It took Bremer-Kamp and Mongol four days to get down the mountain to base camp at 17,000 feet. She recalls, "When they saw only two of us coming down the mountain, everyone thought that I must have died."

She was given gallons of hot tea and other fluids and bathed in hot water to try to counteract the big white patches of frostbite that covered her body. Later, she was carried by stretcher to Pele at 11,000 feet and taken by helicopter to Katmandu, Nepal, where she was flown to Bangkok, Thailand. There followed four days of hospitalization in Anchorage, Alaska, and five months in Seattle.

In the past two years, Bremer-Kamp has endured guilt and depression and 10 operations to amputate all her fingers and toes. (Mongol survived but also suffered the loss of parts of his fingers and toes.)

But with the small stumps grafted on her hands just above the knuckle, she managed to write—in longhand—a manuscript about her life with Dr. Chandler. She drives a stick-shift Volkswagen about the hills of San Francisco. She plans to get her captain's license to sail the *Laylah*. She can't run, but she rides a bike up and down Mount Tamalpais. She is planning a return to nursing, hands-on critical-care nursing.

She says simply, "I want to go back and be what I was."

She desperately misses her husband, saying, "I believe in reincarnation, and I know that Chris and I will find ourselves together again. Sometimes, I get the urge to be with him, but I'm not ready to leave just yet. I used to think about it, but I realized that if I go into that black void, there is no guarantee that I will find him."

She tries again to explain why she climbs: "My father was a pilot for Qantas Airlines and he instilled in me a sense of adventure. I remember as a kid seeing photos of him on a camel in Egypt or with a yogi in India. I was always very athletic and into ballet and water-skiing and other sports, but the first time I did some rock-climbing in New Zealand I was hooked. The feeling of my body moving with the environment and my mind exercising discipline over my body really turned me on. For me, climbing was the ultimate sport.

"When Chris and I were on the mountain together, we felt that this was what we were meant to be. I really cannot describe it fully. The beauty, of course, is stunning—looking down on clouds and glaciers and villages and river valleys. But it's more than that. Chris and I were not conventionally religious people, but being on the mountain is as close to a religious experience as I've ever had. You lose yourself in the environment, and when you see a rock you realize that it's not only a rock but that it's part of a grand design. . . ."

She sighs. "It's a very powerful insight you get."

She continues, "Chris and I always had a plan. After Kanchenjunga, we were going to climb K2 together again and then we were going to sail to Antarctica. The voyage to Antarctica was going to be our last really big adventure and then Chris was going to settle down a bit and write about some of the adventures.

"Chris? What I remember is his charm. His charm and his nourishing. I am the introvert of introverts and Chris, although he appears outgoing and extroverted, was also an introvert. He was a deeply reflective man.

"On the mountain, we had plenty of time to talk and it was during one of our 'tent talks' that we decided that on our next trip to Nepal we would try to construct a building that would be part school and part medical clinic. You cannot imagine the poverty of some of these Nepalese villages. I consider myself a hardened traveler, and I've hitchhiked throughout Asia, but the poverty you will see in Nepal—amid all the natural beauty—will break your heart.

"It is sad but true that the Nepalese literally need to clean up their own shit." The total disregard for public sanitation in Nepal is appalling. This is why diseases caused by amoeba, roundworm, *Giardia,* and other parasites such as hookworm and pinworm, are common in Nepal, Bremer-Kamp notes.

She continues, "To the Nepalese villagers, he was always 'Dr. Chris,' and we always brought along extra medicines to help the sick. Chris would treat bronchitis, conjunctivitis, ear infections, abscessed teeth, and gastrointestinal disease. We tried to lace the medicines with as much health care teaching as possible, stressing the simple act of washing hands.

"Some people may think that this is like throwing a grain of salt into the sea, but we never felt this way. We intended to go back and build the clinic. If I ever make any money, that's what I'll use it for—to build that medical clinic in Chris' honor."

She has come to terms with his death as "something that was meant to be."

"It could have happened to me. I had a transient stroke in 1981 on Kanchenjunga, also while I was melting snow over the butane stove. Mine quickly passed; Chris' was catastrophic. I believe that it was meant to be."

Still, there is sadness. Over lunch at the Casa Madrona Hotel in Sausalito, high above the bay, she confides: "I'm planning to go on an expedition next summer to K2. I don't know how much climbing I can still do, but I am going to find out." And, as the tears come, she adds, "And, after that, I'm going back to try to climb Kanchenjunga myself. To find Chris, I'm going back."

In the meantime, when the nights grow long, she can turn to her manuscript, *Living on the Edge*, which will be published next March by the Australian publisher Mead & Beckett, and look for solace to the poetry she cherishes and which she has used to grace the manuscript. Dr. Chandler and Bremer-Kamp were married in 1980 near Seattle in a simple American Indian ceremony. The chapter describing her husband's death begins with the anonymous American Indian verse:

Do not stand at my grave and weep.
I am not there. I do not sleep.
I am a thousand winds that blow.
I am the diamond glint on snow.

Dr. Seat Belt

Family physician and public health officer Robert Sanders, M.D., forced a kiddie seat belt law into legislation and saved thousands of lives across the country

Tennessee leads the nation in country music, good fishing, and, thanks to one doctor's crusade, child safety. Seventeen years ago Dr. Robert Sanders of Murfreesboro, Tenn., began a campaign against the leading killer of children—automobile accidents—with a simple prescription: mandatory car seats. In 1977 he persuaded the state legislature to pass a law requiring the use of car seats for small children; 49 other states soon followed suit. With his efforts, Sanders may have done more to save lives than any physician in the country.

But back in 1975, when he embarked on his crusade, there was no guarantee of success. All Sanders knew was that as a pediatrician, he'd seen one too many death certificates for young accident victims. He wasn't alone. Car accidents across the country were killing 1,000 children under four every year—making them far and away the number one killer in that age group. As chairman of the state pediatric society's accident-prevention committee, Sanders knew why it was happening. A baby's head is both large and very fragile, and when a child becomes airborne, as it does quickly in an auto collision, it goes headfirst. In a 30 mph crash, a 10-pound baby becomes a 300-pound projectile, and a 100-pound woman exerts a 3,000-pound force—more than enough to crush the baby in her arms against the dashboard. Sanders figured that more than 90 percent of the deaths and 70 percent of the 70,000 annual injuries to children could be prevented with restraints. Clearly, legislation was the only way to get people to use car seats.

Sanders's neighbors didn't take kindly to his message. Murfreesboro is a town of 40,000 located 30 miles south of Nashville in the buckle of the Bible belt; among the locals, the conservative value of self-reliance prevails. "They didn't like being told what to do by some meddlesome do-gooder," he recalls. When he told a fellow pediatrician that 15 other nations (the number is now up to 50), including the Soviet Union, had mandatory seat-belt laws, his colleague responded, "Well, if the Soviet Union is for it, I'm agin it!"

Sanders persevered, though he was an unlikely figure to take on the legislature and the news media. Bald, bespectacled, gaunt, long-nosed, and a victim of stage fright, the mild-mannered fifty-year-old flat-out froze on camera the first time he did an interview with a local TV station. His wife, Pat, gave him some saving advice. "Forget about how you look on camera and concentrate on all those babies who are being killed," she said. "That will see you through."

It did. Sanders soon graduated to an appearance on *Good Morning America* and disciplined himself to testify before state legislative committees in Nashville. One year later he got his law passed. After the vote, Tennessee governor Ned Ray McWherter, who was then the speaker of the state house of representatives, asked, "Is Dr. Seat Belt in the house?" Sanders was—and the name stuck.

Sanders was pleased with the 1977 law but not satisfied. His bill had been watered down by a "babe in arms" amendment offered by a grandfather-legislator who didn't want to deny his daughter the "thrill of carrying her newborn home in her arms." Sanders termed it the "child crusher" amendment and launched a new battle.

During the years the amendment was in effect, 12 children in the state were killed in auto accidents because they were held by a passenger rather than secured in a car seat. One of those young victims was five-month-old Jason Davis of Murfreesboro, who in 1980 was crushed and killed because he had been sitting on his mother's lap when their car collided with another auto on a wet road. In another crash a few days later, a child who was securely strapped into a car seat escaped injury during a serious collision. The Nashville *Tennessean*, a strong supporter of car-seat legislation, ran front-page stories and photos of the two mangled cars beneath the compelling headline LUCKY—AND UNLUCKY.

With Sanders's prodding, the unlucky driver, James Davis, later went before the Tennessee legislature and in a soft, halting voice testified, "I made a big mistake. . . . We should have strapped our son into a car seat." The "babe in arms" amendment was repealed.

In 1981, when Terri Davis gave birth to another son, Phillip, one of her husband's first calls from the hospital was to Dr. Sanders: James Davis wanted to borrow an infant car seat for Phillip's first ride home. The pediatrician had lobbied for the adoption of a program to provide "loaner" car seats to parents; he subsequently encouraged the state troopers to lend car seats to drivers who'd been ticketed for not having them. If the driver subsequently bought a seat, the ticket was voided.

Sanders, now sixty-four, says the legislation he inspired has not been as effective as he'd hoped. "Probably only half the infants under four are buckled up, and only half the adults, too. Plus many of the car seats are not properly used.

"Still, we're seeing five times as many users as before the laws," he says. "Deaths are way down and injuries are less severe, even though we have more cars on the road driving much faster."

Around home (a 370-acre working farm outside Murfreesboro), the Sanderses referred to their crusade as "The Subject." Pat Sanders played an indispensable role by mobilizing physicians' spouses and wielding an unfailing memory for legislators' faces—and votes. "I was willing to work hard in 1977 in the hope that we wouldn't have to work on it in 1978!" she says. "We were consumed by this thing."

There is much more to the Sanderses, of course, than their seat-belt campaign. Sanders recently retired as medical director of the Rutherford County Health Department, where he regularly dispensed advice that sounded a little like the dark side of a Beach Boys tune: Sex can be bad (because of AIDS and other sexually transmitted diseases); the sun can be bad (because of skin cancers, including the potentially fatal melanomas); and, of course, driving fast (with or without a belt) can be bad. Sanders spent much of his time at the county health clinic attending patients and supervising nurse-practitioners. His latest crusade is educating schoolchildren that too much sunlight can be hazardous to their health.

Sanders is a native of Tennessee who grew up in Tullahoma and graduated from Vanderbilt University School of Medicine. As a pediatrician, he found he couldn't make it in solo practice. "I used to give university-style workups," he says, "and I wasn't seeing enough patients to pay the bills. Plus my collection rate was only sixty percent: I just couldn't bear to squeeze blood from a turnip. When the public health job opened up in 1966, I jumped at it."

Now, 26 years later, Sanders says he'll miss all the fuss. "And I'll miss the crying of the children," he muses. But he leaves a proud legacy.

In an upstairs attic of the town's austerely furnished health department, a few "loaner" car seats are neatly stacked. Sanders himself etched a serial number into every one and proudly notes, "So few are left because the idea caught on and people are using them." (It's now a state law that all newborns must leave the hospital in a car seat.)

In his cluttered office at the county clinic, next to plaques commemorating his contributions to his profession, is a 1971 cartoon from the *New Yorker* that captures Sanders's philosophy of life. Across the green ground I AM is inscribed; above the ground, strung between two poles, is a swaying clothesline draped with rickety objects that spell out I HAVE; in the bright sky above is a shower of lights proclaiming I DO.

"That's what my life is all about," says Sanders. For the thousands of infants whose lives were saved because of his persistence, Sanders has done plenty.

Mr. Lean

Amateur cardiologist Phil Sokolof is making food giants see the lite with his advertising campaign against fatty foods and high cholesterol

Phil who?

Exactly. In America, one man can still make a difference, especially if he is a workaholic with a highly personal mission, an expert in show-biz advertising techniques—and a multimillionaire. This is Phil Sokolof the anticholesterol crusader from Omaha, the man who has used full-page newspaper ads to make "cholesterol," "saturated fats" and "tropical oils" into household names for bad nutrition.

The "cholesterol era" is only seven years old, dating from 1984, when Time magazine put two eggs on its cover and sounded the battle alarm. Sokolof has caught the wave. Armed with passion, deep pockets, a telephone and the ability to write his own ads in a compelling style and pay to have them published from coast to coast, he has helped lead the charge.

Almost single-handedly, he has taken on this nation's food giants and created a "reformulation revolution" —that is, a change from traditional high-cholesterol, high-fat offerings to the new low-cholesterol, low-fat substitutes, a swap that promises to help keep people's blood vessels clear and to reduce the incidence of heart disease—the nation's No. 1 killer.

In recognition of this act of magic, Sokolof, 68, was honored in 1989 by the trade publication Food Business, and he has become a minor celebrity, appearing on network TV and showing up in publications ranging from Advertising Age to USA Today.

Dr. William Castelli, the director of the famed Framingham (Mass.) ongoing study of risk factors for heart disease, calls Sokolof "my folk hero. He has made Americans aware that too much saturated fat leads to too high cholesterol."

Indeed, Sokolof has redefined the terms "saturated fat" and "tropical oils" to the nutritionally illiterate and has driven home the saving truth that high fats convert to high cholesterol, even in foods labeled to have "zero cholesterol."

Sokolof's finest hour, perhaps, came last spring when McDonald's announced that it would begin offering the "McLean Deluxe," a hamburger developed by researchers at Auburn University to stay tasty with only 9 percent fat, way down from the 20 to 30 percent found in most burgers.

The new lean hamburger replaces the extra fat with water that is bound to the beef with carrageen, a seaweed derivative. The low-fat burger still tastes good, according to early reports, but the final verdict remains unknown. Persuading the fast-food chains to offer low-fat beef had been Sokolof's No. 1 goal.

Capitalizing on this apparent capitulation by industry-leader McDonald's, Sokolof promptly wrote an ad and a press release praising the change that he had helped force.

He paid for full-page ads in newspapers across the country to mimic his earlier ads that had trumpeted, "McDonald's, your hamburgers have too much fat!" He repeated the arresting heading, but this time he added a big black overlay proclaiming: "*not any more!* McDonald's new low-fat hamburger has only 9 percent fat! Burger King, Wendy's and Hardee's. We are calling on you to follow McDonald's leadership and offer the public this revolutionary lean, only 9 percent fat hamburger!"

Pressing on, Sokolof's message added: "We are also calling on the U.S. Dept. of Agriculture, which administers the National School Lunch Program, to introduce this revolutionary product into all our schools. Forty-four percent of the meat we eat is in the form of hamburger. This innovative ground beef will substantially reduce the cholesterol levels of the American public as it replaces greasy hamburger."

Sokolof's press release, mailed to food-industry opinion leaders, noted: "Sokolof and McDonald's are working in tandem to promote this breakthrough in low-fat nutrition. The public need makes strange bedfellows."

It was a typical performance for the former song-and-dance man who quit his entertainment career to make millions in the construction industry and the stock market. Sokolof has spent the last six years—and $3 million of his fortune—to take his cholesterol crusade directly to the American people through a series of hard-hitting ads headlined, "The poisoning of America." The campaign, targeted at the big food firms and at the congressmen who can help force labeling changes, has proven that it pays to advertise.

In July 1990 Sokolof paid for ads telling McDonald's that "Your hamburgers have too much fat!" and "Your french fries are cooked with beef tallow." Days later, the chain announced that it would cook its french fries in vegetable oil, though company officials emphatically denied any connection to the ads, contending the change was the result of eight years of research.

In the fall of 1990, Sokolof took on Congress in a series of ads that thundered: "It's wrong, America! Special interests are trying to deprive you (of the benefits of a food labeling bill)." Legislation to tighten food labeling was passed, and Sokolof was named an honorary cosponsor. He was exultant. "Let's say that only 15 percent of the population are label-readers," Sokolof says. "Well, to please those label-readers, the manufacturers are going to have to improve their products, and everyone will benefit!"

Sokolof has been the right man at the right time for the right trend before. In 1955, he also had a bright idea.

"Drywall was replacing plaster in the construction industry at that time," he recalls, "and I was astounded to learn how much was being charged for the metal strips that protected the wall boards. I decided that I could build a better corner beam."

He rented a building for $75 a month, bought a $15,000 machine and was turning a profit by the second month. "I went on the road to sell the product," he says, "and returned home to manufacture it. I even typed the sales orders."

In short order, Phillips Manufacturing was a major manufacturer and distributor of steel components for the construction industry, and Sokolof was a millionaire. "I gave the company my first name," he adds, "because it sounds a little zippier than 'Sokolof's!' In the early days, I was a one-man band."

Before that, Sokolof sang for the big bands. "My father had wound me up early to be an aggressive go-getter," he explains. "I learned how to tap-dance when I was 6, and as a kid I did a song-and-dance act across the state of Nebraska. Later, instead of going to college, I went on the road as a singer with the big bands. My favorite song was 'Embraceable You.'

"It was quite an education. This was the 1940s, and I was making, maybe, $100 a week—big money then. Still, I was mature enough at 21 to realize that I was never going to be a star and to get out. I knew that life was much more than hats and horns."

Today he is applauded for his dietary crusade, but, his newfound celebrity aside, Sokolof remains a modest and soft-spoken man, deeply committed to his crusade, which is strongly rooted in two personal events—his heart attack and the death of his wife, Ruth Rosinsky, from cancer.

On October 27, 1966, Sokolof suffered a heart attack. He couldn't believe it.

"I was only 43," he says. "I was thin. I did the Royal Canadian Air Force exercises every day. I ran a mile every day—under seven minutes. My blood pressure was low. I didn't smoke. I knew how to handle stress. I had a wonderful wife and a happy marriage. I was a millionaire many times over."

Sokolof recovered and resolved to become an "amateur cardiologist," reading everything he could find about heart disease. He learned that he had only one known risk factor—a cholesterol level of 300, a level that even in 1966 was recognized as high. "I had never heard of cholesterol before," he says, "and I loved greasy food. I was always eating things like hamburgers and hot dogs and chili, especially chili. My ignorance almost killed me."

Today, believing that awareness is therapy, Sokolof is determined that others will not be as ignorant about cholesterol as he once was. Still, almost 20 years passed before he acted. The heart attack had made him rethink his life, but he had rationalized, "Well, my life may be shortened, but it'll come when the years are less sweet."

The turning point for his activism came in 1982 when his wife died after a long fight against cancer. Sokolof says: "My wife's death is the one true sadness in my life. She had an indomitable spirit, and she is the inspiration for everything I do." Ruth Rosinsky Sokolof developed an incurable tumor of the parotid gland (a salivary gland found in front of the ear) when she was 26 and, despite 15 surgeries over the next 30 years, died at age 56.

"To have a terminal illness at 26," Sokolof says, "well, that's pretty young. Ruth could have taken to bed and loaded up with painkillers, but she was determined to lead a full life. She became an expert teacher of the blind and the handicapped and helped found a school for the handicapped. These kids were shut off from the world, and to see Ruth crack through to them and draw them out and make them a real person, or, in the Yiddish word, a *mensch*, well, that was unforgettable. She taught me how to help others."

By 1985, Sokolof decided it was time to crack through with his fight against cholesterol. In January of that year he wrote a check for $1 million to establish the National Heart Savers Association (NHSA), an enterprise he runs out of his office with two employees.

The NHSA membership card, free to anyone who asks, contains the somewhat simplistic incentive, "For every 1 percent you lower your cholesterol, your risk of heart attack drops 2 percent."

The card's handy informational chart plays the "good" foods (grains, salads, vegetable, fruits, pasta, skinless poultry, fish, skim milk, low-fat dairy products, lean meats) off against the "bad" foods (fast-food hamburgers, fatty meats, organ meats, egg yolks, butter, 2 percent milk, sour cream, bacon, ham, hot dogs, ice cream, cheese, chips, chocolates and any food made with butter, lard, beef tallow and palm, palm kernel and coconut oils).

In October of 1985, working with the local health department, Sokolof underwrote a free city-wide cholesterol testing program in Grand Island, Neb., and was astounded to see 8,500 people show up—many of whom registered high cholesterol.

"The portable cholesterol testing machines come in for criticism," he concedes, "but they're very reliable at the high end of the scale. The first time we found a person with a cholesterol over 300 and were able to counsel him to reduce his dietary intake of fats, well, that was a real high. To think that we might be able to save a life is the reason I'm in this business." Sokolof was off and running.

Next he created "National Know Your Cholesterol Week" in April 1987, expanding it in April 1988 to "National Know Your Cholesterol Month."

More than 20,000 congressmen and staffers had their cholesterol tested by NHSA on Capitol Hill. Sokolof, the little guy from "Podunk, Nebraska," as he likes to describe himself, was photographed with all the congressional movers and shakers, including a rotund Sen. Ted Kennedy, who pinned a "Know Your Cholesterol" heart on Sokolof's lapel.

After these educational efforts, Sokolof decided to launch a "nationwide assault" (his phrase) on the nation's food firms.

In late 1988, he paid for the first "Poisoning of America" advertising blitz to indict companies for their use of coconut and palm oils, both of which are high in saturated fats. The campaign worked.

Though they are loathe to credit Sokolof, nine giant firms—Kellogg, Sunshine Biscuits, Pepperidge Farm, Keebler, Quaker Oats, Ralston Purina, Borden, General Foods and Pillsbury—agreed to remove tropical oils from their products. Sokolof's press release explained, "Food giant 'Goliaths' bow as 'David' perseveres in battle against cholesterol."

Emboldened by success, Sokolof next set his sights on the big game—the dairy and meat products that constitute 75 percent of all the saturated fats eaten in America. The prime target was McDonald's, where some 250 people worldwide queue up every second.

"McDonald's has been so successful," Sokolof says, "that their attitude is that they don't have to listen to or work with anybody. I tried to talk to them, but all I got was a statement that they were 'disappointed' in me."

Indeed, when Sokolof's "Poisoning of America—III" ads took on the fast-food giant in 1990, McDonald's initial response was a letter of warning written to ad-carrying newspapers by high-powered Washington attorney Joseph Califano, who, ironically, had been President Jimmy Carter's secretary of Health, Education and Welfare.

The fast-food firm made a mistake, however, in striking back at the man from Podunk. A Gallup poll commissioned by Advertising Age reported that 57 million Americans were aware of Sokolof's ads and that 21 million of these readers were cutting back on fast-food hamburger chains.

McDonald's had also vigorously challenged Sokolof's claims that its hamburgers were 21 percent fat. They were right—tests commissioned by the New York Times in independent labs found that the standard McDonald's burger was only 19.5 percent fat!

Sokolof used this new information to intensify his ad attack, blaring, "McDonald's, your hamburgers still have too much fat!" He was driving home his message that the chain was a "fat factory."

For its part, McDonald's downplays Sokolof's impact. Michael Goldblatt, a nutritional biochemist who is the firm's assistant vice president for nutrition and product development, says: "Criticism that our food is a 'fat factory' is utter nonsense. Our menu is constantly evolving to satisfy consumer demands, we use only the finest ingredients, and our hamburgers are lean by government standards. . . . We're driven by the long-term goal of enhancing nutrition in accordance with consumer tastes."

As the nutrition world holds its breath over the McLean Deluxe, Goldblatt concludes: "As always, we will let the customer make the choice. That's why we market-test."

In the meantime, Sokolof "lies awake nights" planning his next moves. Remember, we're talking total dedication. "I don't have a set schedule," he says, "and I probably spend 80 percent of my time on business for National Heart Savers." That's 80 percent of a work week that usually runs 100 hours—or more.

At 5 feet 10 and 145 pounds, Sokolof's own cholesterol is 150—"or less." His typical diet includes orange juice, one slice of melba toast and tea for breakfast; a packet of soup mixed with hot water at 4 p.m.; and a late-night snack "whipped up with a can opener, frozen foods and my microwave."

Once a month, the widower will drive his white Mercedes sports coupe out to a favorite restaurant and indulge in a steak, but, he adds, "On many days, I doubt if I eat more than two or three grams of fat." He urges people to eat frequently and lightly throughout the day, rather than one or two heavy meals.

Sokolof says that his new fame has forced him to do his supermarket shopping at 11 p.m. or so. "Before, people were coming up to see what I had in my shopping cart," he says. "After checking it out, they'd tell me, 'Gee, it's good to know that I can eat that!'"

Sokolof's dietary "hit list" for the future includes:

• "Low-fat" milk. "This is a misrepresentation," Sokolof charges. "The milk being sold as 'low-fat' actually is 2 percent fat, which is not much less than the 3.6 fat content of whole milk. True low-fat milk should contain less than 1 percent fat or, better yet, it would be like skim milk, with only traces of fat."

• Girl Scout cookies. "I like the Girl Scouts," he says, "and I know that their cookies go for a good cause, but they're using the wrong manufacturer. The Girl Scout chocolate-mint cookies are made with three kinds of tropical oils—coconut, palm and palm kernel. That's no good."

• Theater popcorn. "It's made with coconut oil, not the healthier vegetable oil," he explains. "I called the executive director of the National Association of Theatre Owners, and he was sympathetic.

"The reason theaters serve oily popcorn is simple: They have a cleaning problem! Since vegetable oil is more porous than coconut oil, it leaves a residue of grease on the bottom and sides of the popcorn kettles. The kids that theaters employ to make popcorn don't have the time or the inclination to clean the kettles, so it's simpler to use coconut oil, which keeps all the grease in the popcorn kernel!"

• Hostess Twinkies. Sokolof says: "They're made with lard and are loaded with saturated fat. The manufacturer basically told me to go away, arguing that the cupcakes are an 'indulgent' food and are going to stay the way they are."

• Cool Whip. Too much coconut oil, Sokolof says, but the manufacturer says it's needed for "acceptable" taste.

• Restaurants that refuse to provide healthier menu choices. "They're not in tune with the mood of the consumer," he says.

• School lunches. If Sokolof has his way, all the nation's schools will serve the low-fat hamburger for lunch, and this change will become the cornerstone of an expanded school educational program on nutrition. The USDA has purchased 300,000 pounds of the new low-fat beef for use this fall in selected schools, and Sokolof is confident "the kids will love this beef. Then we can use it in all the schools."

As he takes aim at his targets, Sokolof often unwinds at home by pedaling furiously on his exercise bicycle. Of course, to make maximum use of time, he watches pre-recorded TV programs. He is especially fond of sports, and he loved watching Michael Jordan and the Bulls win the NBA title.

He also enjoyed watching the McDonald's ads during the NBA playoffs. "The McJordan Special," which was advertised in Chicago spots, "is a horrible product," Sokolof says, "but Jordan is the perfect man to pitch the new McLean Deluxe, as he did in McDonald's national spots."

Sokolof is a student of advertising, and he couldn't help but notice McDonald's tagline for its McLean Deluxe ads: "Our critics call it revolutionary."

The crusader allows himself a sense of satisfaction. Phil Sokolof concludes, "I wrote that commercial!"

June 6, 1944

Among the many heroes on that fateful D-Day when Allied troops invaded Hitler's Europe were two 30-year-old American doctors—Treadwell Ireland, M.D., and Charles O. Van Gorder, M.D.

"Never before had there been a dawn like this. In the murky, grey light, in majestic, fearful grandeur, the great Allied fleet lay off Normandy's five invasion beaches . . . a phalanx of ships bore down on Hitler's Europe—the might and fury of the free world unleashed at last. They came, rank after relentless rank, ten lanes wide, twenty miles across, five thousand ships of every description. . . .

"Suddenly, a new sound throbbed over the fleet. Slowly at first, like the bumbling of some giant bee, and then building to a great crescendo of noise, the bombers and fighters appeared. They flew straight in over the massive fleet, flying wing tip to wing tip, formation after formation—nine thousand planes . . . the air cover."

—Cornelius Ryan,
The Longest Day

H-Hour was 6:32 AM at the coast of Normandy, France, first at the strip of sand called Omaha Beach, quickly followed by attacks on four other beaches. All were defended by heavily fortified German guns. Hours before the coastal invasion, Allied airborne troops had landed behind the enemy lines.

There were many heroes on that fateful D day 50 years ago, and two were 30-year-old American physicians, both of whom were members of the Third Auxiliary Surgical Group:

Treadwell L. Ireland, M.D., arrived about noon as part of the assault waves on Omaha Beach. He was a member of the surgical team accompanying the 37th Engineer Combat Battalion of the U.S. First Division.

Charles O. Van Gorder, M.D., arrived hours before the main invasion began, crash-landing in a glider at 4:02 AM in an area near Hiesville, France, 12 miles behind the beaches. He was attached to the U.S. 101st Airborne Division.

Ireland ran into his first crisis 5 minutes after wading ashore when a large German shell exploded about 100 feet from where he was standing and seriously wounded a general. Van Gorder's crisis came even earlier when the glider in which he was flying crashed into a tree and then was hit from behind by another skidding American glider. The loud landings stampeded a herd of cattle toward the American paratroopers and also alerted three German tank drivers who were poised across the hedgerows.

Both physicians survived these scares—and many more, both on D day and throughout the war. Their experiences were typical of the hellishness of war. Cornelius Ryan described the men in the boats in the early assault waves this way: "These were cold, miserable anxious men, so jam-packed together, so weighted down by equipment, that often there was no place to be seasick except over one another. One young soldier, covered in his own vomit, slowly shook his head in abject misery and disgust and said, 'That guy Higgins ain't got nothin' to be proud of about inventin' this goddamn boat!'"

Ireland summarizes, "Everybody was scared and everybody who survived was lucky." Van Gorder says, "It was something we had to do and nobody thought much more about it."

Today, both men, though struggling with various ailments of age, have vivid memories of D day, which they shared with this reporter. Ireland, who is retiring this year from his practice in Pompano Beach, Fla, visited Normandy in 1984 and plans to return again this year for the 50th anniversary. Van Gorder retired in 1981 from the hospital that he and his D-day Airborne surgical buddy, John S. Rodda, M.D. (now deceased), created and ran for 35 years in tiny Andrews, NC. He returned to the battlefields in 1986, but will not be going back this year, explaining, "It's way too crowded."

Here are their stories.

The Third Auxiliary Surgical Group was created as a World War II experiment to see if there would be any advantage in having a surgical team, composed of four physicians and four medics, attached to a fighting force so that wounded soldiers could be treated right on the battlefield, rather than having to be transported to the rear to evacuation hospitals.

A history of the group, *Front Line Surgeons,* was written and published in 1950 by Maj. Clifford Graves, the surgeon who commanded the outfit in England. This limited edition of 225 books, intended only for members, describes Third Auxers this way:

"For an auxiliary surgical group, there is no precedent in man or nature. It is strictly an illegitimate orphan, dependent on charity, deprived of privilege, cursed by many, praised by few, understood by none." Graves' dedication is to the "stout-hearted, high-spirited, red-blooded outfit."

Ireland, who graduated in 1939 from the former Long Island (NY) College of Medicine and was subsequently trained as an internist, was assigned to the surgical group in 1943 while recovering from dysentery and jaundice in Palermo, Sicily, during the Italian campaign. He explains, "Since all the crack surgeons were assigned to the beachhead in Anzio [Italy], I was recruited into the surgical group simply to fill out their roster. I had lost so much weight and had spent so much time lying in a hammock that my buddies were calling me 'canvas back.'"

On June 6, 1944, he was the officer in charge of the forward cargo hold of the assault transport *SS Empire Anvil,* watching over several hundred young American soldiers to make sure everything was in order. "Most were only 20 years old or so," he says, "and they all slept like babies."

In the early morning hours, watching from the prow of the transport ship, Ireland was able to clearly see the vast armada approach its target. A fellow observer was novelist Ernest Hemingway. "We were alone together," Ireland recalls, "and I've always admired his writing, but both of us were so awed by the sight that we never exchanged a word. Hours later, Hemingway waded ashore, wearing a trench coat and stocking cap—no helmet—and carrying binoculars."

For his part, the unarmed Ireland was decked out with red crosses on both arms and both sides of his helmet, but he was well aware that "artillery shells do not recognize red crosses." He also had only one pair of glasses to correct his extreme nearsightedness, which he puts at "20/400—without glasses I was legally blind."

On this day, 2000 Americans would be killed in the water, never to reach the sand. Wounded soldiers would be fished from the waves by medics, who then dodged German fire while trying to bring them ashore in pontoons.

Ireland recalls, "As we got closer to the beach, I saw 40 armored vehicles trying to make it ashore on pontoons, but German shells sank all but one. It was like watching a failed cavalry charge. Our men fished from the waves two survivors of a boat which had been exploded by a mine. We gave each a good belt of whisky and they were soon fighting mad to hit back at the enemy."

At about 11 AM, Ireland's surgical team, commanded by John P. Peyton, joined several dozen amphibious engineers and climbed down into a landing craft infantry (LCI) for the final ride to the beach. The battle was on, and each man was left with his thoughts—and prayers. Ireland notes, "There are very few atheists in foxholes."

He continues, "Our LCI floating box was getting pretty badly shot up as we approached the shore and the Coast Guard navigator backed it away from the target beach and also a nearby landing area. Then, an Army sergeant gave the sailor a direct order: 'Land!' We grounded our boat at about noon on Omaha Beach, about 50 yards off the sector called Dog Red.

"We all had been hugging the bottom of the boat and when the landing ramp was dropped, everybody ran out into waist-deep water. This was the moment the German gunners were waiting for and the fire was intense. We all raced for shore and hit the beach, trying to hug and hide behind the rise of sloping sand right at the water's edge, hoping that the shots would fly over our heads. The beach was littered with dead and wounded Americans—some say it was as bad as a body every six feet or so.

"A shell exploded about 100 feet from where I was lying and seriously wounded a general from the engineer brigade. Maj. Francis M. Findlay, commander of Surgical Team 16, crawled over and tried to help. The rest of us scrambled for cover. The heavy fire forced us to stay at the water's edge.

"Another doctor and I found temporary refuge behind a disabled tank, but I knew from my experience in Sicily that this was a bad idea. The Germans like to zero in on tanks. I persuaded the other doctor to leave our 'shelter' just in time—moments later the tank was hit and blown away."

The waterline was a dangerous place, Ireland says, "but we couldn't advance." While pinned down, Ireland witnessed the action, heroic and otherwise:

"With shells bursting all around him, a young soldier took his bulldozer and tried to clear a path up one of the little valleys heading inland from the beach. The vehicle and its driver were blown up.

"A wounded soldier in a minefield was shouting, 'Help me! Help me!' An infantryman yelled to a medical corpsman, 'You're medics, why don't you help him?' The medic replied, 'You go in with your mine detector and clear a path and we'll follow.' No one accepted the medic's offer.

"Suddenly, a disabled ammunition ship just beyond the surf started to throw off explosions. We had to move."

Deliverance was in the form of a bombed-out German pillbox. Ireland explains, "After the ammo ship started to blow, we all crawled east toward Easy Red Beach. Eventually, we found ourselves below one of the reinforced concrete blockhouses that guard each of the little valleys cutting through the cliffs that ran all along this part of Normandy Beach. They'd been built with captive labor a year before; this one overlooked the road to Colleville-sur-Mer.

"Our bombers had failed to knock out most of these blockhouses, partly because they did not want to hit our own incoming troops. This one, however, was easily visible from the sea and one of our destroyers had been able to lob a shell directly into the pillbox opening and to destroy its big gun. The German commander moved everything left in the way of manpower and equipment outside the pillbox and tried to resist with machine-gun fire, but our troops had forced them to abandon the place."

The Germans had called the blockhouse "Resistance Nest 62." Ireland and his fellow medics would call it a "hospital," the first medical installation on the beach. At 5 PM or so, he recalls, "we took possession with a whoop and a holler."

Their excitement soon faded. In the pillbox, discarded German and American military equipment and clothing were randomly strewn among the medics' meager medical equipment. Ireland and his fellow Third Auxers felt sick at heart. True, they had small quantities of the new wonder drug—penicillin—but few had a clue as to how to use it. With nothing else but morphine, plasma, and dressings, how could they hope to do the job they were supposed to do? How could they treat patients with peritonitis, with fractured femurs, with deep chest wounds?

Ireland agrees with this vivid description provided by Major Graves in *Front Line Surgeons:*

"The pillbox became the focal point of all the suffering of the invasion beach. It was little more than a shelter of the most primitive sort and equipment was wholly lacking. There were only four walls and a roof and the litter haul from the beach was a gruelling journey for the strongest men.

"Inside, the little space was quickly filled . . . as the casualties accumulated, they were placed wherever there was room: on litters, on blankets, or directly on the cement floor. For the most part, they lay there very still. Some had crude splints; others had bulky, bloody dressings; the majority had neither splints nor dressings. Their wounds were covered with layers of ill-smelling, gas-impregnated clothes and heavy, sticky combat jackets.

"As daylight vanished from the interior, confusion became compounded. Prostrate forms were everywhere. Dead and dying lay next to those who still might live. To reach a litter in a far corner required sharp eyes, steady feet, and a strong stomach. The task of creating order was superhuman."

Still, there was heroism. Ireland recalls, with tears in his eyes, tending a dying soldier "who talked about how lovely life had been with his wife and who then sang with his last breaths the words of 'I'll Be Seeing You.'"

As a nonsurgeon, Ireland mostly diagnosed wounds and performed preoperative and postoperative procedures, including the removal of shell and wine-bottle fragments from arms and legs. "Some soldiers were drinking as they hit the beach," he notes.

He also assisted in what was probably the first lifesaving procedure on the beach—the successful attempt by Findlay to treat a sucking chest wound that was causing a soldier to suffocate. Ireland recalls, "While Findlay inserted a needle in the man's chest to allow the excess air to escape and then gave plasma, one medic held a blanket to cover the opening to the pillbox and another held a lighted candle so we all could see."

Shortly afterward, the medics heard the peculiarly dangerous sound of a German Messerschmidt, one of the few enemy planes able to reach the beach. A bomb was dropped almost at the blockhouse door. The blast knocked Findlay, Ireland, and others off their feet and sent great clouds of sand billowing into the pillbox. The wounded moaned. The medics cursed. Plasma bottles were upset, sand seeped under dressings, blankets were blown away. The patient, however, lived.

It was midnight.

Twelve miles inland from Ireland's pillbox-hospital, Captain Van Gorder and the members of his medical team were equally hard at work in much better facilities—the spacious second floor of a large castle known as Chateau Colombiers. It was a tough time getting there, though.

Van Gorder, a 1939 graduate of the University of Tennessee College of Medicine at Memphis, had spent 2 years in surgical internship at Hackensack (NJ) Hospital. He was already a veteran of the North Africa and Sicily campaigns when he volunteered for the risky job of flying with the Airborne troops. He recalls, "We went to our preassigned gliders about midnight June 5. We all had powdered charcoal on our hands, face, and neck to blend in with the darkness. We were each given one tablet of a new drug—Dramamine—to prevent airsickness."

Van Gorder was assigned to Glider No. 2, which was right off the wing of the lead glider piloted by Col. Mike Murphy, who had drawn up the plans for the entire Airborne operation. Murphy was the top glider pilot in the European Theater of War and his glider carried the assistant commander of the 101st Airborne Division—Brig. Gen. Donald F. Pratt.

It was a 3-hour trip across the English Channel for the massive formation of C-47 planes towing their cargo of gliders. Van Gorder says, "Each glider had a pilot and copilot and each man had a flak suit. My glider carried myself and four or five enlisted men, all seated around a lashed-down jeep trailer containing sterile supplies for 75 operations." He recalls looking back toward the rear of the column and being impressed with the view. "When we were in a curve," he says, "you could see the blue formation lights on the top of the planes' wings, stretched back through the sky for miles and looking like a graceful strip of ribbon."

However, the Dramamine soon put him to sleep ("still does," he says). Suddenly, he was awakened to a new view. "As we flew over the coast, a German Messerschmidt strafed our plane and this woke me up," he says.

"Below, the night was lit up with anti-aircraft fire. It was like an enormous bonfire all along the beach. The light from the fire was so concentrated that it looked as if you could step out and walk on it. We were flying at 600 feet—above the small-arms range and below the antiaircraft guns—and our pilots bravely held their course throughout this explosive outburst. Our plane took 91 bullets, but fortunately, none hit our five-gallon gas tank."

The landings were perfect—with one exception. "We hit the right spot," he says, "but nobody had thought to factor in the dew on the grass. After landing, 40 of our 51 gliders skidded 1000 feet or so at 70 mph and crashed into hedgerows. My plane crashed into a large tree, 10 feet from where Colonel Murphy's glider had also crashed. Seconds later, another glider crashed into the tail of our plane. We all tried to scramble out as quickly as possible. It was scary.

"The noise had set off a stampede of frightened cattle. I thought, 'Oh, boy, this must be a German trick and they're coming at us behind the cows!'"

The paratroopers had been given four ways to distinguish friend from foe—a popping cricket ("One blip was to be answered by two," he explains); the D-day password, "Geronimo," ("everyone was too scared to make any noise, though"); a luminous button under the lapel of the jump jackets ("damn hard to find in the dark with all the equipment we were carrying"); and an orange patch on the jackets ("for daylight"). It didn't take Van Gorder long to realize that he was among Germans.

"Fortunately," he says, "our glider had stopped in an area shaded from the moonlight by the large tree we had struck. I went up to the hedgerow and looked over into a road. The earthen bank was about 5½ feet high, and I could see over it well enough to identify three small German tanks, stopped on the road, with Germans sitting on the sides of the tanks, with their rifles across their laps, trying to see into the field where we had landed. I was so close to them that I thought they saw me and would soon throw a grenade over the hedge. That would have been the end of the war for many of us."

Unlike Ireland, Van Gorder always carried a weapon—an eight-shot, .32-caliber pistol ("everybody in my outfit did," he explains). However, he quickly removed it from his web belt and dropped it on the ground, figuring, "There was no way I wanted to get into a shootout with a tank; better to have them see I was an unarmed medic." The Germans craned their ears and peered into the darkness, but were unable to figure out what was going on. Soon, they drove away and a grateful Van Gorder "scampered down the hedgerow bank."

He was the first doctor to find the injured Colonel Murphy, who was trying to work his way out of the wreckage of his lead glider. Murphy had fractured his femur, but he warned Van Gorder, "Don't give me any of that morphine. It'll make me sleepy and I want to stay alert so that if I see any Germans, I can shoot the SOBs." Van Gorder replied, "'Mike, you can't shoot at anybody because you can't run.'" Murphy told Van Gorder that he would be OK until the doctor could check the inside of the badly smashed glider and see how General Pratt and the copilot were doing.

The doctor continues, "By now, we had found some paratroopers to guard the glider, so I took off my gear in order to get in through the wreckage. I found the general sitting in the front seat of the lashed-down jeep, with his head bent forward on his chest. I couldn't get a pulse anywhere—he was dead. I assumed that when the glider struck the hedgerow, he had been instantly killed by his helmet coming forward and snapping his neck. He was the first general to be killed in action.

"The copilot, who had taken the brunt of the force of the crash, was also dead. I got out and, somehow, we got Colonel Murphy squared away and comfortable. Then, I saw a figure coming across the other side of the field. This turned out to be Maj. Albert J. Crandall, the leader of our surgical team. He had landed down the way and worked his way to our location."

By dawn, the surgical team had rounded up several wounded soldiers from the landing fields. Crandall commandeered a jeep and set off in search of the preselected Chateau Colombiers, which was only a few hundred yards north of the headquarters of Gen. Maxwell Taylor, the commander of the 101st Airborne. Van Gorder says, "Our preparation was so precise that I felt like I had been in this area before. Crandall soon found the chateau—the French owners had moved their personal belongings out and reserved only one room for themselves—and returned to collect Colonel Murphy, the other wounded, and myself."

By 9 AM on D day, the chateau was in business as an operating room—the first Allied hospital in Normandy. Van Gorder describes:

"We went right to work, and by late afternoon there were 400 wounded collected in the castle courtyard, mostly from shell fragments to the abdomen, chest, and legs. Our OR was on the second floor of the chateau, which was previously used to store milk. We created six operating tables by placing a litter across two medical supply chests standing on ends.

"The three surgeons—Crandall, myself, and Rodda—alternated from table to table. Our anesthesiologist was Capt. Saul Dworkin, who had the use of intravenous sodium pentathol, much of it collected from the dentists in the company, and a few anesthetic machines for specific cases. We all wore our helmets while operating because bullets were flying in through the windows and striking the walls."

Among the first patients was Colonel Murphy, who became the first casualty to be successfully evacuated to the United States for treatment. Van Gorder not only worked throughout D day, he also continued to operate until 9 PM on June 9—84 consecutive hours. The others did the same—"always on our feet, never able to sit down." He explains:

"The army had issued 92 quarts of Scotch whisky to the medical company for use during the invasion. I could not understand why until we started to operate. The only thing that kept us going was sipping that Scotch! Oh, as the hours dragged on, we were acting like zombies, but the wounded had to be treated and we were still doing good surgery. Finally, though, on the evening of June 9, I got so tired that my head fell down into an open abdomen! Crandall ordered me to go down to one of the tents in the backyard and get some sleep.

"On the way down the stairs, I passed a young soldier who asked, 'Some hot chocolate, sir?' I said, 'No, thanks,' and went to the tent. Then, I thought, 'You know, that hot chocolate might help me sleep.' While I was back on the chateau stairwell, drinking hot chocolate from my canteen cup, I heard the familiar whine of the

Messerschmidt. The Germans mistook our chateau for General Taylor's command post and they were zeroed in. The bomb demolished an entire wing of the chateau and the crumbling walls did serious damage to our hospital. The tent where I would have been sleeping had disappeared into a 60-foot crater—there wouldn't have been a piece of me left!"

Van Gorder and the others went back to work.

Within 1 year of D day, Hitler put a gun to his head (taking no chances, he also took cyanide) and Germany surrendered on May 9, 1945.

The Third Auxers treated 900 American casualties on the beaches of Normandy ("we saved two out of three," Ireland says proudly), and the U.S. cemetery there lists 9386 names.

After D day, Ireland and Van Gorder soldiered on into Europe, with Ireland getting the softer duty. He ended up stationed in Paris, where, in 1945, he married a Parisian lady (he subsequently divorced, and married his current wife, Esther). Van Gorder was captured by the Germans at the Battle of the Bulge on December 19, 1944 ("my birthday"), and spent 5 months as a prisoner of war. All in all, he figures, "I might have been killed on 30 or 40 occasions. I kept hoping that my luck would hold."

He was force-marched for 10 days without food and water, imprisoned in both Germany and Poland, and escaped into Poland and Russia when frightened German troops fleeing the Soviet onslaught of Marshal Zhukov tried to march the Americans back from Poland to Germany.

He was to "find that our so-called Russian allies really hated us. I can still recall them saying, 'Amerikanski!' and spitting at the ground." Van Gorder told a friend, "If this is Russia, let's go back to Poland!" His final deliverance was theatrical. "With dogs and weapons," he says, "the Russians—most of them standing only five-foot four, all with tommyguns, mostly rusty—rounded us up, marched us within 100 yards of the port at Odessa, and then disappeared. Suddenly, a band struck up with the 'Star Spangled Banner' and a British Cunard liner was waiting to take us home in style."

Both Ireland and Van Gorder have bum knees from old war injuries. Although Ireland is partially disabled from lung disease and requires a cane and a hearing aid, and although Van Gorder suffered a small stroke last month that has temporarily impaired his vision, both remain feisty and optimistic at age 80. And both remain in awe of their wartime memories.

In 1984, while visiting his pillbox-hospital at Omaha Beach, Ireland met a German, Franz Gockel, who in 1944 was a 17-year-old soldier who was in the pillbox firing at the American assault troops. The two have struck up a correspondence and this summer, while revisiting Normandy, Ireland and his wife, Esther, will stay with Mr. and Mrs. Gockel. They will lay flowers at both the American and German cemeteries.

In 1986, while revisiting his chateau-hospital near Hiesville, Mr. and Mrs. Van Gorder ran into a French lady who had been 17 in 1944. "She told us," Van Gorder recalls, "that she had been studying English for 32 years for this moment—to be able to escort us around the area where the paratroopers had landed to liberate France!"

Ireland concludes, "When I think about the American cemetery near Colleville, with its beautiful statue of *Spirit of American Youth Rising out of the Waves*, I always get a lump in my throat [he now has tears in his eyes]. All those young men dying on the beach . . . so young. All I can do is cry."

TOMORROW'S MEDICINE

The Double Helix

In exclusive interviews, Nobelists James Watson and Francis Crick explain their "freak find" of the double-helix structure of DNA—the building block of life and heredity

Saturday, March 28, 1953:

President Dwight D. Eisenhower is determined to honor his winning campaign pledge to keep the Korean War truce on track, despite a new flap over the exchange of POWs. Senator Joe McCarthy's Red-baiting Senate investigative committee is bullying 242 Greek commercial ships into cutting off all trade with China. Jim Thorpe, the athlete of the half-century, dies of a heart attack. An unknown Elvis Presley is preparing to graduate from Humes High School in Memphis, Tenn. Queen Elizabeth is preparing for her June 8 coronation. Her oldest son, Prince Charles, is age four; his wife-to-be, the future Princess Diana, is seven years away from being born.

And at the Cavendish Laboratory of Cambridge University in Cambridge, England, Jim Dewey Watson, 24, and Francis Harry Compton Crick, 36, are trying to persuade Watson's pretty younger sister, Elizabeth, to give up her Saturday afternoon to type a 900-word article that begins this way:

"We wish to suggest a structure for the salt of deoxyribose nucleic acid (DNA). This structure has novel features which are of considerable biological interest."

Elizabeth Watson is persuaded after being told that she is participating in perhaps the most famous event in biology since Darwin published his theory of evolution in 1859. In point of fact, she is. As she types the handwritten scribbles into legibility, the era of molecular biology and molecular medicine is born. Our genes are made of DNA, the secret of heredity is now known, and the dream of understanding and preventing genetic diseases is under way.

Watson and Crick are an unlikely pair to have launched this revolution. The Chicago-born Watson is angular, intense, wild-haired, and a former bird-watcher. Watson, holding a bachelor's degree in zoology and a doctorate in biology, had his interest in learning how the genes transmit heredity ignited at Indiana University when he joined the "phage" group of Salvador Luria, himself displaced from Mussolini's Fascist Italy. The bacteriophages, viruses that attack bacteria, are a form of naked gene and Watson's curiosity was piqued. Now he knows he must move fast because his March of Dimes polio fellowship is running out and he is an innocent abroad. When not holding madcap arguments with Crick, he spends his time playing tennis, complaining of stomach pains from the wretched English food, watching the "popsies" (as the Cambridge coeds were then known), and taking side trips to Paris and the Italian Riviera.

The British-born Crick is debonair, flamboyant, urbane, and very loquacious. He was a highly frustrated physicist during World War II, spending his time developing torpedoes for the Royal Navy. A lover of dinner parties and non-stop conversation, Crick is new to biochemistry, and while intrigued with finding the secret of life, he is also still desperately in search of a project practical enough to gain his PhD. He alternates attacking the theoretical problem of protein synthesis, an attack he carries out in a booming voice to anyone who will listen, with impulsively conducting manic experiments that usually torpedo his theories. His time, too, is running out because, as Watson observes, the Cavendish director, Sir Lawrence Bragg, finds it very upsetting to have conversations with Crick because "the sound of Crick's voice was often sufficient to make Bragg move to a safer room."

Together, however, the two bustling, happy, comic antiheroes are making history. Working with little more than bold theories and Tinkertoy building models, they pull a rabbit out of a hat:

The startlingly simple secret that the master DNA molecule is a gently twisted spiral ladder, a double helix, that carries the genes, the messages of heredity, and that is capable of endlessly copying itself.

Complementary base pairs of the nucleotides adenine (A) and thymine (T) and guanine (G) and cytosine (C), always bonded in these specific pairings by hydrogen, form the step plates that are linked to outside rails of sugar and phosphate to form the double helix ladder. Splitting the spiral ladder down the middle produces two separate strands of A, T, G, and C. Enzymes acting on the DNA match each A with a new T and each G with a new C from a reservoir of bases within the cell, forming new pairs that reconstitute two complete copies of the original double helix. This is all there is to the process of how like begets like.

Philosopher-scientist Peter Medawar would later describe this 1953 discovery as a "blaze of understanding. . . . The great thing about their discovery was its completeness, its air of finality." Referring to Watson and Crick's later work to analyze the genetic code and to understand how the genes direct the synthesis of proteins, Medawar added, "It is simply not worth arguing with anyone so obtuse as not to realize that this complex of discoveries is the greatest achievement of science in the 20th century."

In March 1953, however, Crick and, especially, Watson were not so sure. In writing their elegant, spare paper, the euphoric Crick gave in to the jittery Watson in favor of understatement. He did, however, insist upon writing the 12th of the 14 paragraphs comprising the paper, stating: "It has not escaped our notice that the specific pairing we have postulated immediately suggests a possible copying mechanism for the genetic material."

On Tuesday, March 31, 1953, the short paper, encumbered with only six footnoted references, was sent to Bragg, himself the winner of a Nobel Prize for his role in founding the science of x-ray crystallography. Two days later, Bragg submitted the paper to the British journal *Nature*, which published it on April 25. In the interim, on April 6, Watson turned 25.

Soon Crick and Watson were cultural icons, their names jointly resonating in the collective consciousness like Ike and

Nixon, Desi and Luci, DiMaggio and Monroe. This permanent pairing in the public mind was only enhanced by their winning of the Nobel Prize in 1962 (shared with Maurice Wilkins, whose long, patient work at King's College in Cambridge had preceded Watson and Crick's rapid, brilliant solution) and by the publication in 1968 of Watson's ground-breaking scientific memoir, *The Double Helix: A Personal Account of the Discovery and Structure of DNA*.

A man of few but telling words, Watson wrote his slender memoir in a style that made it both a classic and a controversy. In the foreword, Bragg admonished that Watson "writes with a [Samuel] Pepys-like frankness and those who figure in the book must read it in a very forgiving spirit." Watson's original working title was "Honest Jim." In describing his impressions of a very suspenseful scientific tale, Watson bared the contradictory pulls of ambition and fair play that mark modern science and portrayed a competitive world of scientist vs scientist, with knowledge often an accidental by-product. He also made many tactless appraisals of what he considered the foibles and frailties of others.

Crick, among others, threatened to sue over descriptions considered to be unflattering and unseemly. Critics thought the book would be better titled "Lucky Jim" or, even, "Base Pairs." Some informed readers were put off by Watson's unabashed glee in beating out famed chemist Linus Pauling in the race to discover the structure of DNA; others thought he unfairly portrayed and squeezed out the valuable contributions of Rosalind Franklin, a top x-ray crystallographer and an ardent feminist.

Still others thought Watson revealed himself to be cold, calculating, childish, and cruel. The unperturbed Watson had a different perspective. In 1953, Watson had celebrated his great achievement with a trip to Paris, and he closes his book by recapturing the feelings he had then: "But now I was alone, looking at the long-haired girls near St. Germain des Prés and knowing they were not for me. I was twenty-five and too old to be unusual."

At the time of the book's scheduled publication in 1968, Watson was a professor of biochemistry and molecular biology at Harvard, but after much agonizing, the Harvard University Press reneged on a commitment to publish the book. When the dust cleared, the book was promptly published by a commercial house, Atheneum, and quickly became a surprise best-seller.

Gerontologist, novelist, and eventual fellow best-seller Alex Comfort (*The Joy of Sex*) wrote in the *Manchester Guardian*, "We could do worse than give Watson a second Nobel gong for literature."

Another best-selling scientist, Jacob Bronowski (*The Ascent of Man*), writing in *The Nation*, saw it as a "classical fable about the charmed seventh sons, the antiheroes of folklore who stumble from one comic mishap to another until, inevitably, they fall into the funniest adventure of all: they guess the magic riddle correctly. Though the traditional parts of Rosalind Franklin as the witch and Linus Pauling as the rival suitor have been toned down (from Watson's original unexpurgated version), they are still unmistakably what they were—mythological postures rather than characters." Bronowski also saw Watson as playing Boswell to Crick's Dr. Johnson—"monumentally admired and, every so often, scored off."

In his review in *The New York Review of Books*, Medawar attributed Watson's apparent failure to give proper credit to his scientific predecessors not to lack of generosity but to "stark insensibility," arguing that highly creative scientists like Watson view an interest in the history of science "as a sign of failing or unawakened powers."

In time, all was forgiven, including Crick's displeasure with Watson, and, 40 years after the fact, this remarkable book remains the best description of *how* the secrets of the double helix were pierced. The Watson-Crick sparring has been relatively genteel and they remain very good friends, despite exchanges like the following:

In 1968, Watson began his book, "I have never seen Francis Crick in a modest mood. . . . Although some of his closest colleagues realized the value of his quick penetrating mind and frequently sought his advice, he was often not appreciated and most people thought he talked too much."

Crick got his turn in 1974, writing an essay for *Nature*, entitled, "The Double Helix—A Personal View." In Crick's view, Watson's book was "a rather vivid fragment of his autobiography, written for a lay audience. As to a [self-written] book, I confess I got as far as composing a title, 'The Loose Screw' and what I hoped was a catchy opening ('Jim was always clumsy with his hands. One had only to see him peel an orange . . .'), but I found I had no stomach to go on."

That was then. Now, in 1993, 40 years after Elizabeth Watson sat behind a typewriter, it is time to both celebrate the seminal 1953

Crick-Watson discovery and to look to its future impact. As Crick observed in that 1974 *Nature* article, "Rather than believe that Watson and Crick made the DNA structure, I would rather stress that the structure made Watson and Crick. After all, I was almost totally unknown at the time and Watson was regarded, in most circles, as too bright to be really sound. But what is really overlooked . . . is the intrinsic beauty of the DNA double helix. It is the molecule which has style, quite as much as the scientists. . . ."

The scientists, too, retain their style and, although they are now on the last laps of their distinguished careers, both are still running hard. In recognition of the planned republication in *JAMA* of the 1953 *Nature* paper to celebrate its 40th anniversary, each agreed to an exclusive interview with this reporter. The elusive Crick, 76, remains a pure scientist, now studying the brain at the Salk Institute for Biological Studies in La Jolla, Calif. A continent away, the enigmatic Watson, 64, is marking his 25th year as the director of the Cold Spring Harbor Laboratory in Long Island, NY.

Resplendent in a cranberry sport coat and matching floral-patterned shirt, the silver-haired Crick cuts a striking figure. A contemporary who knew both Crick and Watson well once wrote under the pseudonym "F.X.S." in the British monthly, *Encounter*, and described Crick this way: "The voice is pitched high but incisive and the mind moves with an obvious, bewildering celerity, beside a fusillade of rather campy laughter. It is the kind of voice one goes grouse-shooting with. Crick is a dandy in the precise, strong sense."

Crick does little grouse-shooting in Southern California, but he does love the climate in La Jolla, a cheerfully eccentric community just north of San Diego. A U.S. resident alien since 1976, when he joined the Salk Institute, Crick and his wife are building a second home in the nearby desert and one son has become an American citizen, but Crick plans to remain a Brit, as do his two daughters, who live in England. He has to be prompted to reminisce about the double helix.

"I've left all that stuff behind," he begins. "I'm not like Jim [Watson], who is still deeply immersed in the field. Today, I only understand molecular biology at the level reported in the *Scientific American*. My interest now is in studying how the brain processes visual stimuli. Jim and I stay in touch as friends, but we don't stay in touch scientifically. Jim is an administrator and manager; I'm still caught up in research."

"Basically, I'm trying to figure out what goes on in our heads when we see something? How do our brains store information? My long-term interest is understanding both human conscious and unconscious processes. It is much tougher work than understanding DNA because it is on a much more difficult level."

Joining his past and present research interests, Crick jogs his memory back to the early days of DNA. "I don't remember very much," he says, "and the human memory can be very unreliable. I recently saw a documentary about the discovery of DNA and, now, I have to think hard to remember what I actually remember from 1953 and what I remember from watching the documentary!

"Our first paper was written in such a simple style that it was a little like pulling a rabbit out of a hat. I suppose if we had done the usual scientific paper—overly long, poorly written, unnecessarily polysyllabic—it would not have had as great an impact. In many ways, the double helix was a freak find. It was so revealing of deep biological secrets that it gave the game away.

"More importantly, people and money were available to exploit the discovery, leading to new techniques to create the new breakthroughs to understand the genetic code, to clone and recombine DNA, and to greatly amplify DNA through polymerase chain reaction. These later developments are the important thing, not that Jim and I found the double helix. I doubt if it made all that difference that Columbus discovered America. What mattered much more was that people and money were available to exploit the discovery when it was made."

Crick says that in March 1953 he was much more optimistic than Watson about their find. "Absolutely," he exclaims. "Jim was nervy and jumpy, afraid we might overstate the case. People tell me I was euphoric! I remember writing a letter to my son and allowing as to how we had 'discovered something interesting.' I was so excited that my wife didn't believe we had what I thought we had."

Crick is reminded of his 1974 description in *Nature* of how he happened to write the famous 12th paragraph of the paper and decides he cannot improve upon it now. He wrote:

"The first [April 25] *Nature* paper was both brief and restrained. Apart from the structure itself, the only feature of the paper which has excited comment was the short sentence: 'It has not escaped our notice that the specific pairing we have postulated immediately suggests a possible copying mechanism for the genetic material.' This has been described as 'coy,' a word that few would normally associate with the authors, at least in their scientific work.

"In fact, it was a compromise, reflecting a difference of opinion. I was keen that the paper should discuss the genetic implications. Watson was against it. He suffered from periodic fears that the structure might be wrong and that he had made an ass of himself. I yielded to his point of view, but insisted that something be put in the paper; otherwise, someone else would certainly write to make the suggestion, assuming we had been too blind to see it. In short, it was a claim to priority."

Crick adds that after reading the other two papers published on April 25, 1953, in *Nature* by Maurice Wilkins and collaborators and Rosalind Franklin and collaborators, and seeing how strongly their x-ray data supported the Watson-Crick helical structure, that things changed. He says, "We were sufficiently emboldened to author our more speculative May 30, 1953, *Nature* paper, in which we made it clear that we thought we were on to a very good idea."

Asked if Watson's *Double Helix* is an accurate account, Crick takes a rare pause. "Well," he responds, "parts of it are little more than sketches and caricatures, but the science is accurate. When I reread it recently, I was impressed with how much science Jim got into it. The book was very cleverly done, very suspenseful, and it is told in such a way that you can't put it down.

"In 1968, though, I thought, 'Who will possibly read all this ivory tower stuff?' I was also very cross with Jim for the chitchatty style and gratuitous descriptions of people. There was a school of thought in England in those days that you didn't write about your living friends. I objected to its being published at Harvard because it was not scholarly. I also made some vague legal threats about blocking publication elsewhere, but I didn't have a leg to stand on. In fact, Harvard become cross with me because the book was a best-seller and would have made them a lot of money! So, yes, I went through a period when I was cross with Jim, but that was ages ago."

Asked to advise today's researchers in molecular biology and medicine, Crick says, "If research money is made available, the returns will be enormous. Gains in the search to understand cancers, for sure, but cancer is too narrow a view. There will be tremendous changes in the neurosciences, developmental biology, and social and ethical areas, too, though I try to avoid these. In the long run, there will be even more scientists working on molecular biology than there were in the years immediately after the discovery of the double helix.

"Things are going fairly well, now, and you can see progress, but the best is yet to come. In five years, the impact upon medicine will be big. In 10 or 15 years, it will be overwhelming. Ask Jim."

Asked his feelings upon discovering the double helix, he sticks to his *Nature* essay of 1974: "If Watson had been killed by a tennis ball, I am reasonably certain I would not have solved the structure alone . . . As to how we did it, I cannot do better than quote from a brilliant and perceptive lecture I heard years ago in Cambridge by the British painter, John Minton, in which he said of his own artistic creations, 'The important thing is to be there when the picture is painted.' And, this, it seems to me, is partly a matter of luck and partly good judgment, inspiration, and persistent application."

On this day, Crick concludes, "I've always been cool to the media and rejected all interview requests, if possible, because I have never wanted to be a celebrity, a person who is made and unmade by the media. But I've been able to remain hidden away and mysterious and, yet, have my publicity, too. That's because I've always had an extremely good press agent—Jim Watson!"

By all accounts, among Watson's many talents is also one for finding the best researchers. During his 25-year tenure as its director, the Cold Spring Harbor Laboratory has received universal acclaim as the top independent biology lab in the United States and one of the best in the world, as measured by citations of published papers. Data from the Institute for Scientific Information's *Science Citation Index* for the years 1973-1987 found Cold Spring Harbor far and away the top lab; running a distant second was the Salk Institute for Biological Studies.

Watson's sunny office is in a research building commanding the highest ground on the laboratory's campus and it offers a panoramic view of the harbor, an inlet of Long Island Sound. The harbor was first developed by the descendants of a British pirate and it reached its commercial peak as a whaling port, before being turned into a "summer camp for biologists" and then the premier research facility known as "DNA Town." Dominating his view opposite the harbor is a 65-story bell tower, each face of which bears a granite plaque inscribed with the initial of one of the four nucleotides that make up the backbone of the DNA molecule—A, T, G, and C—the alphabet of the new genetics. Running up the center of the tower is a spiral stairwell.

Watson's tie is askew beneath a rumpled sweater and a rumpled sport coat, the pocket of which bulges with pens and pencils. He speaks very softly and his words are punctuated by long pauses. His wispy white hair appears electrified. Prominent behind his desk are framed photos and plaques and an enclosed model of the double helix. Fresh in the reporter's mind is the published description of Watson by the pseudonymous "F.X.S.," who used *his* Pepys-like frankness to report:

"Professor James D. Watson is a very intricate person. A lemming of a being, with luminous yet strangely evasive eyes and lemming's ears. Watson's shyness, his arch withdrawal from most interlocutors, do not shut *him* out; they shut out those who bore him (you and I, sir), whose plod of spirit or lack of elegance fail the test of his fastidious *hauteur*."

Not to worry, though. Watson is a man willing to tackle most questions fairly put. Brought up to speak the truth as he sees it, he has always done exactly that. He is also a gracious host, honoring his guest with a coffee-table pictorial history of the Cold Spring Harbor Laboratory assembled by his wife, Elizabeth, who is an expert in historical preservation. The book highlights many of the buildings she has helped to preserve on the laboratory's 95-acre campus. It is also graced with the prose of Jim Watson, who in eight spare essays manages to tell the history of molecular biology from Darwin right through the federal Human Genome Project he headed from 1988-1992. Molecular biology has come a long way. Before Darwin published his theory of evolution in 1859, Watson writes "The most educated people took for granted that each form of life had been created *de novo* by some almighty body, possibly even as recorded in the Bible." Smack in the middle of this story is the discovery of the double helix.

Asked if his landmark 1953 paper was peer-reviewed, Watson smiles and says dryly, "It was submitted by Sir Lawrence Bragg, so there was no reason for peer review. If your goal is to publish fast, peer review can be overemphasized. Of course, *Nature* was right to publish it immediately. Why not?" He adds, "I was in favor of understatement, because what did we have to lose by it?"

Asked if he were overly combative in expressing his views in *The Double Helix*, Watson responds, "I wasn't bothered by the controversy. Up to that time, no one had ever written a book like *The*

Double Helix. My goal was to write an awfully good story with fascinating characters. And you have to stand up for your rights, or people will squash you down, as Francis was squashed down by the government in his early life. Sometimes, the bad guys will get you unless you get the bad guys first."

Francis Crick remains much on Watson's mind. He asks, "Did Francis show you his white Mercedes coupe? His license plates are ATGC. Did he show you the printed cards he keeps on file checked off to read, 'Dr. Crick does not do TV shows . . . Dr. Crick does not accept honorary degrees.' Francis has remained the pure scientist." This summer Watson will accept an honorary degree from Cambridge University in celebration of the 40th anniversary of the discovery of the double helix. He says, "I'm accepting because I feel it is only proper to express my thanks to the university. Francis has refused the same honor." He shakes his head in admiration or exasperation or both.

He continues, "Francis always tried to look after me and was enormously supportive. Of course, I tried to look after Francis, too. We're very good friends because we think alike on scientific things. Given the same set of facts and assumptions, we . . ." He breaks off and stares out at the harbor during a long, long pause. "It's hard to say," he continues, "and I'd probably have to write an essay to fully describe my relationship with Francis, but he's very sensible, he's the rational mind. Given the choice between a simple solution and a complicated solution, he'll look first for the simple solution, even if the problem is very, very difficult. Francis always believed that science will come through with answers and I was very lucky to meet him because I feel the same way. Francis and I were never dogmatic. If a theory didn't work when we checked it out, we changed our assumptions and checked again. Science can be a very frustrating business and we were often frustrated, but Francis less so because he is truly extraordinary. I've always felt that Francis is much more clever than I, that his brain works much faster. Of course, Francis now chooses to study the brain; it's a bigger unknown than genetics. If I were 20 again, I would also study the brain."

Looking to the future of genetics, Watson says, "Solving the structure of DNA was immensely simple, but understanding life, well, that's immensely complicated. The double helix was a great discovery because it told us how DNA replicated and how it controlled protein synthesis. We knew that it was a great discovery at the time and we also knew that the passage of time was not needed to establish it as a great discovery. Still, even after 40 years, we do not completely understand how DNA works, especially in its regulatory functions.

"And understanding cancers and genetic diseases is proving to be very complicated. I'm encouraged by the new techniques we have—recombinant DNA and DNA amplification through polymerase chain reactions. I'm discouraged because solving the riddle of cancers is so much more difficult than we hoped. We'll probably understand cancer only *after* we understand the entire workings of a single cell and that's a big challenge."

Still, he's optimistic. "The impact of genetic medicine will be brought home very soon because researchers are closing in on the gene that predisposes women to develop breast cancer. The answers should come in two years, maybe two months, and it will hit like a bomb. Cystic fibrosis and other isolated single-gene defect diseases are seen as 'the other person's disease,' but one of nine women acquires breast cancer. Once this gene is discovered, my wife will be screened for it, every woman will be screened for it, and those at higher risk will be screened for this disabled gene much more frequently."

For four years, Watson directed the federal Human Genome Project, an ambitious 15-year, $3-billion effort to map and sequence all of the estimated 100,000 human genes. If completed, this will be the ultimate script of life, the complete genetic instructions for human existence. (Right now, only 100 of the genes have been isolated and sequenced.) Watson relinquished this directorship last year, a topic he does not choose to discuss, except to say, "Bernadine Healy [the director of the National Institutes of Health, the agency coordinating the genome project] and I are not exactly compatible."

He shares the project's goals. "Mostly, I was staying on only until they could find a replacement. It was very demanding for me to hold down two full-time jobs and it required a lot of sacrifices. The genome project is so demanding that it requires the leadership of a younger scientist and I hope they find one soon. The question all comes down to how much the nation is willing to pay to understand the genome. If we're going to succeed, I think that the nation needs to become much more genetically literate and the current amount of federal funding needs to be doubled over the next 10 years. Given the benefits that are going to come out of this program, not in 200 years, but probably in our lifetimes, I feel it's essentially unethical not to pursue it."

Asked if the discovery of the double helix has made him religious, Watson smiles. "No, I've never had a religious streak," he begins. "The story of human life is the story of DNA and its time on earth. We're all the products of evolution. Even if we had enough time and manpower to understand it, though, we can't go back billions of years to study the original molecular relics. Understanding the chemistry that transformed RNA into DNA into the process of evolution poses some very big questions.

"What intrigues me is the tension between the messages we get from genetics and the messages we get from society. I'm a total Darwinian, believing that human beings are totally a function of evolution. Yet, all our cultural values were formed long before the world ever heard of Darwin or Crick and Watson. Mankind has always yearned for a moral authority and science cannot offer moral authority."

Asked about today's climate of "politically correct" expressions of thought, Watson actually raises his voice. "It's all a pile of manure," he says. "I'm not interested in what is 'politically correct,' I'm interested in what is correct—period. What the truth of the matter is.

"We're told that men are created equal, but we're not. There are terrible genetic injustices, especially in terms of susceptibility to diseases. Would it be better if everyone thought they were equal, that it's God's will if they get cancer? We're told that if there are conflicts between two cultures we should try to merge the differences. Well, I don't want to merge with the Moslem culture. We're told that we should love animals, but do we want to cozy up to the scorpion that can kill us or get affectionate with a tick? We're told that because we are descended from the apes that the monkeys must have rights, too, and we shouldn't be able to do research on them. We're told that if amniocentesis discloses a baby will be born with cystic fibrosis that the mother should not be able to have an abortion. This kind of 'politically correct' abortion and animal rights nonsense is nothing more than kookdom. And there are a lot of kooks out there."

He doesn't have all the answers, either. "If we put all our faith in science and take away a sense of moral authority, then we will have nothing but chaos. People have always looked for their answers in gods and tried to find them in the sky or in the sea. Well, it's unlikely that there's anything up on the moon except moon dust, so I believe you may as well base your life on the truth, as you understand it."

Watson plans to soon take a six-month sabbatical in England to write his autobiography. "I'm a better writer than I am a scientific manager," he says. "Yeah, I know how to write. I want to try to convey the mood of my scientific times, the vast hidden life of a scientist."

And what is that mood?

"A mixture of everything," he says. "Boredom, excitement, frustration. For the most part, you're frustrated, dissatisfied because you don't know how to take the next step. You're always trying to find the next step, the final piece of the puzzle. You spend a lot of time reading up on others' works to find encouragement."

Does he enjoy writing?

Sharing his final smile, Watson concludes, "When it's done."

So, the question remains: should *The Double Helix* really have been titled "Lucky Jim." Perhaps. Sure, Watson was lucky. So was Crick. Luckiest of all are those of us who will benefit from their collaboration. The philosopher-scientist Peter Medawar summed it up best in his review of *The Double Helix*, writing:

"Lucky or not, Watson was a highly privileged young man. . . . Almost at once (and before he had done anything to deserve it), he entered the privileged inner circle of scientists among whom information is passed by a certain beating of tom-toms, while others wait the publication of a formal paper in a learned journal. Because it was unpremeditated, we can count it to luck that Watson fell in with Francis Crick, who (whatever Watson may have intended) comes out in this book as the dominant figure, a man of very great intellectual powers.

"By all accounts, including Watson's, each provided the right kind of intellectual environment for the other. In no other form of serious creative activity is there anything equivalent to a collaboration between scientists, which is a subtle and complex business, and a triumph when it comes off, because the skill and performance of a team of equals can be more than the sum of individual capabilities.

"Watson's and Crick's was a relationship that did work, and in doing so brought them the utmost credit."

The Cancer Revolution

Top genetic researcher Bert Vogelstein, M.D., is helping to prove that cancer is caused by defects in our genes. His next goal is to develop therapies to prevent and cure it

Bert Vogelstein, M.D., arrives at his office at Baltimore's Johns Hopkins Oncology Center at 5:30 in the morning—6 or 7 days a week—and he often finds one of his laboratory researchers already at work. With time out only for a lunch of bagels, toasted in the room next door, he usually stays at work until 7:30 at night. It adds up to 85 to 90 hours a week. His wife got used to it long ago. He, too, shrugs it off.

"There's a lot to do," Vogelstein told this reporter last month. "Sure, I work hard, but so does everyone in my lab. Molecular genetics requires a lot of hands-on work and most lab investigators work long and hard."

The 44-year-old Vogelstein and his team of 12 to 16 young scientists (co-supervised by Kenneth W. Kinzler) are seeking the secrets of cancer in a warren of small cramped offices that were converted from the former Brown's Supermarket in a high-crime downtown area of Baltimore hard by the Hopkins hospital. Among the reasons to stay in the laboratory is the fact that it is not very safe to walk in this neighborhood.

Vogelstein adds, "As a resident [in pediatrics at the Johns Hopkins Hospital], I used to shop here. The office we're sitting in used to be the fruits and vegetables section." In the "lunch room" outside his office, several young researchers are fortifying their enthusiasm with skimpy offerings from the fridge and the microwave.

Thanks to the work of Vogelstein's laboratory and hundreds of similar molecular genetic laboratories throughout the world, there is now new hope for the understanding of what causes cancer and, eventually, for improved therapies. He summarizes, "In the last 10 years and, especially, in the last 5, there has been a revolution in cancer research. I can sum the revolution up in one statement:

"Cancer is, in essence, a genetic disease."

He elaborates, "Cancer is driven by a series and accumulation of mutations in genes that normally control growth—either positively or negatively.

"The automobile is a good analogy of what happens. The oncogenes are in normal cells but have mutated and gone awry, acquiring the potential to trigger abnormal cell division. The oncogenes act as accelerators for cell growth. It is like having the car in top gear with the accelerator stuck to the floor. But just like the driver of a car can reverse a floored accelerator by stepping on the brakes, so can other genes brake the oncogenes.

"The cell's brakes are called tumor-suppressor genes, and just like an auto has more than one brake, foot and emergency, so does the cell have more than one kind of tumor-suppressor gene.

"It is only when each of the cell's accelerators and each of its brakes have been dismantled by dysfunctional genes that the process of cancer begins. And it is only when all the cell's accelerators are stuck to the floor in high gear and all the cell's brakes have been knocked out that cancer spreads to its final stages."

"This is a reasonable analogy to what appears to happen in a cancer cell. When the oncogenes are always actively turned on, as opposed to only on cell demand, and when the tumor-suppressor genes cannot inhibit cell growth, the result is cancer.

"It is an aggregate of mutations to the oncogenes and to the tumor-suppressor genes, the cell's accelerators and brakes, that causes cancer. Though it is a bit more complicated, we can now say that this sequential accumulation of mutations in several oncogenes and/or suppressor genes causes cancer, just as polio is caused by the polio virus and AIDS is caused by the human immunodeficiency virus."

However, he qualifies, "All scientific assertions are hypotheses. Right now, most cancer researchers—including me—believe in this hypothesis of what causes cancer."

Thus, the revolution of discovery. As for the next hoped-for revolution, the revolution of dramatically improved cancer treatments, Vogelstein says:

"The great hope is that the discovery of what causes cancer will lead to the development of new drugs that are targeted specifically to mutant genes—drugs that will restore the function of tumor-suppressor genes and will inhibit activated oncogenes without destroying other normal cells. The targeting of cancer-causing mutant genes is a great hope for the future, but it is impossible to know if it will happen or not. Progress will be measured in decades."

He is more hopeful about efforts to assess high-risk patients, catch their tumors early, and improve their treatment with the aid of new prognostic markers. He adds, "To make any of this happen, we need higher levels of research funding, and physicians must support efforts for higher funding."

Still, the first revolution represents a great leap forward. It was only 50 years ago, during the 1940s, that demons like "cancer" and "mental illness" were spoken of in whispers. It was during this time that famed philanthropists Mary and Albert Lasker, for whom this nation's most prestigious scientific awards are named, had to use all their persuasiveness to convince David Sarnoff, then the powerful head of the Radio Corporation of America, that it was OK to even mention the word "cancer" on the airwaves.

As recently as 1974, when Vogelstein received his M.D. from Johns Hopkins University, cancer was, in his words, "still a black box. There were a lot of theories about aging and the immune system and possible genetic changes, but very little was really known. Also, cancer was still sort of a taboo—you couldn't say the word for fear you might catch it."

That's why Vogelstein decided to make cancer genetics his life's work. "Back then," he says, "they were two separate areas. I became interested in studying cancer because it was a completely mysterious disease and presented a tremendous medical and scientific challenge.

"And I became interested in studying genetics because of my work caring for children during my residency in pediatrics. Kids get cancer, too, and there was so little known about what causes their diseases and so little that we could do for them that I thought that the study of genetics might provide a few answers and that this would be a worthwhile way to spend my life."

Today, one of the few breaks Vogelstein allows himself from his laboratory is to teach a course in cancer genetics to Johns Hopkins medical students. "It's very exciting," he says. "With the powerful new tools we have, like gene cloning and sequencing, the study of genetics opens up a whole new way to see disease. Today's medical students have a completely new perspective on killers like cancer and heart disease."

At conception, human beings have about 100,000 genes, located in 46 chromosomes—half from the mother's egg and half from the father's sperm. It requires a million billion cell divisions to turn a fertilized egg into an adult human being, with the descendants of those original 100,000 genes residing in each and every body cell. It is an awe-inspiring work of biological xeroxing, but although mistakes are relatively rare, nature did not design the process to be perfect. And this helps to cause cancer.

Vogelstein says, "In a sense, cancer is a side effect of evolution. The cells are designed to make mistakes when replicating, because that is nature's way of driving evolution—the 'wrong' gene can sometimes confer a survival advantage upon the species. Unfortunately, however, these mistakes can also represent a step toward cancer. Although mistakes are very rare at the base-pair level, even rare mistakes can create a significant step toward cancer."

Gene mutations have three primary causes, Vogelstein explains—heredity, exposure to environmental carcinogens, and mistakes in the cells' duplication of DNA, the building blocks of life. He elaborates:

"Some mutations in the genes are inherited and can predispose to cancer. Since it only takes four or five gene mutations to cause colon cancer, having one at birth gives a person a head start on cancer and can have an immediate impact on health.

"Most mutations, however, occur after birth, either because of exposure to environmental carcinogens like tobacco or the ultraviolet light in sunlight, or because of mistakes in the way the cells copy their DNA. DNA mistakes in oncogenes and tumor-suppressor genes can lead to the initiation or progression of tumors. The ratio of environmentally caused mutations vs. replicating mistakes is unknown, but we can now assess specific carcinogens, like ultraviolet light, in terms of the genetic mutations they cause."

In recent years, the Johns Hopkins Oncology Center investigators have pinpointed the precise nature of several cancer-causing gene mutations.

Vogelstein and Kinzler reported in the January 16, 1992, issue of *Nature* that "[c]arcinogens leave fingerprints. . . ." In the case of one such carcinogen, ultraviolet light, they noted, the fingerprint is in the form of mutations to skin-cell p53 genes that will prevent that gene from suppressing tumor growth. They added that this type of "molecular epidemiology" may help prevent cancer, noting, "It is one thing to tell a tanning champion from California . . . that epidemiological and animal evidence suggest certain preventative measures. It is quite another to say we know that light of 300 nm induces mutations at pyrimidine dimers in skin-cell p53 genes which will prevent that gene from suppressing tumor growth . . . [thus] providing a coherent picture of how a specific agent contributes to the development of human cancer in molecular detail."

The two reported in the August 21, 1992, issue of *Cell* that alterations of the tumor suppressing p53 gene "appear to be involved, directly or indirectly, in the majority of human malignancies," fulfilling the "long-standing hope that the same biochemical pathway for controlling growth is disrupted in many different kinds of cancers, despite their biological heterogeneity, [providing] a common denominator for understanding, treating, and preventing these diseases." They added that this has "stimulated an intense search for the biochemical functions of p53 and the effects of mutations on these properties."

In the March 18, 1994, issue of *Science,* Vogelstein, Kinzler, and a team of international researchers reported the last in a series of discoveries about gene mutations that cause colon cancer. The researchers said that "defects in any of several mismatch repair genes can cause hereditary nonpolyposis colorectal cancer."

Vogelstein summarizes his laboratory's work this way: "We have made contributions to the understanding of the pathogenesis of cancer, primarily colorectal cancer and, especially, cancer of the colon. We have learned that these cancers are caused by an accumulation of mutations in both oncogenes and tumor-suppressing genes and we have precisely defined the mutations within the genes. These discoveries provide a backbone or outline to help improve the care of cancer patients."

For 10 years now, Vogelstein and his research team have primarily concentrated on the study of human colon cancer. "Colon cancer is a very good model," he says, "because it progresses from a small benign growth to an intermediate size to a larger precancerous size to actual cancer to the metastasis of cancer. We can study all stages of growth and analyze tissue from each stage to assess the progressive mutations of the genes and to try to find the straw that breaks the camel's back. Understanding the disease process itself is the first step in improving treatment."

He adds, "We made human cancer our focus because we believe that any findings will have more relevance to human health. Plus many other labs are doing animal studies. It's very important to us that our findings improve the care of patients. Cancer is not just a scientific puzzle; it's a disease that kills many people. As many as one in 200 people have hereditary colon cancer, accounting for 15% or more of all colon cancers.

"The first major clinical impact of our research will probably be in improving the medical management of these millions of people who are at high risk for familial colon cancer. We are looking for ways to screen these people for risk; to detect tumors as early as possible; to improve their survival odds by better assessing markers for tumor progression; and, thus, to better determine the form of treatment; and, ultimately, to develop new treatments.

"Our major focus right now is to allow presymptomatic diagnosis of the risk of cancer among these individuals and we are working very hard toward this goal; this knowledge can be lifesaving. Hopefully, a blood test can be developed in the near future to test colon cancer families for the presence or absence of mutant genes. If an individual does not have the bad gene, that's great news; if he or she does, they can receive strict surveillance and benefit from the earliest possible treatment. Such tests will be invaluable to the physicians' management of patients.

"A knowledge of the science of genetic mutations can help physicians do a better job of managing these [cancer-prone] families in terms of assessing risk, detecting tumors early, and monitoring and treating tumor progression, but it is the last area, developing better treatments, that is the hardest. Progress in this area will probably be measured in decades."

Asked his research hopes for the next 5 to 10 years and his suggestions for scientific papers in *JAMA's* special theme issue on cancer, Vogelstein says, "The answer is the same—the same four key areas we have been discussing:

• "Genetic tests for the presymptomatic diagnosis of people who are at risk of inherited cancers—breast, colon, prostate, ovarian, and others.

• "Genetic tests for the earliest possible diagnosis of cancer and the earliest possible treatment—such as colonoscopy and removal of polyps to control colon cancer.

• "Improved prognostic markers to measure tumor progression and to improve treatment by determining if surgery alone is enough, or if additional treatments are needed.

• "The beginnings at least of some ideas for better therapies and drugs and experimental systems of treatment."

He thinks that the first three goals are "doable, at least to some degree, within the decade." He doubts if any new therapies "will be clinically testable within a decade, but I hope that we at least see some signs of progress."

Vogelstein says that his laboratory is typical of hundreds of others in terms of its young investigators working long hours against great odds. And in contemplation of the first revolution of the discovery of the cause of cancer bridging over into a second revolution that will bring better ways of detecting and treating cancer, he warns:

"We have a golden opportunity during the next two decades to translate the discoveries of the lab into new cancer therapies, but this will happen only if the nation continues to support research. We have trained hundreds of brilliant young researchers and given them powerful new tools, and yet we are barely paying them minimum wages. The explosion of research has not been accompanied by an explosion of research dollars for young investigators. Current levels of funding for research are not adequate—period!"

In regard to the contentious issues of whether everybody should be screened for cancer risk, whether there are enough skilled counselors to advise patients who carry mutant genes, and whether insurance companies will use genetic information to deny coverage, Vogelstein summarizes:

"Society is just starting to come to grips with the implications of the cancer-causing genes that have been discovered in the last few years. Genetic screening tests are very labor-intensive and very difficult and there is no way to find the resources to do all the tests to manage all families at risk. Since the presence of a mutant gene is very important information, it must be transmitted in the right way, and there are nowhere near enough skilled counselors to do this. As for insurance, I don't know. That's not my area. I do know that genetic tests will be invaluable in the management of cancer patients."

He concludes, "Walking through the Hopkins cancer radiation unit and seeing the suffering that patients have to endure is a powerful motivator for all of us. People have to suffer because current cancer therapies are not specific for cancer cells; they also destroy normal-growing cells.

"I hope that we can some day target specific drugs to specific cancer-causing genes. You can't predict revolutions, but it can be predicted that the next revolution of better ways to treat cancer will require at least as much creativity, hard work, and good luck as did the revolution of discovery!"

Altered Fates

Genetic researchers Barbara Weber, M.D., and Francis Collins, M.D., are in the thick of the race to find the gene for breast cancer. Meanwhile, they help counsel those who carry this devastating gene

The modern era of genetic counseling began last August on a bright, sunny Friday in Ann Arbor, Mich., when the director of the breast cancer clinic at the University of Michigan (UM) School of Medicine made a snap decision in "oh, maybe, 5 minutes, tops."

Barbara Weber, M.D., recalls, "One of my research patients, a 33-year-old woman who we'll call Susan, walked in and announced that she was going to have both her breasts removed a week from Friday. She was part of an extended family cluster that had been devastated by an inherited form of breast cancer and she had decided that she could no longer live with this cloud hanging over her head."

Weber and her colleagues had been studying blood samples of the family and had isolated and identified genetic markers for the fateful gene that means an 85% lifetime risk of developing breast cancer, as well as a significantly higher risk of ovarian cancer. For members of this family, finding the marker meant the same grim prognosis as finding the gene. Serendipitously, however, Weber had obtained only that week the results of sophisticated DNA-typing tests that disclosed that *this* woman was unlikely to be a carrier of the gene, BRCA1, located on the short arm of chromosome 17, the mutations of which make women highly susceptible to potentially fatal breast and ovarian cancers.

"This woman's story blew the whole area of genetic counseling wide open," Weber says. "Previously, we had thought that we would wait until the actual cancer-causing gene was identified before we would give information to individual members of any one family about their carrier status. Now, I thought, 'Under the circumstances, can any reasonable person withhold this information? Of course not!'

"Susan had come to the clinic with her older sister, Janet [another pseudonym], who had been diagnosed with breast cancer only 2 months earlier, and with each of their husbands. I told Susan, 'I have this information about your carrier status and I need to know how you want me to give it to you—alone or with your family?' She insisted that the other three remain in the room because she was convinced that she did carry the bad gene.

"When I told her that in all likelihood she did *not* carry the gene—I was 98% sure—she was simply dumbfounded. I can still see that look of complete and utter shock on her face. Then, the four of them jumped up and hugged and cried and danced about the room. I felt like crying myself. She canceled the surgery, of course. In the months ahead, however, she would be overcome with feelings of guilt that she had been spared while her relatives suffered."

Weber adds, "I tried to consult Francis about my sudden decision to release our research results and although I couldn't reach him, I knew he would be in agreement."

"Francis" is Francis Sellers Collins, M.D., who less than 2 years earlier had recruited Weber to work with him on the linkage and mapping of breast cancer to chromosome 17. A professor of internal medicine and human genetics at the UM and a principal investigator for the Howard Hughes Medical Institute on UM's Ann Arbor campus, Collins is the newly named director of the National Center for Human Genome Research at the National Institutes of Health (NIH), Bethesda, Md (his appointment was announced this month).

Elsewhere in the April 21, 1993, *JAMA* theme issue on molecular genetics, Collins, Weber, and colleagues have published an article on their protocol for counseling Susan's family about their inherited susceptibility to breast and ovarian cancer. In interviews last month with this reporter, the genetic researchers emphasized that their experiences are an early warning of a coming revolution.

Weber says, "These issues are soon going to land right in the laps of practicing physicians." Collins adds, "As soon as we find the gene that causes the inherited form of breast cancer—and we may find it this year—the impact will be enormous. It is estimated that up to one in 200 American women may be carriers of BRCA mutations and it is not inconceivable that every woman in America may want to be screened for this gene. The economic, ethical, and counseling issues will be very daunting."

It would be unwise to bet against Collins' prediction that the gene may be discovered this year, either by the UM group or one of many others now in a furious race to be first. Hanging above his Ann Arbor office door is a banner reading, "Three down, three to go." Down are Collins' electrifying discoveries of the genes that cause cystic fibrosis (1989), neurofibromatosis (1990), and Huntington's disease (1993, as part of a consortium effort). To go are the hunts for the causes of inherited breast cancer, a form of leukemia, and a form of sudden cardiac death due to ventricular arrhythmia.

The entire field of gene hunting is moving very rapidly and Collins' decision to run the federal genome project is expected to accelerate the pace. Breast cancer strikes one of every 10 American women and will kill 50,000 this year; the inherited form of the disease accounts for about 5% of these cases. The identification of the gene that causes inherited breast cancer and that may very well also play a major role in the more common noninherited, or sporadic form, of breast cancer is expected to bring the value of molecular medicine home once and for all to the nation.

This is amazing because it was only in November 1990 that Collins and everyone else first learned of the landmark paper by University of California, Berkeley geneticist Mary-Claire King, which used genetic-linkage analysis to identify chromosome 17 as the location of a gene, now termed BRCA1, providing convincing evidence that single genes are the cause of the inherited forms of breast and ovarian cancers. Excited, Collins signed on as a collaborator with King. A few months later, as the result of a casual conversation between mutual friends at a 1990 Christmas party, Weber, an oncologist turned geneticist, signed on to help Collins.

By August 1992, less than 2 years later, Collins and Weber had gained all the information they needed to change the life of the 33-year-old woman who was saved at the 11th hour from unnecessary breast surgery. Conversely, they also were able to tell the woman's unsuspecting 40-year-old cousin that she *was* a likely gene carrier and to persuade her to have a long-delayed mammogram that detected a small cancer that had not spread to the lymph nodes. Subsequently, she elected to have prophylactic surgeries to remove her breasts and ovaries, so "she could live without fear."

Since their stories (both briefly mentioned in the scientific paper) are likely to be repeated in the years ahead, the two women agreed to grant their first face-to-face interviews to this reporter. Susan, 33, and Emma, 40 (both are pseudonyms), arrived last month at a Michigan hotel to describe their decisive encounters with Weber, Collins, and genetic research.

Susan begins by apologizing for being a little late. "I had a bad morning," she explains. "Thinking about this interview brought back all the painful memories and my tears kept ruining my makeup.

"The day they find a cure for breast cancer will be the happiest and saddest day in our family's life. Happy because we can live without fear. Sad because a cure wasn't available earlier to spare us the suffering we've gone through.

"For 15 years we've all lived a nightmare. My mother was diagnosed with breast cancer in 1978. Six months later, my aunt was diagnosed. Both were in their 40s, both had mastectomies, and both survived. As their children, we younger women thought, 'Well, this is something we may have to deal with when we're in our 40s and 50s.' No such luck. The younger generation was hit much earlier and harder.

"My oldest sister, Faye, died in 1988 at the age of 36. She had been diagnosed with breast cancer in 1986 and everyone thought she would be fine. It was a small tumor that had not spread to the lymph nodes and the doctors recommended against chemotherapy. If you have to have breast cancer, this seemed to be the perfect scenario and, yet, everything went wrong. The cancer spread to her brain and lungs and within 18 months she was dead.

"That same year, my cousin, Renee, died of ovarian cancer. She was only 29. About 6 months later, another cousin, Renee's sister, Audrey, also died of ovarian cancer. It was a very virulent cancer that was stage III at diagnosis. She was only 32.

"Next, in June 1992, my sister, Janet, was diagnosed with breast cancer at the age of 41. By then, my mother and both sisters had come down with breast cancer and my oldest sister was dead, as were two cousins. I knew that this could not be a fluke and I was scared to death. Previously, I had trouble working up the guts to have a mastectomy, but no more. I was so petrified that I wanted my breasts off—like yesterday.

"It was pure luck that I stopped in to see Dr. Weber only a week before having my breasts removed. The only reason I dropped by was because I was at the medical center to give blood for my surgery. Since my sister, Janet, had an appointment that day at the breast cancer clinic, we all went together.

"We all went into an office and I took a deep breath. I was sure my tests would turn out really bad and I wanted to be prepared for the worst. I didn't want any false hopes like my sister Faye experienced. My only thought was, 'Let's hurry up and take off these breasts, so I can have some peace of mind.'

"When Dr. Weber told me that I didn't have the gene, that I should cancel my surgery, I couldn't believe it. My mouth fell open and I felt faint. I said, 'Are you sure?' She was sure. We all jumped up and hugged and cried. For the first time since the nightmare began, there was hope in our family, hope that maybe some of us would escape the curse. We're a very religious Catholic family, but for years I had wondered, 'God, are you listening?'

"Now, it all seemed too good to be true. And, when I was told that the identifying markers had been discovered only that week and that I did not have them, I thought, 'Well, there must be a God!' However, I did insist upon a second test just to make sure they were right!

"And, Dr. Weber is my favorite person in the world. I had been everywhere seeking help and everyone told me the same thing—to have my breasts removed. My gynecologist felt very frustrated about our family history, but there was nothing he could do. I had been seeing a surgeon every 3 months to have my breasts examined and at my last appointment he had told me, 'Why are you here? What are you doing? Get in there and get your breasts off!' If Dr. Weber hadn't given me the good news that day, I would have followed through with my surgery and learned later, 'Well, I missed it.'

Despite her good fortune, Susan is still battling feelings of anxiety and guilt. "After you've lived with constant dread for 14 years," she says, "this type of thinking will never go away. Every month, when I would check my breasts, I would get nauseated before I stepped into the shower, fearing that I would find, 'Oh, my God, here's the lump!' I got to the point where I didn't like my breasts, didn't think of them as being very friendly. Now, I'm a little more relaxed about examining them, but I'm still very nervous, very fearful. When my gynecologist told me that he could change my annual breast exam to once every 2 years, I thought, 'WELL, I don't know about THAT . . .'

"Before I talked to Dr. Weber, I was also very frightened for my daughter, Chrissie, who is only 10. One day, she had asked me, 'Mommy, am I developing?' I told her, 'No, not yet.' She said, 'Well, I don't want to, I don't want breasts. Why do we have to have breasts, anyway?'

"It almost broke my heart because all I could say then was, 'Well, in our family they don't seem like such a good thing.' Later, when I learned that since I didn't have the gene Chrissie wouldn't either, I explained to her that she didn't have to worry, that her risk of breast cancer was only that of every other woman—one in 10 (if a woman lives to be 85; the risk is much lower for younger women). She said, 'That's great—I have only good genes!'

"Today, my feelings are all mixed up—anger and relief and sadness. I'm happy for myself and Chrissie but I'm angry, too. I can't help but wonder, 'Why weren't my sisters spared, too?'

"At least, with our knowledge of the gene, we can now act. It's a terrible thing to have your breasts and ovaries removed, but when it comes down to your life or your breasts, there's no choice. You can live without breasts."

The choice was an easy one for Susan's cousin, Emma, who, tears in her eyes, has been patiently listening for more than an hour to Susan's story.

"My story is different than Susan's," Emma begins. "The blood work for my side of the family wasn't completed until last October, and I never dreamed that I was at risk. Neither my mother nor my grandmother had breast cancer and I was sure I didn't, either. At the time, we were ignorant of how the gene is passed on. We thought it was only carried by females. It turns out that my grandfather and father both carried the disease gene and it was passed on to me, two of my sisters, and three of my brothers." (The full pedigree of this Michigan family includes nine of 19 men with the gene and 11 of 23 women; no family member is tested until he or she turns 18.)

"Our side of the family came to Ann Arbor to be tested, thinking we were going to a picnic or a family reunion. Nothing to worry about. I guess I should have been worried, though, when I walked in the room and *both* Drs. Collins and Weber were there to talk to me. They started going through a lot of details and explaining this and that and I couldn't stand it. I said, 'Wait, STOP. Before you go any further, I have to ask—do I have the gene or not?'

"When they told me, 'Yes, you have the gene,' it blew my mind. I was numb and I really didn't hear much more of what they said. I mean, my life had been turned upside down and backwards and forward. I was in a fog. Still, I could understand my options—either regular mammograms to catch any cancer early or preventive surgery. Removing my ovaries and having a hysterectomy was OK with me, since I already had my children [two teenaged sons]. I had been having mammograms only every 2 years and my next one wasn't scheduled until January 1993. Barb [Weber] asked if I would like to have one done immediately and I agreed to do so. The technicians thought everything looked fine, but Barb studied the film carefully and told me, 'This doesn't look quite right to me.' I think we should do a needle biopsy to make sure.' She did the biopsy and then I drove home to await the results.

"As I drove, all I could think of were images from the funerals for Faye, Renee, and Audrey. I felt like I was living a nightmare and I prayed, 'Please, God, have this end.' I was crying the entire trip.

"When I got home, the house was empty. My husband had taken the boys to a football game. When he returned, he took one look at me and said, 'My God, what is wrong?' I started to cry all over again. But you can only cry so much. Then, you gotta make some decisions. I have to tell you, though, that, first, you go through all the 'why me's?' After my husband and I had talked and talked and I had cried and cried, I finally hit rock bottom. At that point, I made a decision:

"I was not going to let the stress get the best of me. I decided that if the biopsy found cancer—no matter how small—then it was out of my hands and I was going to *act*. I was going to have both breasts removed and a hysterectomy and be done with it. I would not live with constant fear that the cancer would strike again."

The biopsy found cancer and, last December, Emma had a bilateral mastectomy, ovariectomy, and hysterectomy. She says, "Thank God for Barb [Weber] and for the science of gene testing. Otherwise, I probably would have cleared my mammogram and my cancer would not have been caught until 2 years later—when I would have been in big trouble. Gene testing saved my life and it may have saved the lives of my two sisters as well. They now both plan to have preventive surgeries, whether they have cancer or not. There's no point in having a mammogram every 3 to 6 months when it's almost certain you're going to come down with cancer. You're just waiting for it to happen—a time bomb ticking to go off. I couldn't live with that fear.

"Everything worked out well for me. The breast cancer had not spread to the lymph nodes and I didn't need chemo or radiation. There was no cancer in the ovaries. Still, I know that the best outlooks can turn bad and the worst ones good. I'm a little worried because of what happened to Faye (Susan's sister). She had a really small breast cancer, but it spread everywhere. So, I'm a little bothered by not having chemotherapy, but I've put my life in Barb's hands and she tells me that I don't need chemotherapy. Whatever happens next, I'll be prepared. I'll never let myself be as unprepared as I was last October, when I was told I had the gene for breast cancer and I thought, 'Wow, you gotta be kidding.' I'll never be shocked like that again. And, once the gene for inherited breast cancer is found, no other woman will have to be, either."

She concludes, "Our real hope is that medical science will be able to offer a life without dread for our children and grandchildren."

Susan and Emma say the villain in their dark drama is the health insurance industry.

Susan says, "After Janet was diagnosed, I thought I had to have my breasts removed immediately, but the health insurer (through her husband) refused to pay for it. A mastectomy and breast reconstruction, plus removal of the ovaries, can cost $45,000 to $50,000. Before they agreed to pay, we went around and around:

"The benefits adviser asked me, 'Why do you think you need this surgery?'

'Well, because of my family history. My mother, my aunt, my two sisters, my two cousins, all had breast cancer—and three are dead.'

'That doesn't mean you will get it.'

'How can you say it doesn't!'

"Finally, a sympathetic supervisor who had cancer in her own family fought for me and got approval. Then, of course, thanks to Drs. Weber and Collins, I found out that I didn't need the surgery, after all. No thanks to the health insurer, though, for putting me through a lot of misery. And over the years, my health insurance also refused to pay for my mammograms and Pap smears. Their lack of interest in prevention is maddening. And when they do pay, it seems that every doctor's fee is unreasonable and uncustomary and not to be paid in full."

Emma adds, "The insurance industry is the enemy. We've had almost more stress in dealing with them than with the cancers. Because I did have a diagnosis of cancer, I was able to get my surgeries reimbursed. But my two sisters who have the gene are still fighting to get approval for prophylactic surgeries. They're in a Catch-22. If they tell the insurer the scientific reason of why they know they are at high risk of cancer—because they have the gene—then our whole family runs the risk of losing its health insurance because we have this genetic defect. Yet, when my sisters tell their insurers about the family history, they're told. 'So what? The family history doesn't mean that *you* will get cancer.' It's infuriating.

"If it weren't for our fear of losing health insurance for everybody in the family, Susan and I would not be using pseudonyms with you and we would be on TV in a second to tell our story. The public needs to know that our experiences prove that for the first time there is hope for the future."

Dr. Weber adds, "The predicament of one of Emma's sisters is a classic case of why we need health care reform in this country. Her husband is self-employed and doesn't have health insurance. She works three part-time jobs and none provides coverage. The only insurance she has is a limited health policy she was forced by the school district to buy so her son could play soccer. It doesn't cover her, of course.

"The solution to these kinds of problems is to convince governments and insurers that it's cheaper to pay for preventive surgeries for people with cancer-causing genes than to pay for the cost of the cancer."

Asked about young women, like Janet's daughter, who are diagnosed at age 18 as having the cancer-causing gene, Weber says, "We tell them their options as they grow older—mammograms every 3 months or preventive surgeries. My bias is for the surgeries, but I keep this out of the consultation. I do tell women this young that they don't have to live hurry-up lives, that since their breast cancers usually won't strike until they're in their 30s and their ovarian cancers until they're in their 40s, that anyone under 25 doesn't have to worry about breast cancer and anyone under 35 doesn't have to worry about ovarian cancers. They do have time to get married and start a family before worrying about surgeries."

Weber, who says she works a 60- to 70-hour week—"easily"—thinks that the imminent isolation and identification of the gene that causes inherited breast cancer "will have an impact that is absolutely enormous—the greatest of any scientific find in recent history. It will cause a flood of women to come in for screenings and prophylactic surgeries. It also opens up the long-range possibility—maybe as soon as 5 to 10 years—of understanding what goes wrong and being able to repair the defective gene."

She describes it this way: "What we've been able to do with our Michigan family and what other researchers have been able to do with other family clusters is to identify a marker that means with 98%-plus accuracy that the cancer-causing gene is there. Right now, identifying the marker is a little like walking into a room filled with members of a given family and knowing that every person in that room who is wearing a red sweater has the bad gene. The red sweater is the marker. In another room, filled with members of a different family, the marker might present as a green sweater. When we isolate the actual gene, to continue the metaphor, it may turn out to be a white silk blouse underneath all those sweaters. The white silk blouse will be the gene, and it will be the same for everyone, meaning that we can screen every woman in the U.S. to see if she is wearing that white silk blouse. If so, she has the inherited gene and is at very high risk of breast and ovarian cancer. And, I think some researcher is going to find that white silk blouse very soon."

Weber is a good example of the growing importance of genetic research and the federal effort to map the entire human genome. "Only 3 years ago," she says, "before I began my collaboration with Dr. Collins, I thought the genome project was absolutely stupid. I mean, why spend $15 billion for this information. Now, I'm totally immersed in the effort.

"However, we're going to have to educate a lot of practicing physicians. One of the surgeons right here at the university of

Michigan Medical Center told me that he would continue to perform mastectomies on women who request them because of their family histories—even if our research shows that, like Susan, they don't have the inherited gene and are not at high risk. I guess this is his way of saying he doesn't believe us."

Weber says her science is strong, but that mistakes can happen. "Last year," she recalls, "I thought that I had made a mistake in identifying two of the male members of our Michigan family cluster as carrying the gene and I almost had a breakdown. It was a very, very scary feeling, but Francis and I went over everything again and again and we proved that we had it right the first time. When you're working with a large family cluster and looking for markers, you can always go back and check your findings. The future problem will be testing individuals for the actual gene and avoiding mix-ups in blood samples. As in any high-volume testing by commercial labs, there will be human errors and the answer will be for patients with positive results to have a second test."

She concludes, "This is the most fun I've ever had. It's a chance to combine research and clinical medicine with molecular genetics, epidemiology, and ethics."

Dr. Collins, 43, a 90-hour-a-week worker, is another physician who is very excited about his new job—running the Human Genome Project. Interviewed on March 30, he confirmed that his "first official day as a federal employee will be Monday, April 5." He will split his time 50-50 between Ann Arbor and the Bethesda, Md., campus of the NIH until September, at which time he will move his research lab and 10 researchers from Michigan to Maryland.

The appeal, he says, "is enormous. This project is absolutely revolutionary, the most important organized scientific effort in the history of mankind. It dwarfs the space program and the superconducting super collider in terms of the potential benefits to mankind—and it is only going to be done once. There is no way I could pass up this chance."

Raised in the Shenandoah Valley on a Virginia sheep farm, Collins' early education came from his mother, a playwright, and father, a teacher of drama. He started out as a chemist because he found biology "too chaotic and descriptive and I wanted to study a physical science based on nice, clear mathematical models." Chemistry filled the bill until it "became emotionally sterile and medicine began to beckon." He soon acquired expertise in both internal medicine and human genetics and stamped himself as a rising star with his discoveries of the disease-causing genes for cystic fibrosis, neurofibromatosis, and Huntington's disease.

Now, as the chief actor in the Human Genome Project, he is asked how he sees the drama unfolding. He is reminded of Federico Fellini's comment at the previous night's Oscar awards—namely, that "the visionary is the true realist."

Collins chuckles and takes over the stage. "Well, if this is a five-act drama," he begins, "then we're now near the end of act II. I don't know how the rest of the story will develop, but based upon the start of the play, a lot is going to happen. This is a drama with humor and a few edges with the potential for tragic outcomes. It could represent either a golden revolution in history or it could prove to be a Pandora's box with genetic information gone awry. I've intentionally posed the tensions provocatively, but I really don't fear a bad outcome. I believe that our research gains will greatly decrease the possibility of any tragic aspects.

"When the curtain falls after act V, I hope that two things will have been shown:

- We can assess the specific risks of individuals for various medical conditions, with an overriding emphasis on what can be *done* to prevent an unnecessarily bad outcome.

- We can develop new treatments for diseases by using genetic therapies that are effective and nontoxic.

"That would make a very nice ending. It could all come true within 30 to 40 years—hopefully before the complete end of my career."

The Human Genome Project will change the face of medicine, Collins believes. "It's very possible," he says, "that in the future a physician will give an 18-year-old patient a physical exam that includes a test of his or her DNA for hundreds of diseases with known genetic components. Family histories are useful, but genetic exams will give the doctor a much more precise tool to assess risks and give advice. The physician will be able to tell the patient whether the risk is high, low, or average for a given condition and to make lifestyle recommendations based upon known risks. There will be personalized schemes for a new kind of preventive medicine and I think that it will prove very appealing."

Asked about his remarkable success in quickly tracking down three disease-causing genes, Collins replies, "It didn't seem quick when we were in the middle of the hunt. Cystic fibrosis took 2 years. It was 5 years before the gene for neurofibromatosis fell. We started to hunt the gene for Huntington's disease in 1985 and we found it only a few weeks ago. When we were banging away day after day in search of these genes, it seemed like forever."

He expects to find soon the gene for inherited breast cancer and he believes that every American woman should be screened for it. "Women carrying this gene run an 85% lifetime risk of cancer," he says, "and I think it is ethically and economically justifiable to give them a chance to do something about it, although many of the things are not pleasant." He worries about the potential need for counseling. "I can't think of any information that is more emotionally charged," he says. "We have less than 1000 qualified genetic counselors in the nation. Where will we find the people to counsel these women the way we have been able to counsel our patients?"

As the new head of the Human Genome Project, scheduled to run through the year 2005, Collins succeeds Nobelist James Watson, PhD, a man for whom he has "enormous respect." Still, the two are, in Collins' phrase, "like day and night." The caustic Watson is outspoken, even vitriolic, and a total Darwinian. The soft-spoken Collins is given to consensus building and describes himself "as a serious Christian."

He adds, "It's sort of a taboo for a scientist to discuss his religion, but, after a period of atheism, I have now, through a process of rational thinking, arrived at the belief that there is no conflict between what I know as a scientist and what I know as a Christian. Science has augmented and reinforced my religion and helped me to understand what God has created. I know that there are some people out there who are slightly nervous about this kind of talk, but I can say to them with complete confidence that my Christianity will not interfere with my scientific work."

He describes his feelings toward his scientific work as "very complex. I'm exhilarated and gratified at the vote of confidence from my colleagues, but I'm also a bit daunted. I'm being really stretched by my responsibilities in three areas—supervising the entire genome project; recruiting new scientists to run the intramural genetic research program at NIH; and continuing my own research. Right now, they're equal thirds, but once I hire the intramural researchers, I should be able to achieve a 50-50 split between supervising the overall project and hunting genes on my own."

Collins' successful gene hunting was greatly facilitated by the techniques he developed called "positional cloning" and "chromosome jumping." While it is beyond the scope of this article to describe the techniques of molecular genetics, Collins is asked to describe what it is that he does to find the defect in a gene that causes disease.

"I like the map analogy," he explains. "Let's say you're looking for a very small object within a very large territory, like trying to locate a single burnt-out light bulb in the basement of a single home in the entire U.S. and you start with absolutely no clues.

"Well, by doing DNA probes on blood drawn from family clusters with linkages to certain diseases, like the linkages of the Michigan family with inherited breast cancer, we can locate which chromosome has the defect. This is a little like narrowing our map search down to a state, say Kansas.

"Well, Kansas is a pretty big place. So, we do more DNA probes to narrow down the specific area of the chromosome where the defect always seems to appear. This is a little like breaking Kansas down into its various counties.

"Next, we have techniques to distinguish genes from non-genes, which is a little like distinguishing Kansas towns from the countryside. The towns look different. That leaves us with the need to catalog all the genes in the chromosome, or towns in the state.

"Finally, we search for that single burnt-out light bulb, which may turn out to be a single base pair within a very large gene. To find it we may have to hit every basement in every town in the entire state.

"Of course, it helps if the defect is a gross rearrangement of genetic material, rather than a subtle mutation. This shortcut is a little like learning that the light bulb we want is in the basement of a house that has been bombed to the ground."

Sobered by the difficulties just described, this reporter reminds Collins of the description of the current status of the genome project reported by Stanford geneticist David Botstein, who once said:

"Much of the opposition to the Human Genome Project is based on the fact that just knowing the sequence of base pairs doesn't mean anything in itself. The genetic code lets you turn the base sequence of a gene into the amino-acid sequence of a protein, but even that doesn't mean anything by current technology. It's as if you had a row of hieroglyphics and a way of transcribing them into Urdu—but you don't understand or speak Urdu. That's pretty much the situation we're in."

Collins smiles before relying, "David is always comparing the genetic code to some unheard-of language. It's true that the sequences are not valuable per se. If I could print them all out today on the computer in this room, they would not tell us how things work. However, these sequences will be the fodder for the next centuries of science, as we try to learn the rules of how some genes work. Someday, the sequences of how the genes for Huntington's and other diseases do their damages will be translated to our understanding."

In the meantime, Collins relaxes by playing the guitar and piano, usually on Sundays at the small Baptist church he and his wife, Mary Linn, helped found on Ann Arbor's northwest side. Now in the middle of a divorce, Collins also spends a lot of time with his two daughters and rides his motorcycle as often as the weather will allow (his helmet is festooned with stickers representing the genes he has bagged so far, and he emphasizes that he always wears it). He also likes to practice medicine and, for that reason, will return to Africa this June to do medical missionary work in a small village. "After I talk to a patient," he says, "I almost always feel good, because I can usually offer some help. This is a lot different from doing research, where you're usually led up a blind alley."

Collins has done much of his own best research under funding provided by the estate of eccentric billionaire Howard Hughes, who died in 1976 after almost total neglect of his own health even as his fortune endowed state-of-the-art medical research across the country. Now, as he prepares to leave the Howard Hughes Medical Institute at Ann Arbor for the unknown challenges of government service, Collins muses:

"You know, I think that Howard would be quite pleased. He always loved wild and crazy frontiers."

Index